THE

DANGEROUS

ANIMALS

CLUB

Stephen Tobolowsky

SIMON & SCHUSTER

New York   London   Toronto   Sydney   New Delhi

Simon & Schuster
1230 Avenue of the Americas
New York, NY 10020

First Simon & Schuster hardcover edition August 2012

SIMON & SCHUSTER and colophon are registered trademarks
of Simon & Schuster, Inc.

For information about special discounts for bulk purchases,
please contact Simon & Schuster Special Sales at
1-866-506-1949 or business@simonandschuster.com.

The Simon & Schuster Speakers Bureau can bring authors
to your live event. For more information or to book an event,
contact the Simon & Schuster Speakers Bureau at
1-866-248-3049 or visit our website at www.simonspeakers.com.

Designed by Renata Di Biase

Manufactured in the United States of America

10 9 8 7 6 5 4 3 2 1

Library of Congress Cataloging-in-Publication Data

ISBN 978-1-4516-3315-3
ISBN 978-1-4516-3317-7 (ebook)

Photo Credits:
Photograph by Ann Hearn Tobolowsky: 16; Photographs by Helen Runge: 38, 64;
Photograph by David Chen ©2011: 336; All other photographs courtesy of the author.

For my boys Robert and William.
As dear and dangerous as they come.

CONTENTS

CONTENTS

THE
DANGEROUS
ANIMALS
CLUB

1.

THE DANGEROUS ANIMALS CLUB

ON'T ASK ME, "How are the kids?" I never have any idea. I know they eat and get dressed and go to school, but as to what is going on in their lives and in their heads, forget it. It is the secret world: the world that every child has and that no parent gets to see.

Ann and I are active parents. We try to meet all of our kids' friends and their parents and ask questions and look under the bed, and check in the closets, tap their phones—but we still don't know the various deals with Satan they may make when they leave the house. We're not unique. Every parent is in the dark.

When I was five, I had an invisible monster that lived alternately in my closet and under my bed in a kind of winter-home/summer-home arrangement. His name was "Eye the Monster." Eye would come out of hiding when I was alone and we would talk.

I had an up-and-down relationship with Eye. I often appreciated his middle-of-the-night visits. We would talk about school and about girls I had crushes on. You would think that Eye the Monster didn't care about the opposite sex. But he did. He always argued for patience and honesty. He urged me to be more aggressive with the ladies on square dance day. It was hard advice to take. I was never a player. I thought five years of age was too young to be married. But not Eye. He thought I could be a trailblazer and be married and have children before I was in fourth grade. And this was years before MTV.

Besides being a confidant and an advisor, Eye had another side. He could be angry. There was a period when his opening my closet door and coming into my room at midnight terrified me. I snuck a steak knife from the kitchen and kept it under my pillow as a last line of defense. I hid the knife in the morning so Mom would never see it when she made my bed. Love, terror, and steak knives were all part of my secret world.

Eventually, my parents became aware of Eye the Monster. On a car trip to San Antonio, Eye came out from under the backseat. He told my dad, who was driving, that we had to go back home. Davy Crockett was at the Alamo, and we could get killed by Mexicans. Dad didn't listen. I started crying. Eye the Monster started screaming at Dad.

Dad was not pleased. He had to work hard to get a few days off to go on a family vacation. Being a pediatrician, he realized that what he wanted was a vacation from screaming, crying kids. By the time we got to Waxahachie, Dad turned the car around and we came home.

The big secret my parents never knew was that I was also a member of a club across the alley at Billy Hart's house. I would kiss Mom on the cheek and "go out to play." In reality I ran down to Billy's for a meeting of the Dangerous Animals Club.

Billy already had a clubhouse in his backyard so it was only natural that he should be the president. He was also older than I was. He was almost seven, and I was content to put myself in his capable hands.

The purpose of the Dangerous Animals Club was straightforward. Both Billy and I were big fans of dangerous creatures. We made a list of all the dangerous creatures we wanted to catch. Being in Texas, there were a lot of them. The list included: rattlesnakes, copperheads, water moccasins, black widows, scorpions, tarantulas, centipedes, leeches, and the deadly coral snake, which we were hoping lived in the woods nearby.

We went out into the fields and hills and creeks carrying jelly jars and burlap sacks. We used broken broomsticks and umbrellas as tools of capture or weapons, if necessary. We would lift rocks and roll over rotten trees, hoping to find something horrible, catching it alive and bringing it back to the clubhouse, effectively making Billy's backyard the most dangerous place in Texas.

Charlie Harp, another neighborhood boy, a little younger than I, became aware of the Dangerous Animals Club. He heard our mission statement; he saw the clubhouse. He wanted in. Billy and I refused at first. What good is a secret club if everybody is a member? Charlie ran home and came back with a brown paper bag. Inside was a genuine rattlesnake skull. He said we could display it in the clubhouse if he could be a member. He was in. And we were now three.

So I kissed Mom good-bye and told her I was going out to play. I ran over to Billy's where we met and swore that if we told anyone about the club, we would be put to death. We had a disagreement as to whether it should be a blood pact. Charlie Harp argued it had to be a blood pact if punishment for telling was death. There was a logic to that, but I was opposed to any kind of bleeding that happened on purpose. Billy, being a natural leader, said the blood oath wasn't necessary. The activities of the Club were already dangerous enough.

We agreed and went out for our first task: to find a scorpion or a centipede. Billy was sure that if we went down to the creek we would find a scorpion. He heard that they liked rotting wood. There were several dead trees lying on the ground.

As I think about it, Billy was a damn good president. His instincts were right on. We went down to the creek and found a fallen tree. We moved a decaying branch with our bare hands—and wha-la, there was a scorpion!

We slapped a jelly jar over it. The scorpion started slashing at the glass and our hands with its tail, as scorpions are wont to do. We righted the jar and filled it with rubbing alcohol. The scorpion started swimming furiously. We screwed on the top and we headed back to the clubhouse. One day, about thirty minutes of time invested, and something nasty in our possession. Priceless.

I ran home for dinner. Mom asked me if I had fun playing with Billy. I said emphatically, "Yes!"

The next day we headed down to the creek where Billy hoped we could catch some leeches, and if we were lucky, a water moccasin, one of Texas's four poisonous snake species. Billy told me that water moccasins weren't as deadly as coral snakes—which was disappointing—but they were more aggressive. That encouraged me. I didn't want to be wasting my time with something that wasn't potentially lethal.

We started wading through the creek water. Leeches swam up and tried to attach themselves to our legs. How great was that! We just scooped them up in a jar and we had leeches. Another creature to check off our list. Too easy.

Now we were on to the snakes. Water moccasins apparently love stagnant water—so we were in the right place. The water had a thick green foam on top of it and you could see the mosquito larvae swimming under the murky surface. Billy suggested we start turning over rocks by the bank of the creek.

I flipped over a big piece of limestone and there was a baby water moccasin. It opened its little mouth and showed its baby fangs. Billy reminded me that the babies are just as poisonous as the grown-ups. I nodded and reached down to get it. Billy yelled to me to remember to grab it behind the head. Not to worry. I knew that. Everyone in Texas knows you grab a poisonous snake behind the head.

But the water moccasin didn't want to be caught and it took off through a field of tall grass. I ran after it shouting to Billy that it was headed toward him. I could see the snake making a rippling trail in front of me. It seemed to stop for a second. There was movement near my feet. I reached down quickly and pulled up—the mother water moccasin! She was four feet long and angry. In all of my haste, I hadn't grabbed her behind the head but around the fat middle of her body. She hissed and readied an attack, showing her trademark white mouth and huge fangs.

I screamed and started swinging the snake over my head. I used the centrifugal force to keep her from bending back and biting me. I was now holding her by the tail, swinging her around my head and walking around wondering what to do. Billy came up to me to give me advice. He assured me that as long as I could spin the snake fast enough, the g-force would keep her from striking. I told him I was getting tired. I needed to throw the snake. He told me I couldn't. He said the water moccasin was not only aggressive, but it had a good memory and would follow me home.

I started to cry.

I told Billy that I had to let it fly, to let him get a head start for the clubhouse. Billy started running. I screamed after him, "If I throw the snake and run, will she be able to follow me?" Billy stopped and shouted back, "She'll track you by scent. It could take days, but she'll find you." He took off like a jackrabbit. I stood in the middle of the swamp grass, swinging the snake over my head and crying.

I couldn't do this forever. I decided that the snake was probably dizzy and disoriented. That would buy me some time. I slung the snake. She twirled, helicopterlike, several yards through the air and landed in the creek. I took off. I ran as fast as I had ever run in my life. To confuse the snake, I didn't run directly home, but took a circuitous route in the opposite direction. I ran over to Driftwood Street and down the alley behind Mark Henley's house. There was a terrifying German shepherd that always barked at us when we rode our bicycles. I figured if the snake tried to track me, she would have to deal with the dog first.

I got home in full gallop. I blasted through the kitchen door. Mom was putting supper on the table. She asked if I had a good time playing with Billy. I said "yeah" as she spooned some lima beans onto my plate. I asked her if we lock the doors at night. Mom looked at me with a touch of surprise and answered, "Yes, honey. Always. Why?" I started eating and said, "Oh, just wanted to make sure no one could break in." Mom rubbed my back. "Oh, don't worry. I always lock the doors." I smiled. I was as safe as I possibly could be in an unsafe world.

———

BILLY HART AND I had a cooling off period of about three days, waiting for some sign that the mother cottonmouth hadn't tracked me down. When she never showed up, we figured the DAC could begin its full-scale operations once again. Billy produced a huge Whitman pickle jar from the Wynnewood Movie Theater, our local Saturday matinee hangout. He had a sly grin on his face. "Know what we're gonna do with this jar?"

"No," I said.

"We're going to catch us a tarantula."

This was the best news I had heard since I found out the tooth fairy paid more money for bigger teeth. A real tarantula. The clubhouse would be a showplace with a tarantula next to the leeches, next to the scorpion, next to a real rattlesnake skull.

"When do we get the tarantula?"

Billy thought for a moment. "We have to get some supplies. My brother has to go to the drugstore and buy denatured alcohol."

"What is that?"

Billy again showed his expertise. "It's deadly poisonous. They only sell it to adults. My brother will buy some and give it to us. Then we go out and find a tarantula hole. And then we find its escape hole and put the pickle jar over it. Then we pour the denatured alcohol down the main hole and when the tarantula tries to escape out the back, we got him."

Let me just say right now, Billy Hart was a genius. He was right about everything, except for maybe the bit about the mother snake following me home. Anyway, Billy's brother bought the awful stuff and gave it to us, and we wandered into the hills behind our homes.

For the uninitiated, the way you find a tarantula hole is to find an arid locale (most of Texas), then you look for a hole in the ground that looks kind of like a gopher hole but with some telltale webbing around the entrance. Once you find the main hole, you walk in small but ever-widening concentric circles until you find another hole with a slight trace of spiderweb around the outside. This is the escape hole. It's usually about twenty to thirty feet away.

Billy and I found a hole that looked suspicious. It was three inches in diameter with some cobweb blowing in the breeze. We walked around the hole, and sure enough, about twenty feet away on the other side of a scrub oak was a second hole. I put the Whitman pickle jar over the escape hole. Billy pulled out the denatured alcohol. He handed me a thick piece of cardboard for phase two of the operation.

He said, "We don't know if the hole is deserted or not. I'll pour this in and if a spider jumps in the jar, you slide the cardboard under it and we'll have us a tarantula." We laughed. We would have done a high five if it had existed back then. Billy unscrewed the cap, turned his head, and held the can as far away from him as possible so as not to be poisoned by the fumes. He poured the entire contents down the main hole. He threw the can away and then ran to join me behind a boulder, where I was stationed, watching for any action in the pickle jar.

We waited an eternity, which was probably more like ninety seconds, when—*plop*—a huge, brown tarantula popped into the jar. We screamed with glee. We had a giant, reddish brown, hairy spider with a leg span of about eight inches in the pickle jar. Billy nudged me to slide the cardboard under the mouth of the jar. I ran up and reached down to slide the cardboard in place when *plop*. Another large spider popped into the jar. And then *plop*, another, and *plop*, another. I ran back to join Billy.

Another plopped into the jar and then *plop. Plop. Plop. Plop.* A half dozen more. The jar was about half full with angry, squirming spiders. *Plop. Plop. Plop. Plop. Plop. Plop.* It didn't stop. They kept filling the jar. There had to be fifty tarantulas in there. The entire pickle jar was filled and more spiders kept jumping into it from the escape hole.

Billy and I started to panic. "Now what are we going to do?" I asked him. Billy thought about it and said, "We can't take the jar back to the clubhouse and we can't leave them in the jar. That would be cruel." Billy thought about it some more. After due consideration, he said, "We have to knock the jar over and run."

Remembering my recent run-in with the snake, I asked, "Will they follow us?"

Billy shook his head, "No. Spiders are stupid. But we have to make sure we never come back to this part of the woods again. We poisoned that hole so there'll be tarantulas everywhere." We knocked over the pickle jar. Once again we bolted.

I got home and Mom was in the kitchen. "You're back early," she said.

I walked over and grabbed a chocolate-chip cookie she had just pulled from the oven.

"You and Billy have a good time?"

I grunted with a mouthful of cookie, "It was okay," and went into the den to watch TV.

The next day Billy and I met at the clubhouse to discuss future missions. We didn't have a lot to show for our trouble. Things got worse when Charlie Harp, who had never joined us on any excursions, came over and said he had to take the rattlesnake skull back home. It was a major setback for the club.

The real blow came when Billy decided we had to mount and display the scorpion, which was currently floating near the bottom of the jelly jar we caught him in. I took the top off, reached in, pulled the scorpion out, and placed it on the table when it flashed its tail at us. It was still alive! It ran off the table and into the clubhouse. Billy and I screamed and ran into the yard. Miraculously, the scorpion had lived for days in an environment of pure alcohol, much like I did in the 1980s.

With the scorpion on the loose, we had to abandon our clubhouse. Billy pointed out that since the clubhouse was made of rotten wood, which scorpions love, it would never leave. We didn't dare go back inside.

There was something poetic about the scorpion taking over the Dangerous Animals Club clubhouse. If there were such a thing as a "scorpion poet," he may have sung of the Beowulflike heroism of one of their own who survived so many trials for such a rich reward.

We never talked about it, but these were dark days for the DAC. Billy and I still played together, but it was hard to continue without a clubhouse, a rattlesnake skull, and all of nature turned against us.

There was one brief moment when the DAC thought of staging a comeback. One afternoon a large, beautiful box turtle was sitting on my patio. Just sitting there! As if dropped from the heavens. I ran over to get Billy to show him my find. I asked him if we could include the turtle as a trophy for the Dangerous Animals Club. Billy pondered and furrowed his brow. It was doubtful, he said. The turtle could hardly be considered dangerous. It just sat there. But it could be a part of a new wildlife club: the Wildlife Club of Texas. The purpose of the club would be the same as the DAC, but its reach would be more ecumenical.

I called Mom outside to see the turtle. She was impressed. I asked her if we could keep it. Mom looked unenthusiastic, but agreed to take me to the pet store to buy it a proper home.

I described the size of the turtle to the man at the pet store. I should mention that in those days, the late 1950s, pet stores were not staffed with the young enthusiastic animal lovers that work at pet stores today. The people who ran pet stores back then were just one cut above carnival people, the scariest people on earth.

Our pet store man, who had no bottom teeth, said we would need a tub for the turtle. We would need bags of gravel for the bottom of the tub. He sold us two large bags of colored pebbles. He said the turtle might appreciate a couple of the plastic palm trees he sold as turtle tank decorations. Most importantly, we would need snails.

"Snails?" Mom asked.

"Yes, ma'am. They eat the feces and keep the tub clean. You don't want to be cleaning that tub yourself."

Mom made a face and looked at me. She bought two snails. We headed home with the tub and the gravel, two palm trees, and two snails. The ride was joyous as we tried out different names for the turtle. They ranged from the dignified like "Sam" or "Tom" to the ironic like "Speedy" or "Lightning."

We got out of the car brimming with enthusiasm. I ran onto the patio. The turtle was gone. Never to be seen again. Mom and I unpacked the tub and the gravel and palm trees. We filled it with water. And that's how we ended up with two pet snails.

The Dangerous Animals Club had officially slipped into the realm of memory. Fade-out.

Fade-in, some forty years later. I was married, just as Eye the Monster had urged me to do. Annie and I, and my two boys, Robert, age twelve, and William, age seven, took off on an adventure one summer to live in a three-hundred-year-old farmhouse in the little Alps of southern France. It was late afternoon in this wild place of mountains and forests and dirt roads and ruins that date back to Roman times. I was sitting at our kitchen table drinking a glass of wine when my seven-year-old son, William, came running into the house. "Daddy, Daddy, come quick. I just saw a giant lizard on the hillside. We could catch him and take him back to America if you come quick."

I was up in a flash. I found myself laughing in a most peculiar way as I ran out the door, grabbing an umbrella to use as a tool of capture or, if necessary, a weapon. I ran with William into the mountains at dusk, honored to be invited into his secret world and proud that yet another member of the Dangerous Animals Club had stepped forward to do the job so few are willing to do.

———

I WAS NOT up for much when we arrived in France. I fell into a near-terminal case of jet lag. I would sleep on the couch. I would sleep on the floor. I slept while Ann explained to me how I had to force myself to stay awake to stop the sleep cycle. I had become Snow White in the story of my life, but even the kiss from my beloved couldn't help.

One afternoon while I was sleeping on the kitchen table, William came running inside to tell me to come quick—he had learned to talk to the bats.

I muttered, "Talk to the bats?"

William said, "Sure, Dad, they're everywhere. Now that I know their language, I can make them our friends."

Parents know that occasionally children will utter a sentence in which every word can make you question the fabric of sanity. But I believe that it is in these moments when you get a peek at the secret world your children have had all along. I had no idea we had bats at our house in the country, let alone that they "were everywhere." I had no idea William was working on breaking the language barrier. I had no idea what being friends with a bat would entail, and if it was a road I was willing to travel.

I got up and followed William outside the farmhouse. He ran about ten yards away from me and started squeaking. It was loud. It could be heard for miles. If there were any glass nearby, it would have broken. Overhead I saw a dark circle forming. I couldn't believe it. It was clear that my son was doing something that engaged the bats on a critter level. He continued the call. Occasionally a bat swooped out of the sky and landed on his shoulder. My reaction was a strange mix of pride and nausea. He was a genius. Kind of like the young Mozart, except instead of playing the piano blindfolded, he was a vermin magnet.

Like any good father, I tried to calculate ways I could monetize this ability. The only options that came to mind involved the circus or the military. I called out, "William, this is great." Ann came outside. I whispered to her, "Baby, can you believe this? Our son can talk to bats."

Ann was not amused. She said, "Stephen, the bats could have rabies." I said, "I know. I know. You're right. You're right. They probably all do. This should stop."

I turned to William and congratulated him on his accomplishment and asked if there was a safe way to get the bats off of his head. William said, "I'll just ask them to go away." He started turning in circles and squeaking again. As if by magic, the bats began to disperse. I promised Ann I wouldn't encourage William in his bat-talking experiments anymore.

But you can only keep that kind of light under a bushel for so long. One afternoon I was in a deep coma, when the bat signal awakened me once more. I dragged myself out of bed and saw William down the road calling the bats at our landlord's home. My son Robert was displaying him to our neighbors and asking for contributions. Our eighty-year-old Iraqi landlord was impressed with William's talent. Robert came alongside of me and whispered conspiratorially, "What a scam. It's just a sound frequency. Not William."

"Yeah," I said. "But he's the only one doing the frequency."

Robert rolled his eyes. "Yeah. Who else would want to? He's just weird."

"I have to agree with you there, Robert. It's a weird thing to want to do."

Robert got serious. "Any way we can make some serious money off of this?"

I shook my head. "Already thought about it. I doubt it."

"What about *America's Funniest Home Videos*?" Robert asked.

I hadn't thought of that. That was far more practical than sending William off to the circus. Robert added, "Only thing wrong is that he would probably have to get bitten for us to win."

After the bat-calling session, our landlord suggested we go down the mountain a ways. A Pakistani chess master and his eleven-year-old son were living on a farm over the summer. They might enjoy the bat calling.

William was thriving with his newfound notoriety. He had even perfected the blush of false modesty.

A big factor in any fascination is proximity. If you're close to the object of your passion, it can blossom. Fantasy can turn into romance. That was the case with William and the black bull snake. This snake was about four to five feet long and he lived on our mountain. We would find snake skins all around our house and pool. We had little doubt that our home was ground zero in the bull-snake world.

One day I was passed out in the living room when William ran inside and asked me, "Daddy, if I capture a bull snake, can we bring it home to America?" I mumbled, "Doubt it," before I rolled over and continued to sleep it off. Robert came in and said, "Hey, Dad. The pool is filled with snakes."

I roused myself and staggered out toward the pool area. There were several snakes in the water swimming. Several sunning on the bank. It didn't look safe. It was starting to resemble something from an Indiana Jones movie. I called our landlord to come and take a look. He drove up about five minutes later. He looked in the pool. He looked up at the mountain. He checked the angle of the sun in the sky and then felt the temperature of the water. He nodded and said, "Yes. Yes. This is about right. They like to spend the summers in the pool. It gets so hot."

"I understand. We like to spend the summers in the pool, too, which is why we rented your house. It would be nice to do it without the snakes. Is there someone we can call?"

Our landlord laughed and said, "Who would you call? There are hundreds of snakes in the mountains. They love it here. They come down and have sex in the pool. The big lizards come down here, too. You may find them mating here in the morning and evening. They won't hurt you. They just want to have sex and eat the rats. The rats are everywhere."

I gathered my thoughts. "So you are saying our backyard is the Playboy Mansion for the reptiles of Europe?"

"No. Just for the bull snakes. They are the only ones who go in the pool. I promise you there will never be a rat inside the house. After a while, you will get used to it. I have come to find it amusing to watch them court. The dance of love. It is beautiful."

I avoided getting misty-eyed and stayed on point. "Do they bite?" Our landlord looked at me like I was crazy. "Only if you get in the pool with them," he said. I was feeling too sleepy to stand my ground on any sort of rent reduction. I was just able to ask, "Any other snakes around here? I read you have poisonous snakes, too. Vipers."

Our landlord's countenance grew serious. "Yes. The viper is very dangerous, but they are not around here. They are short, only about a foot or eighteen inches long. You can't miss them. They are bright yellow with a black diamond pattern down their back. They have a triangular head."

I puffed up with a certain amount of authority and said, "Yes, I know. Poisonous snakes have triangular heads. When I was a little boy, I was in the Dangerous Animals Club in Texas. We tried to catch poisonous snakes alive and bring them back to our clubhouse." Our landlord looked at me and smiled. "That is really crazy," he said. "But if what you say is true, I would think a few bull snakes in the pool shouldn't bother you." He headed off to his car. "I think your son has a gift with those bats. He really impressed our neighbor from Pakistan."

———

A FEW DAYS later we headed out on a day trip to visit something else you don't see every day. The Pont du Gard. This is the ruin of a Roman aqueduct built in the first century AD. Ancient graffiti covers the stones. Looking at all of the inscriptions you see that the power of humanity isn't always found in great art. Over the centuries, lovers, soldiers, poets, and scoundrels have met here and left behind messages to the world: "Max and Emma—Love—1806" or "To God—1640" or "Freedom 1783." You don't need much more than that to understand the history of mankind.

We crossed the Gard River and started exploring the other side. Ann wanted to take in the beauty of it all. She sat down on the bank while Robert, William, and I set out to see what we could find. We got to a place where the river was narrow enough and we could throw rocks across to the other side. We started firing at will when William said casually from the log behind us, "Daddy, look. A viprish."

"A viprish?"

"Yes, a cute, little, beautiful viprish." I turned and looked back at the log where William was hunting for rocks. Coming out to check on the commotion was a short snake with a bright yellow body and a distinctive dark diamond pattern. I froze. "William, walk toward me now. Walk slowly and steadily, honey," I whispered.

"No, Daddy, let's catch him and take him back."

For some unexplainable reason, it sounded like a good idea. "Wait. I know how to grab him. Behind the head!" I said.

Robert and William and I started chasing the terrified snake. At one point it crawled over my foot just out of my clutches. The viper disappeared in some tall grass on a low-lying hill. Robert quieted us down and said, "Let me take a look." We waited in silence, afraid to breathe too loudly. Robert lifted himself to look over the crest of the hill. His face turned red. He tried to squelch his laugh as his eyes filled with tears. I said, "Robert, what is it? Did you see the snake?"

"No. Worse. Nudies. Lots of nudies."

I lifted myself over the hill and he was right. Several heavyset nudists were sunbathing. Some had apparently never heard of sunblock. William ran up for his look and started to laugh hysterically. The nudies looked back at us in disgust. The three of us turned like madmen and ran back to Ann. We arrived breathless from the run and the laughter. She waited to hear what the commotion was all about. We began our stories. Her face changed as most women's do when they listen to their men: from amusement to horror to incomprehensibility. We told her about the viper and our brush with death and the cluster of nudies. I lay down on the shore with the Gard River running beside me, and as I started to fall asleep, I smiled with the knowledge that the human being is still the most dangerous animal of all.

William in the wilderness on the trail of something awful.

2.

FAQ

MY IQ INCREASED dramatically in 1995. I'm not talking about my intelligence. That was cooked in 1968. I am talking about my "interview quotient." Before 1995, I was rarely interviewed. I didn't become more interesting in 1995. I just finished shooting a television show called *Dweebs* for CBS. It was going to be put on the fall schedule. The network arranged for all of the actors to take part in what is referred to as a "satellite tour."

The satellite tour is like a lot of things in acting. It sounds far more interesting than it actually is. The actor shows up at a nondescript location. A room. Even a hallway will do. He or she sits on a metal folding chair and is sequentially interviewed by several dozen reporters from all over the world in about two hours.

The members of the press were always the same. They were affable and had no idea who I was. I was nervous. I couldn't help but wonder what handful of questions they would ask me. Were they intent on boiling me down to my essentials like my mother with a chicken? Did they have questions honed by time and experience that would pluck out the heart of my mystery? No. Not even interested. To a man (and woman), they smiled and said, "It will be painless. A few softballs. All routine. Nothing tricky." They would just hit me with some *fak*.

I nodded as if I understood, but I had no idea what *fak* was and if it was appropriate for them to hit me with it. Used in a sentence, *fak* sounded dirty. It sounded like something you would find at the bottom of a monkey cage. After an hour and a dozen reporters, I got the idea that *fak* was *fak*. It wasn't going to change. Its purpose was to reveal nothing. Sitting on my folding chair, the interviews began to feel like a curious exercise in indifference.

I was disappointed. I always imagined being interviewed would be a defining moment in my life as an actor. If it didn't mean I had arrived, at least it meant I had been cast.

During hour number two, I muscled up the nerve and asked a friendly and partially intoxicated interviewer from Australia what *fak* was, thinking if it was naughty, at least he lived on a different continent. He laughed and explained that *fak* wasn't a thing. It was three letters—FAQ—and it stood for Frequently Asked Questions.

"Really? It's initials?"

"That's right, mate. Shorthand. They call it an acronym."

"Like 'scuba'?"

"Right."

"You're kidding," I said.

The interviewer laughed. "I wouldn't do that to ya."

I was fascinated. FAQ became a mystery. Not the "question" part of it, but the "frequently" part.

"Are these the questions people ask with great frequency?"

"I don't know. I expect so."

"Why?" I asked.

"A way to get to know you, maybe?" His eyes were especially bright from a combination of the Foster's and the fact that this interview was different from the last fifteen he had done.

"But does anyone know me after these questions? 'What's your name? Where were you born? How long have you been an actor? What do you think of your part?' Do people want to know these things? Seems kind of unimportant."

My Aussie interviewer looked at me over the tops of his black-framed glasses as he took notes with more vigor. "What questions would you ask? With frequency?"

I rocked back in my folding chair. I looked at his open face. "If I was the interviewer I would ask you: who was the first person you ever fell in love with?"

The interviewer flushed red. He smiled and shook his head. He thought about it for about half a second. "Lord. That would have to be Sally. Sally Carmichael."

"When did you meet Sally?" I said.

He started laughing and looking at the ceiling. "Ten. I was ten."

"And what was it about Sally that did it for you?"

He looked me in the eye. He leaned forward as if he were revealing an age-old secret. "Her laugh. She had a great, good sense of humor. She brightened up the room. Her hair was blond and always had a perfect little curl to it. I got the nerve one day to walk her home. I have never had such a good time with a girl as on that twenty-minute walk to her house."

"Where is Sally now?"

"Married. Three children. Lives in another town. I tracked her down and wrote her last year."

I started laughing. "Did she write you back?"

He nodded.

"Did you learn anything more about her?"

He nodded again. "Yeah. She still remembers the walk." He blushed.

An employee of CBS came by and said that our time was up and there were other interviews scheduled. We stood and shook hands and wished each other good luck. The afternoon continued. Inundated in a sea of FAQ.

―――――――――

ACCORDING TO THE reporters at the satellite tour, the answers to my most frequently asked questions would be: Stephen Tobolowsky.

Dallas, Texas. Yep. Born there. Yes, Cowboys fan. Six foot three. And I have been a professional actor most of my working life.

Well, stop right there. To be fair, that's somewhat interesting. There aren't many professional actors walking around. And I am an actor that works *in* show business. That's even more unusual. You can never be too sure when an actor says they're working, what they really mean.

Case in point: in 1972, my girlfriend, Beth, and I did summer stock in upstate New York. We were doing a production of *A Midsummer Night's Dream* when Jack (who shall remain otherwise nameless) left our company because he had gotten "a job on Broadway in *Pippin*." We had a big good-bye celebration for him. He said the next time we were in the city, we should see the show and come back to the stage door afterward to say hello.

We took him up on the offer a couple of months later. Beth and I went to *Pippin*, but Jack was nowhere to be seen. We went to the stage door and asked for him. The guard called back for Jack. He showed up wearing elbow-length black rubber gloves. I told him we enjoyed the show but missed him onstage. I asked if he was in the chorus. Beth asked if he was disguised as a mushroom or a tree.

Jack was not amused. He said he never claimed he was *in* the show. He said he worked *on* the show. He was in charge of giving enemas to the animals that appeared onstage so they wouldn't have an accident during a musical number and horrify the audience.

Pause.

There have only been a few times in my life when I have been speechless. In this case it was the combination of horror, surprise, and curiosity as to how much the job paid and if they offered it to me, would I take it.

Jack was rightfully offended by whatever look we had on our faces. He hit us with a now classic rejoinder: "Hey, at least I'm on Broadway." Jack and his rubber gloves taught me never to trust an actor when they say they're working.

For years I have assumed that one reason why I am not frequently asked interesting questions is that I am a character actor. Even though I have been in hundreds of shows, I am not famous by any unit of measure. You would recognize me if you saw me in line at the coffee shop. Not necessarily as an actor. There is a fifty-fifty chance you might think that I was the guy who used to work there. Or a science teacher at your high school. Or the man who sold insurance to your parents. In Canada, one man came up to me on the street thinking we had played hockey together.

I was premiering my film *Stephen Tobolowsky's Birthday Party* at the HBO Comedy Festival in Aspen in 2005. As a sociological experiment, I asked strangers on the street if they had heard of Stephen Tobolowsky. They all had.

One man said he just read about Stephen Tobolowsky that morning. He was a serial killer in Denver about to be released from prison. There was a huge protest. Another man said that he thought that Stephen Tobolowsky was the real name of a popular porn star, someone named Rick "Hot Rod" Rocket. Unfamiliar with Mr. Rocket's work, I moved on. One woman had a kinder but equally incorrect view of the universe. She thought Stephen Tobolowsky was either a financial expert or a physicist who had just discovered something about time.

I liked that one.

Time has always interested me. We always tend to imagine time as a line of past, present, and future. But I don't think we experience it that way. In our lives, memory rarely serves as a measurement of time, but rather as a measurement of meaning. The associations we make are rarely linear. Time and memory combine to create an unpredictable picture. We never can know what moments will rise to the level of significance. The strangest, smallest things can become your evening star.

FAQ will almost always relate to work. I've been asked dozens of times over the years, "What was it like to perform on Broadway the first time?"

To tell the truth, my opening night on Broadway in 1982 is a blur. Not completely. I remember I wore blue boxer shorts. But the play and the applause, nothing. You would think, being an actor, that event would be central to my personal history. But it's not. Unpredictably, two events that happened when I was five years old dwarf my first night on Broadway. These memories are always with me.

I was five and had just proposed to the first girl I ever fell in love with, Alice Nell Allen. She was also five. I ran home and told my mother that I was getting married and would probably be leaving soon to start a family of my own. Mom took the news well. "That's nice," she said.

I dashed out of our kitchen screen door and ran across our backyard into the world. I was as excited as only a young man in love could be. I wanted to give my mother a gift to thank her for her kindness and support during my early, formative years.

Behind our house in Oak Cliff, Texas, was a tangle of wildness. There were fields and woods and a creek. But there was also a meadow that covered an entire block. It was filled with the most beautiful flowers I had ever seen in my life. They were red, and yellow, and orange.

I ran barefoot through the field at sundown to pick a bouquet. I came running back into the kitchen. I put my flowers in a glass with a little water and offered them to Mom. She looked down at me holding my flowers as she washed the chicken. "Stepidoors, those are just weeds. Those aren't nice flowers that you give to someone. Throw them away," she said. I couldn't move. Mom took the wildflowers out of the glass and tossed them into the trash.

I was devastated and embarrassed. My mother, though the kindest person I have ever known, could not have understood what those flowers meant to me. They were the most beautiful things I had ever seen, and I wanted to share that beauty with her.

A week later the land where the wildflowers grew was sold and plowed over. They started building homes on the lots. The flowers never returned. I looked for them for years, but they were gone. That was the last time I saw those reds, yellows, and oranges by our home. They entered the realm of memory, becoming a sort of evening star that warned me to protect what I loved.

Another important story comes from the same distant era. I'm afraid I need to explain some ancient history. Back then, in the early 1950s, kids walked. We walked everywhere. Or we ran or rode bikes. We were on our own a lot. I remember I had walked down to Daughtery's Drug Store to buy a candy bar and read comic books. Thick in the middle of the latest *Batman*, I noticed the sky had darkened. I thought I should head back. Texas was always prone to sudden and dangerous shifts in the weather. I didn't want to get caught in a thunderstorm.

I started to walk down the bumpy, tar-covered, two-lane road that led back home. I saw something about half a mile away that upset me. There was something wrong. I couldn't quite make it out. As I got closer I saw a car was leaning sideways on the shoulder of the road. I could smell smoke in the air.

I ran toward the wreck to investigate. Steam was coming from the radiator. I heard a noise and I saw movement and turned. There was a man lying by the side of the road. I froze.

He was wearing light blue pants and a light blue shirt and he had a black belt with a silver buckle. He whispered to me. "Buddy, come here." I obeyed. He said, "Help me here, buddy. I need to sit up."

I knelt beside the man and put my arms around him and helped him. He didn't have the strength to sit. I kept holding him. He said, "Thanks. I can't be lying there like that." A sudden stream of blood flowed out of his mouth onto his blue shirt.

I gasped. "You're bleeding."

"Don't worry, buddy. I'm okay. I don't hurt at all. So don't be scared. I may need to ask you for a favor."

I was trembling but said, "Yes, sir."

"I may need you to find my daughter. Her name is Diane. I may need you to tell her that I'm okay."

"Yes, sir," I replied.

I heard the sounds of tires screeching on the road behind me and footsteps running. A grown man in a light-colored jacket came up to me and said, "What happened?"

"I found him here," I said.

The injured man looked around at the scene. Other cars stopped.

More help ran over. He turned to me and said, "Buddy, I guess you can go on home now."

"What about your daughter, Diane?"

"Don't worry. It'll all be fine."

I handed my charge off to those more capable. I started to leave. I looked back at the man once more. He tried to gesture to me. I remember his pale blue eyes and his parting words, "Go on home now. And, buddy, don't be afraid."

I am sorry to say I have been unable to honor his request. I have been afraid. Often. When I asked Claire Richards to the prom. When I was held hostage at gunpoint in a grocery store. The first time I made love. Just about every audition I've had. And yes, opening night on Broadway in 1982. The list is too long. But I still see the man dressed in light blue—broken, in need of a doctor, worried for his daughter. Yet he spent a moment to quiet the fears of a child he happened to meet by the side of the road.

Of the many questions I have never been asked, one stands out as being significant. "What were the happiest moments in your life?" There are the obvious answers: when I fell in love, the birth of my children, the second time I married my wife, Ann—but there is one I have never mentioned.

Several years ago, I was in one of those periods in my life when happiness was hard to come by. I returned to Dallas to visit my family. I thought family would make things better—or not. My brother took me out on a bike ride to White Rock Lake and to have breakfast with his friends. I hadn't ridden a bike in ages. It was a beautiful day. I felt like I was flying. We crested a hill, and as if by divine gift I saw something that took my breath away. There, before my eyes, were my wildflowers—the reds, yellows, and oranges—acres and acres and acres of them in every direction. They were never gone. I just thought they were. I smiled for the first time in months, knowing they were probably here all along. I had just never ridden on the right path.

A question I frequently ask myself: why do I tell these stories? My answer: the mystery.

It is a mystery as to what makes us do what we do. It is the other side of the mystery as to what makes us who we are. One of my favorite philosophers, Epictetus, said that the only things we can control in our lives are what we are drawn to and what we are repelled by. Somewhere between the last field of wildflowers and the words of comfort from a dying man, there was something powerful that made me stop and take notice.

Telling a story is my way of living up to the high standards created for me by the woman in Aspen: to be the physicist who has come up with something new about time. It is the only way I know to make sense of the unpredictable. It is the only way I know to search for Diane.

3.

LOCAL HERO

MY FIRST ENCOUNTER with heroism was in the figure of Davy Crockett, ably portrayed by Mr. Fess Parker on Walt Disney's television program. Or miniseries. Or whatever it was. I don't think it was called *Walt Disney's Wonderful World of Color* yet. At that point in time, the world was pretty much in black and white. It was the mid-1950s. It was a time so simple, so innocent, that if you could time-travel and magically run an episode of *Celebrity Rehab with Dr. Drew*, millions of Americans would believe that they had died in their sleep and gone straight to hell.

Simplicity doesn't mean simpleminded. It just meant we didn't have cell phones, or computers, or automatic transmissions. We thought wrestling was real. We liked our symbols like we liked our scotch—straight up. Davy was a symbol. He wore the signature coonskin cap and lived in the woods with his wife, Polly. He had a friend, Georgie, played by Buddy Ebsen, in a pre–*Beverly Hillbillies* role. Through an eerie act of Hollywood precognition, Ebsen, as Georgie, was costumed almost exactly like Jed Clampett.

Davy was a great shot. Always. But when he wanted to shoot really well, he would lick his thumb and transfer the spit to the metal gun sight on the end of the barrel of his rifle. I tried this technique when

I was five, playing Cowboys and Indians. I would carry an imaginary rifle and lick my thumb and swipe it across the imaginary metal sight when I wanted to insure real accuracy with my imaginary bullets.

My father bought me a coonskin cap. I almost broke down into tears I was so happy. The cap and I were inseparable. Most photos taken of me when I was four and five feature me in this hat. But the hat was more than a fashion statement. It was also a symbol. A symbol of the heroic life. Of rugged individualism. Of personal skill. Of manhood.

On television, Davy had to combat men like Mike Fink. You knew they were bad because they had unappealing names and they never shaved. Shaving was a big part of heroism. The one contradiction to the shaving rule was the comic sidekick. For men like Buddy Ebsen and Gabby Hayes, spotty personal hygiene was an indication that despite their good nature and appeal, they had not achieved full hero status.

On television, Davy once had to hypnotize a bear to save a little boy. Even though Davy had a knife and gun, he knew violence was not always necessary. Not always the best way. Not when you had the powers of hypnosis. He knew the ways of the bear almost better than the ways of man.

Like most men, Davy was uneasy on the dance floor, but his wife, Polly, didn't mind. She knew learning bear hypnosis took time. Davy could only muster an awkward two-step. There were many endearing shots of Polly and Buddy Ebsen smiling and shaking their heads at Davy's poor but earnest attempts on dance night.

Davy went to Washington, D.C., as a congressman from Tennessee. They all made fun of his clothes and especially the coonskin cap. He was little more than a savage to those blowhards who were running the country. But Davy had a couple of powerful skills: reason and plain speaking. What could have been an embarrassing episode turned once again into triumph.

The television show was so successful Disney decided to cobble all three television movies into an actual motion picture called *Davy Crockett: King of the Wild Frontier*. Davy Crockett on the big screen.

This was better than butter pecan ice cream. It opened in downtown Dallas at one of the big theaters, the Tower or the Majestic. The line on that cold, cold Saturday morning had to have two or three hundred children, all in coonskin caps. All of us were there to see Davy Crockett. It included a new installment to the story: Davy Crockett at the Alamo! It sounded exciting.

God help us all.

We had no idea. It was like walking into an airplane propeller. None of us were prepared for the Alamo. The movie began innocently enough. There were bears, there was Polly, there were rasslin' matches, there were displays of gunmanship with the signature "licking of the thumb and transferring spit to the gun sight." There were rude, unshaven men bested by Davy.

And then there was more. There was a new character, Jim Bowie. He was well shaven. He carried a huge knife. He also knew his way around a bear. He told Davy about a place called Texas where a man could be a man. Davy listened with interest.

I was uneasy. This didn't make sense. Why Texas? Tennessee was fine. Tennessee had everything a man could need. Then the fever came and Polly died! Polly died! The fever? What was that? That wasn't on the television show! Buddy Ebsen tried to comfort Davy in his grief, but Davy was inconsolable. He left for Texas with Jim Bowie. That wasn't on the television show, either. Something was going terribly wrong.

Davy got to Texas. Frankly, it was not scenic. It looked a lot like the deserty areas of Southern California. There were no bears and no forests. Even worse, there were Mexicans.

The Mexicans were in control of Texas and almost none of them shaved. Davy ended up in a little mission church called the Alamo with a lot of other men. The cleanest of all of them was William Travis. He was almost a sissy he was so clean. He told the men that Sam Houston was trying to get an army together to defeat the Mexicans, and they had to stall the onslaught of Santa Anna at all costs. At all costs. My five-year-old brain could not grasp the significance of "at all costs."

The Alamo was not a good arena for Davy's skills. He couldn't use stealth, he couldn't rassle, bear hypnosis was useless. He was trapped in a little building. My anxiety level was rising. But then, hurray! Buddy Ebsen showed up full of irony and good humor. His presence gave me a sense that everything would be all right.

It wasn't. Buddy Ebsen got shot. In the heart. He died in Davy's arms. He tried to muster a smile as he died—ironic to the end. With his last breath, he said, "I'll say hello to Polly for you." I burst into tears. My little five-year-old heart broke.

Heartbreak was not what I had bargained for when I bought my ticket. Buddy Ebsen, the soul of decency and rural humor, was dead. But it was going to get so much worse. The Mexicans stormed the walls. Davy and Jim Bowie fought back to back. A pile of Mexicans formed at their feet. The camera started to pull away. What? The camera pull-away is what always happened at the end of a movie. Was this the end? Certainly Davy could not survive.

How could Disney do this to me? It wasn't just the end of a story. It was the end of a hero, of a coonskin cap. It was the end of someone I looked up to. Something with real meaning. It was the end of decency, of reason and plain speaking. It was the end of bear hypnosis and all mountain skills lost to the dusty books of time.

Without my hero, what would fill the void? Some of my friends had to wait for *Star Trek*. Others had to wait for *Star Wars*. Other poor souls still play numbly with their remotes, switching between *American Idol* and *Survivor*, hoping for something to replace the coonskin cap.

Two rival thoughts come to mind. One comes from Bertolt Brecht in *Galileo*. The play ends with Galileo renouncing his findings. A disheartened observer comments, "Unhappy is the land that breeds no hero." Galileo answers him, "Unhappy is the land that needs a hero."

Second is the truism from G. K. Chesterton in the early twentieth century: "When a man stops believing in God, he doesn't believe in nothing; he believes in anything."

UNDER THE CATEGORY of those doomed to believe in anything, in March of 1978 an amazing story emerged from Southern California. The story began as the simple escape of a pigmy hippopotamus from a San Diego wildlife park. But this story grew until it gripped the nation. Now, over thirty years later, the event has vanished into the ash bin of history. But these were powerful times to have lived through. I, for one, feel this history deserves resurrection.

One must cast one's mind back to the sunny days of the late seventies. Jimmy Carter was advocating multiculturalism and the neutron bomb. If you don't remember the neutron bomb, it was a weapon whose positive feature was that it killed people but left buildings intact. True to form, Carter is still in the housing business.

Multiculturalism is still with us, albeit in a mercifully limited form. Its main expression today is in the kind of take-out you can get in Los Angeles and New York—and the types of holidays celebrated in the Santa Monica School District.

Back in the late seventies, there was a deep belief that multiculturalism could catch on, like folk music in the sixties. In that fever, there was an attempt to find something African to bring to America. It wasn't going to be slavery this time. We didn't care for the famines, genocides, and plagues. But just about everybody agreed on the animals. We loved the animals.

Problem. We already had zoos. So what could we do? Answer: No cages!! We'd let the beasts roam free!! Like in Africa!! And the wildlife park was born.

The concept had limitations. The animals were dangerous so the park couldn't be near major population centers. It had to cover a large area to accommodate grazers such as rhinos and giraffes and antelope, so the only cost-effective way to create these parks was to grab up huge tracts of cheap, unusable land, like floodplains or the vast acreage under high-voltage towers.

The result was that visitors would have to drive long distances to a deserted, inhospitable area to see lions from the comfort of their cars. I know it sounds crazy now, but this was the late seventies.

The long drive time and ominous high-tension power poles meant a low volume of visitors. Consequently, the bottom line dictated that staff be cut to the minimum. People willing to deal with lions and fifty thousand volts often tend to have personal problems, like mild schizophrenia or heavy drinking.

Shake this cocktail up with a huge perimeter to maintain and you have the perfect prescription for a breakout. These parks were always susceptible to animal escapes. A band of chimpanzees escaped in Arlington, Texas, and lived off garbage for weeks. It was the subject of many crude jokes about the future birthrate in that area. The police weren't laughing. They set up dragnets to haul in the monkeys. It was rumored that not all of the chimps were caught. One of my friends joked that they nabbed a couple of them teaching at a local junior college.

In San Diego it was a single pigmy hippo named Bubbles who made her break for freedom. Bubbles escaped into the nearby suburbs and also lived on trash. The story barely got any play. After all, it was just a single little hippopotamus. How far could she get?

After a week, Bubbles was still free. The Los Angeles newspapers started carrying the story: "Bubbles Eludes Capture Again." "Wildlife Officers Bamboozled by Bubbles." They followed her trail, anticipated the garbage cans they thought she would raid, but she defied expectations again and again. She would double back, jump ahead, revisit old garbage cans right before garbage day. It was as though she had inside information.

They needed help. They brought in a hippo expert from the San Diego Zoo, one of the top zoos in the world. Interviews on television confirmed what we all began to suspect. Bubbles was one smart hippo. And thus she captured the imagination of the nation.

If there is one thing that runs deep in the human soul—if there's one thing that Disney can count on—it is that we are all suckers for smart animals. Television commercials have shown talking dogs and cats for years. Even though they mainly talk about food, litter, and occasionally insurance, we are still amused. A staple of the sitcom has been the pet that is smarter than its family. I was in the pilot of a sitcom in which the lead often talked to his rat for advice. A rat. For advice.

When you think about it, if the only issues that concern you are food and comfort, why not listen to your dog?

Sidenote: our household is no exception. We are beholden to our smart pets and always turn to them in moments of crisis. They are often the focus of our attention and concern. Once I made up an objective list of the relative intelligence in our home from smartest to the stupidest:

1. Blackberry (rabbit)

2. Ann (wife)

3. Bandit (cat)

4. William (eleven-year-old son)

5. Robert (sixteen-year-old son)

6. Thistle (rabbit)

7. Rosie (rabbit)

8. Stephen (me)

9. Campion (rabbit)

10. Fleury (rabbit)

11. Tugger (turtle)

In my defense I need to point out that I *never* have gone to Tugger for any advice or comfort.

But I digress.

Bubbles was not only a "smart" hippo, but a hippo that was

smarter than several humans, including a hippo expert. That was all the press and the public needed. Bubbles was becoming a folk legend.

San Diego TV news stations interviewed locals whose trash cans were knocked over and looted in the night. Bubbles's charm was evident by people laughing and smiling as they cleaned up the mess in their back alleys: "We heard a noise. Thought it was kids or something. Now they tell us it was a hippopotamus, I just don't know. Sounds crazy to me."

Articles about Bubbles appeared on the front page of papers all over California. "Day 12: Bubbles Still on the Loose!"

Apparently there was a system of swamps that Bubbles was ducking into as home base. The park rangers just didn't have the manpower to cover such a large area. And there was too much garbage to cut off Bubbles's food supply. The situation was getting out of control.

That's when the San Diego Sheriff's Department stepped into the picture. The solution? Shoot Bubbles. After all, Fish and Game couldn't handle the problem, the park rangers couldn't handle the problem, and no matter how cute a pigmy hippo was, she was still a wild animal. During the sheriff's interview they showed file footage of high-powered rifles being loaded with very long bullets.

Outcry! Explosion! Chaos! A cute story turned not so cute. It was unthinkable. Shoot Bubbles? The hippo had done nothing. She was just foraging. She had displayed no hostility. She just had a taste for trash. The midnight raids were amusing. To be ransacked by Bubbles was almost a bragging point. It was like hearing Santa on your roof on Christmas Eve. Now they were sending in lethal force?

The story went national. Animal rights activists had a face to go with their cause. And it was the face of a hippopotamus. People who had never protested anything, people who had missed out on Vietnam, were getting ready to march. Phone calls to newspapers, television stations, and houses of government streamed in.

The assassination of Bubbles was put on hold. There was an emergency meeting. Police met with government officials and animal experts. A new plan was hatched. A trap would be set. A tranquilizer dart would be used. If the tranquilizer didn't work, a dozen armed police would be ready to finish the hippo off.

I remember that day. I was doing children's theater with the Twelfth Night Repertory Company. We were driving in a carpool to our first school. All we could talk about was Bubbles. The subject touched on some archetypal nerve connected to our metaphoric midbrain. That responsible people would shoot Bubbles as a first option chilled us like the witch in *Snow White*.

Memories of Davy Crockett and the abusive Disney Corporation hung in the air. Could such horror be possible in a good world? I was the voice of optimism. I told my friends in the car, "Things like that don't happen. The animal park people and the zoo people are in charge. It was on the news. They'll use a tranquilizer dart."

Just the thought of a tranquilizer dart gave us comfort. All of us had grown up with Marlin Perkins and *Mutual of Omaha's Wild Kingdom*. Jim Fowler often used the tranquilizer dart. It was a good thing. He used it to relocate wild pigs that were tearing up a farm in Borneo. Once he used it to get a Bengal tiger to the animal dentist. It was about as close to a sure thing as exists in this world. Bubbles would be fine.

In San Diego the trap was set. A pile of garbage was laid out by the bank of the swamp. Animal control officers stood poised with dart guns a few yards away. Behind them, cops, armed with high-powered rifles.

In Los Angeles we performed at our first school. We ran out to the car afterward to hear the news. Nothing. No word of Bubbles.

The day wore on. No sightings. Not a word on the radio. I got home. My girlfriend, Beth, was in the bedroom switching channels for any updates. We sat on the bed and held hands fixated on the television screen. Finally, there was a news break in the early evening. Bubbles was dead.

My heart stopped. I went numb. Beth exploded into tears. I stared at the set stupidly. I was so sick and so sad. I couldn't even cry. I held my pillow and watched the report.

Bubbles was not shot by the police. She came out of the water and was shot by a zookeeper with a tranquilizer dart. She was scared and disoriented. She began running in panic. When the drug took hold, she fell on a tree stump. Animal Control ran to secure her. But she was heavy. Very heavy. The tree stump pushed against her diaphragm. She suffocated before they could lift her off of the stump.

The story gripped the world. Sorrow filled the hearts of everyone I knew. Children cried in school. Moments of silence were taken for Bubbles.

Protestors who had marched in San Diego to save Bubbles now carried signs: "Bubbles LIVES" and "Bubbles, we will NOT FORGET." One middle school in the area made a resolution to change their name to Bubbles Junior High School. The principal said that this event had stirred the student body unlike any in the school's history. He held an emergency meeting of students and faculty. The name change was voted in by acclamation. The principal said he was behind them all the way. The head of the student body was interviewed by the local media. She said that they felt Bubbles embodied all of the traits they hoped to embrace in adulthood: intelligence, resourcefulness, and the desire to be free. (They left out an insatiable taste for garbage.) The camera panned to rows of children, singing the new school song: "Hail, all hail, Bubbles Junior High."

Life went on in its predictable day-to-day way even though the heart of the day-to-day seemed not to beat anymore. In some way we felt like the world was no longer safe, no longer smiled, and certainly could not take a joke. It was probably the finality of it all—the death, the tears, the singing school children that contributed to the story being buried. Buried for about two months when a remarkable event occurred.

Tending the animals at the wildlife park, a worker saw a pigmy hippo coming out of the water. While shoveling dung he noticed the hippo's ankle bracelet. All of the hippos wore ankle bracelets with their names on it because one pigmy hippo looks like another pigmy hippo.

He called management. He called his coworkers. This news was big. The hippo that came out of the water was Bubbles! Bubbles! Bubbles was alive and still at the park!

All of the experts shook their heads at the apparent miracle. Then reality sank in. The hippo that escaped, that was killed, that was the focus of national news and consequently became a folk legend, was not Bubbles. Never was. After a quick head count in the hippo compound, they realized the escapee was a hippo named Rosie. Rosie was the unintended heroine.

This story slipped onto a back page of the first section of the *Los Angeles Times*. It was never on the TV news again, even though in my opinion, this story was even bigger. There was now a middle school in Southern California named after a *living* hippopotamus. A hippopotamus that had done nothing in particular but swim and eat. Imagine how upset Luther Burbank would have been to know his legacy was bumped for a sea cow, or more accurately, a "river horse."

It was a story that took on the moral power of what heroism is and what it is not. In a post–Davy Crockett universe we have hungered for meaning. In the void, we will hang our affections almost anywhere. The Bubbleses of our world are trumpeted on the front pages of our papers and on television—while the Rosies of our age toil, strive, live, and die unnoticed.

In my grandmother's front yard in Throop, Pennsylvania, with my constant companions: my coonskin cap and Betsy, my rifle.

4.

LAND OF ENCHANTMENT

As an actor I've worked in a lot of different places. I'm not special. It's part of the job. People get into acting thinking that it is a road to comfort. It's usually just a road to a Comfort Inn. The tradition of travel is so much a part of the profession that when I was fired from a television show, they gave me a suitcase as a parting gift.

Where you shoot a film almost never has a connection to the story. Everything depends on the budget. *Cold Mountain*, which takes place in the American South during the Civil War, was shot in Romania. Eastern Europe provided cheaper locations and a nonunion crew that could survive on vodka fumes.

A producer offered me a part in a movie about oil-rig workers in Houston, Texas. I was excited because I have relatives who live in the Houston area. But before the fantasy of visiting Walt and Syma became reality, he told me the movie would be shot in Cape Town, South Africa.

The Time Traveler's Wife was shot in Toronto, not because of any story elements but because the Canadian government gave the movie company money and tax breaks to shoot in some of the state-run insane asylums. I shot in three of them. You had to make sure you got off the elevator on the right floor on that shoot. One night, the wardens came into the dining hall with Tasers drawn and told us to stay in the cafeteria, as there may have been an escape.

Usually, when you work in exotic locales, the producers brief you on any local problems for your safety and to meet the requirements of their insurance policies.

In Jamaica, we were given insecticide to protect our feet and ankles from "cow ticks."

In Thailand, we were warned that feet are profane and can never be pointed at anyone. You can never point a shoe at anyone. You could never put shoes on the pillow of a bed. You could face jail time by going outside the hotel with your shoes on your head. Truth.

In Rio it was kidnappings, in Alabama you couldn't swim in the lake where they dumped medical waste, and my favorite of all was the Houston film shot in Cape Town. The producer told me the only local problem was if you jumped into any east-flowing rivers or streams. There was a small parasitic fish that could swim up your penis and live there forever. I didn't do that movie.

When I got cast in the 2007 film *Wild Hogs*, we were told we would be shooting in Santa Fe for a couple of months. This was remarkable. The movie took place in the United States. It was such a relief we didn't have to fly to Croatia. But the Disney people never called with any warnings about the exotic nature of the locale. I was unprepared. As a public service I'd like to give a brief advisory for anyone planning to spend time in the area.

The first big surprise I had about Santa Fe is that you can't get there. It is rumored to be the seventh-largest tourist destination in America, but there were no flights, not even an airport, or at least not a public one. The best you could do is get to Albuquerque, rent a car, and drive across the desert for an hour.

I drove to the hotel. Within thirty seconds I made my second discovery. There was no oxygen. Or at least not in normal amounts. I would have sold my soul for an Aqua-Lung. The city sits at about seven thousand feet above sea level. I wheezed from my car to my room. I had a phone message that they needed me at the location for a costume fitting. I wheezed back downstairs where a Teamster was waiting to take me to the set.

The set that day was up one of the local mountains at a national park situated at eleven thousand feet. As a point of reference the base camp for Mount Everest is at sixteen thousand feet.

On the way up the mountain, I got dizzy and nauseated at the same time, like when I was fifteen years old and made out with a girl who had just eaten a chili dog. I had been in town less than an hour and already I had altitude sickness. The makeup artist told me not to worry, everyone on the movie had altitude sickness. The assistant director warned me that besides the nausea, I might not be able to sleep through the night. He told me that to counteract this I needed to drink water constantly. It occurred to me that the "drinking water constantly" remedy was directly related to the inability to sleep through the night. I asked how serious the altitude sickness could get.

"Most people acclimatize in a couple of weeks. For some, it takes years. Rarely, someone gets HACE," he said.

My alarms went off. It came from my fear of acronyms. "HACE? What is HACE?" I asked.

"Severe altitude sickness. Marked by disorientation, bleeding in the brain, and death."

"Anything else I need to know about this place?"

"The coffee's great."

After a haircut and a costume fitting, a Teamster drove me back to the hotel. Certain I had a rapidly developing case of HACE, I decided to go out on the town before my brain started bleeding.

I drove to a nearby cluster of restaurants. I parked my car and strolled down the sidewalk. I was surprised by how many women seemed to live in Santa Fe. It was a ratio I could have used in high school. I heard someone shout my name. I turned around and it was Wendy, an old theater buddy from New York. She hugged me and pulled me into a bar for a drink. The bar was filled with women. The bartender was a woman. The busboys were busgirls. I was clearly in the minority. I asked Wendy if she noticed the strong female current. "You're kidding," Wendy said.

"About what?"

"Don't you know?"

"I guess not."

"Santa Fe is the lesbian capital of the world."

"Really? I didn't even know they had an election."

"Stephen, why do you think I'm here? This city is built and nurtured by lesbians. It's the lesbian burial ground."

"I had no idea, Wendy. Thanks for the heads-up."

Wendy finished her drink, gave me a hug, and vanished into the night. I headed back out to explore. The complexion of the city came into focus. It all made sense. Just like in music, when you pluck the fundamental tone, you start a string of sympathetic vibrations. I could see the societal effects of being in a culture dominated by lesbians.

All of the bars had names that paid homage to the empowered female, like "Sister Act" or "Cowgirls," instead of male-dominated bar names that for some reason often refer to playing cards, such as "Jack of Clubs" or "Joker's Wild."

Lots of lesbians in a culture meant lots of Volkswagens and minivans. For some reason, lesbians preferred boxy, slow-moving automobiles. They also seemed to spend a lot of time plastering them with bumper stickers. The stickers were spiritual ("In GODdess We Trust"), musical ("Madonna—Like a Virgin"), and nostalgic ("Kiss My Grits").

Instead of a Starbucks on every corner, there were unisex barbershops or clothing stores that sold sleeveless cowboy shirts.

Just when I thought I knew everything about the sexual proclivities of the city, I came across a building with the sign saying: "HUMAN RIGHTS COALITION: GAY, BI, AND PANSEXUAL."

I almost drove off the road. I stopped my car. I studied the sign to see if I just read it wrong. No, there it was: "PANSEXUAL." What was a pansexual? I'm no dummy. I am a man of the world. I was in the delivery room when my wife had a caesarean. I have a liberal arts degree. Maybe if I broke it down into its component parts. I knew a pan was either something I used in the kitchen to heat sausages or the Greek prefix *pan* meaning "everything or universal"—like pantheist, panorama, or pandemic.

I was reeling. How much sex were these people having? There wasn't enough oxygen here for me to climb a staircase, let alone search for other pansexuals to have pansex with. They clearly didn't want to be lumped in with bisexuals who by definition will sleep with anything that walks on two feet. Pansexuals considered themselves different. They had their own human rights center with their own name on the sign.

I tried to understand the needs of a pansexual. What were they in search of? Here is what I found out for the pan-curious out there. If my research is wrong, don't blame me. My only reference materials were the personal ads in a free newspaper.

If you believe in past lives, as do lots of people in Santa Fe, those past people inside you might have a different sexual orientation than you do. I am a white middle-aged man, but in one of my dream states I could be an aging stripper from the 1930s. If I were to have sex with my wife, it could be the stripper that's having sex with her and not me. My wife would then be having a lesbian affair behind my back. It's all very complicated, which is why they have to have their own human rights center. Bottom line: I'm not secure enough to be a pansexual.

If you are in Santa Fe for any length of time, you will be moved by its beauty, charm, and how uncomfortable the furniture is. The reason for this is the entire city has dedicated itself to celebrating the trappings of Native American culture. Many of the restaurants, hotels, spas, and movie theaters have chairs made of antler horns. You may have to sit on logs. You may have to crawl into stores built like teepees, and interact with salespeople wearing beads and feathers.

For the shoppers, Santa Fe has hundreds of stores. All of them sell turquoise necklaces. The soundtrack in the background of every hotel lobby, of every shopping mall, of almost every restaurant is that irritating, breathy, echoey Indian flute music. Even the original Native Americans got stoned on peyote to listen to that crap. I pleaded with the assistant manager of our hotel to switch to easy listening in the elevator. No avail.

And as the Native American languages were highly nuanced, it is almost impossible to read a menu in Santa Fe because of all of the adjectives.

For breakfast: Geronimo-style enlarged yolk, organic brown Copper Creek hen eggs with pinyon pine chipolata-smoked triage of peppers and fingerling range-wood-seared potatoes with Montezuma greens.

And at two dollars an adjective, it's pricey.

Santa Fe has the strictest drunk-driving laws in the country. And they need them. At several restaurants they didn't put tequila in the margaritas. The owner explained to me, "People would just drink it." I asked at the hotel bar if I could have a glass of wine at nine thirty p.m. on a Friday night. They told me "no." The bartender had a party to go to. This was not an aberration. I went to several bars that closed early. As my waitress speculated, "Most people here don't go to bars on the weekends. They prefer to drink in the privacy of their cars."

And finally, the spa scene deserves a mention. It is big business in Santa Fe. People come here from all over the world for health treatments.

The most talked-about of all the spas was a place called Ten Thousand Waves. They specialize in expensive massages where they put hot rocks on your back or rub you down in sea salt. They give you bathrobes and invite you to enjoy the clothing-optional coed hot tubs where you get to hang out with naked Japanese men.

When you arrive they give you a menu of facials. One of my favorites was a $125 half-hour facial massage utilizing extra-virgin olive oil, avocado, and pureed tomatoes. Why pay? I give myself one of these every time I eat a submarine sandwich. The most expensive massage was a $200 half-hour facial. The active ingredient was organic nightingale poop. For real. One of our makeup ladies got this facial. She reported that it was very nice. Not at all what she expected. What did she expect? I wondered. And if she expected dung to be rubbed into her face, why did she request it? Why did she pay for it? This sweet woman seemed to embody a mental pathology so disturbing that I can only describe it as very "Santa Fe" and just the thing you would expect in the Land of Enchantment. Just on a personal note: if you're going to pay someone to rub bird poop into your face, go ahead and spend the extra money for the organic poop. It's not the time to economize.

THE FIRST SCENE I shot in *Wild Hogs* took place in the desert. We shot it over three excruciatingly hot days. I had no lines. I had to sit on the wooden fence of a corral and watch other actors talk. I was what they call "background." That's a show business term for an "extra." Your purpose is to "fill the frame."

I could see from my lofty perch atop the corral that the camera was over two hundred yards away and pointed in the opposite direction. That's when I guessed I was not even "background." I was what's referred to as "deep background"—a show business term meaning "we probably won't see you in the shot but wear your costume just in case." One of the advantages of being deep background is you can text your friends during a scene and no one will notice.

I was playing the role of Sheriff Charley. I always hope that my character has a last name. There is an unintentional hierarchy in the parts written for actors. At the top are parts Harrison Ford gets: Richard Kimble, Han Solo. These characters have first and last names. Writers have thought about these characters a lot. Consequently, during the movie, Harrison Ford characters do almost anything: eat, sleep, read the newspaper, drink coffee, shower (from the back only, waist up), get dressed, drive to work, shave, run for their lives, shoot guns, deliver stirring oratory to alien warlords.

The next level of characters in a script are called by one name and a job description. Interestingly enough, in comedies you are more likely to get the job description and a *first* name: here I was Sheriff Charley. In my career I have also played Ranger Bob, Ringmaster Bob, Dr. Ted, Dr. Bob, Father Jon, Father Joe (actually, the two Fathers were the same part in two different versions of the same movie: *Trevor*). Once in a TV movie, *Last Flight Out*, I was Tim for the first part of the script and Jim for the last part. Richard Crenna, the funniest man who ever lived, would always call me TimJim during all our scenes. No one noticed.

In a drama you get the job description and the *last* name: Agent MacLaren, Dr. Andross, Detective Keefe. I'm not saying this rule is hard and fast, but it happens a lot. Usually, if the writers have not imagined you with two names, they have also not imagined you with a car, a girl, or a life. They have just imagined you as a vehicle to get someone with two names from point A to point B (or point R to point S, as the case may be).

There is a level beneath the characters with one name. These are characters with no name at all. And I've played these, too. Sometimes it's just the job description. I have played TV Clerk, Professor, Doctor, Hotel Clerk (I almost got fired from that one), and the unforgettable Butt-Crack Plumber.

The only thing worse than characters with just a job description is a character with a job description and a number: for *The Love Bug 2*, I read for and did not get the role of Cop #2. But I have played Homeless Person #2, Teacher #3, Government Man #2. These roles are so low on the totem pole, you are sometimes mistaken for the cleaning crew and chased off the set.

So, as I was saying, in this scene, I was sitting on top of a six-foot-tall circular corral watching our leading characters, played by Tim Allen, John Travolta, and Martin Lawrence, slap a live bull on the ass and try to run out of the ring without getting killed.

A crucial element in shooting a scene such as this safely is the principle that to the human eye all bulls look alike and can be substituted at will.

We had four bulls. Bull One had a name. He was Zorro. Zorro was a huge old bull. He was extremely docile. Practically catatonic. You could hit Zorro in the head with a shovel and he wouldn't move. This bull was put in the ring when the real actors had to be in the same shot with him. I was shocked near the end of day one when the bull wranglers told Walt Becker, our director, that they would have to switch bulls. Zorro was getting tired.

Tired? All Zorro ever did was stand and chew. He would do that off the set. I was curious as to what the warning signs were that Zorro was near exhaustion. I asked the bull wrangler. It turned out to be a matter of science. Because Zorro was black (as were all the bulls), he was absorbing heat (it was 104 degrees that day). The wrangler noticed Zorro was sticking his tongue out farther than usual when he licked his own face. That was a sign of dehydration. It was advised that he be removed from the ring.

I had to agree with the wrangler. I was sitting on the fence in the sun, and I was only wearing brown. I was absorbing a lot of heat, but I never thought to lick my face.

Buddy replaced Zorro.

Designated as Bull Two and termed "slightly more aggressive" than Zorro, Buddy would whirl his head around at approaching actors. So for safety, one of his front feet had to be tied with a length of chain and nailed into the ground with a spike.

We got some usable shots with Buddy until he got tangled in his chain and started to trip over his front feet. At that point the primary actors went to the air-conditioning of their enormous trailers. We resumed shooting with stunt doubles and Bulls Three and Four.

Bull Three had no name other than Bull Three. His minders described him as the "aggressive but smart" bull. He would kick and snort and bellow and then mount a single charge before looking for a way out of the ring. I'm not sure what part of that was "smart."

I should mention that all of the bulls, smart or otherwise, were given commands with a single word: "Bull!" The bull wrangler yelled this at full volume. It meant a variety of things, including "Go," "Stop," "Don't," "Do," "Now," and "Look out, everybody, a bull is loose!"

Bull Three was good for getting the actual footage of a bull charge, but he steered clear of humans so he was not good for shots of a bull nearly goring our leading actors or stuntmen. For that, we needed Bull Four.

Bull Four was the "highly aggressive" bull. He was a full-sized, fire-breathing, murderous, man-eating bull. He bellowed. He roared. There was nothing in his eyes but mayhem.

The scene was going to be the release of Bull Four into the ring with the three stuntmen resembling our lead actors—and me, sitting on the corral fence watching. I was concerned that I was the only person without a stunt double. But then again, I was Sheriff Charley. One of the downsides of not having two names is that usually you don't get a stunt double.

John, the first assistant director, came up to me. "Stephen, I'm not going to tell you anything that isn't just plain old common sense. When we release the bull he's going to see you on this fence. I figure you'll have about six to seven seconds to jump off the fence and get clear before he reaches you. Anything on the inside of the ring will be crushed, fingers, feet, legs, anything."

I looked across the ring at Bull Four. He was looking at me and snorting. I performed a mental calculus like a professional golfer with a thirty-foot putt. I estimated the size of Bull Four, adjusting for his stride when angry, as plotted against the diameter and slope of the bullring. I looked at John and said, "More like five seconds— five seconds before he reaches me." John looked back at the ring and agreed. "Yeah. More like five. Anyway, I just want you to realize that it won't be instantaneous. You have time. Be careful. Don't rush and fall *into* the ring. Five seconds is plenty of time to get clear."

They started all seven cameras, yelled, "Action!" and released Bull Four. I heard the roar. I felt the vibrations through the ground. I saw a cloud of dust and Bull Four heading straight for me. I swung my legs up and over the fence. Three seconds. I landed on a slight down slope and fell away from the fence. Four seconds. Bull Four recognized no barriers like fences and at five seconds, he slammed into the corral where I had been sitting. The force of the impact shattered the four-by-four timbers. Bull Four's impact pushed the entire corral a foot toward me. He eyed me angrily through the slats of splintered wood. He wasn't thinking, "I'll get you," or "Just you wait." It was more vacant like, "Fence. Hard. Oh. You, deep background."

During the shooting, one stuntman was hit by the bull and flung out of the ring. The other two barely made it over the fence. I then witnessed something I had never seen during the shooting of a film.

The stunt coordinator approached the director and said that there was time for another run with the bull. They had enough daylight, the bull was still "fresh," and the injured stuntman wanted to give it another try. Walt Becker considered for a moment and said, "I don't know. The guy can hardly walk, the other two stuntmen barely got out of the ring. I don't know. I have a bad feeling about this. I say we call it a day."

I tip my hat to Mr. Walt Becker, erring on the side of safety. I knew at that moment the movie was going to be a success. The angels were on our side.

The next morning on the way to the set, in the distance I saw a swirling cloud of dust by the corral. Then sheer pandemonium. Extras were running for their lives. I heard screams. Then, through the dust, I saw three galloping cowboys going in every direction at once. The crowd of fifty or so people started running toward our Jeep. Then I saw horns. A bull was loose. It was running wild through the terrified mass of people and tables and camera equipment with three wranglers with lassos on horseback in pursuit. We stopped the Jeep. The bull charged toward us. He had a desperate energy. I recognized the glint in his eye. It was the smart bull. Bull Three.

One of the riders at full gallop lassoed the horns and pulled hard. The bull stopped and turned and gored the horse in the ribs. The horse reared, blood streamed down its side. The cowboy never gave up but continued pulling the rope tighter. Other cowboys got their ropes on the bull's horns. They backed their horses up until the ropes were pulling in three different directions. The bull stopped. The wranglers ran in and led the bull back to its pen. Everything was still, and then everything went back to normal as we started to get ready for the next shot.

I had to find out if the horse survived. I saw the cowboy over by some rocks taking a drink from a canteen. I asked him how his horse was. He turned around and pulled off his hat and a cascade of blond hair fell down like in the movies. He was a she! She was the cowboy bull roper. She smiled. The horse was fine. She had cleaned up the wound and was giving him the day off. She'd be riding him tomorrow. I was relieved. I asked her how she got in this line of work.

"Oh. My granddad taught me how to ride. Been riding my whole life."

"Was your granddad a cowboy, too?" I asked.

She laughed. "No. An actor. His name was Fess Parker. He played Davy Crockett. Maybe you saw him when you were a boy."

I said, "I did. I still have a picture of me in the hat."

"Did you have the rifle, too?"

"Yes, ma'am."

She licked her thumb and moved it across her invisible gun sight.

I smiled and headed back to my trailer, ready for another day of deep background, feeling that the world was a little safer.

Davy Crockett rides again.

5.

THE ALCHEMIST

WE DON'T CHOOSE our memories. Our memories choose us. Why certain thoughts rise to levels of importance and others vanish is not entirely obvious to me.

I will always remember the night in Boston when my father punched a bus. People could remember their fathers for lots of reasons. Dad taught me the alphabet. He would give me a different letter on a small chalkboard every day on his way to work. Then I would ask for something that became known as a "puffed cheek kiss." He would fill his mouth with air and puff out his cheeks, and then I would kiss his cheek while he let the air out with a sort of expelling-air-but-not-quite-farting sound that made me laugh. And then I would demand that we do it again. And again. And again. Until he protested that he "had to go to work."

When I was ten, Dad took me to the Lions Club midget go-cart races and put me in charge of the concession stand. I was ten! In charge of a concession stand! Talk about having the fox watch the henhouse. It may have demonstrated questionable judgment on his part, but it was great. There I was, unsupervised, in charge of taking in money and dispensing candy bars, popcorn, corn dogs, unlimited cola, and soft-serve ice cream. I went through half a box of soft-serve cones within the first hour. I was my biggest customer. And I was free.

The head of the event came over, red-faced, and scolded me. I don't remember ever having been scolded by an adult other than my father or a teacher. It was a good preparation for television directors, but I didn't know that at the time. He told me he was going to "count cones on me." If I was short, I would have to pay him for each ice cream eaten.

Dad was embarrassed. I let him down. I was scared. I was ashamed—for about seven minutes. Then I figured out I could get around the prohibition on eating ice cream by just avoiding the cones altogether and dispensing the soft serve directly into my hand. No cone. No trail. No problem.

But if you were to ask me at a party what event I remembered most about my dad, it would be the snowy night in Boston. We were crossing the street. A bus waiting for the light inched forward into the crosswalk and Dad whirled around and punched it. He punched the bus. To the bus's credit, it stopped. Not from the force of the blow but from the shock of the bus driver that some man would give a right hook to his bus's grill.

Now why has that memory chosen me? Out of all the little, and the big, and the wonderful, and the sad moments I could remember—why this one?

Bertolt Brecht in his book *Development of an Aesthetic* wrote about creating the *gestus* for a character in a play. The *gestus* was the character-logical gesture. It was the single external act that represented the character's hidden inner life. Maybe the swing at the bus was my dad's *gestus*. Possible meanings of the gesture could be: he always felt he was fighting against something bigger than himself, his willingness to protect his family at any cost, his hatred of mass transit. Who knows?

The Talmud, the set of Jewish holy books second in importance to the Bible itself, suggests that you have to use great care in interpreting some dreams, that often the explanation of a dream is more powerful than the dream itself. The interpretation can become true, even if it is wrong. Using that as a caution, I will refrain from trying to divine why the memory of the bus and Dad is so important to me. It is enough to say that it is.

I have two strong memories of my mother. The first was on my twenty-seventh birthday. I was still depressed from the death of Bubbles, the pigmy hippopotamus. I was in Los Angeles where I was doing a children's theater production of California's Spanish heritage for the public school system. I took off the sombrero for a few days and flew to Dallas for the big celebration.

We had a sort of ritual for birthdays. The birthday boy or girl would pick his or her favorite restaurant. Like most families, we went to a narrow range of eateries. Our family was enamored of "all-you-can-eat" restaurants. Texas was big on all-you-can-eat. The idea is similar to the cattle trough. You come in, pay one price, and eat until you rupture your peritoneum. There was The Shed, which was all-you-can-eat steak. Pedro's was another favorite, which was all-you-can-eat Mexican. And Big Chinese Restaurant, which was all-you-can-eat Chinese.

The Shed was rumored to serve what the waiters called *retreads*. These were steaks that were on other people's plates but were not eaten. Rather than waste food, they put the slightly used steak on your plate, rewarmed it, and wha-la, retread. That was the risk you ran if you went to The Shed. I never thought the idea of getting retreads was that bad. It was like eating at home. You would just wait until your sister got up from the table to get something to drink and you would take something off of her plate and eat it before she got back. No harm, no foul.

Pedro's was worse. They got busted for serving dog food in the enchiladas. We had to stop going there. With the temporary closure of Pedro's and the bad rep of The Shed, all of the all-you-can-eat diners headed for Big Chinese Restaurant. They were swamped. What good is a big Chinese buffet if your access to the egg rolls is blocked by several three-hundred-pound people in front of you? It was like playing against the Green Bay Packers without a helmet.

I decided to buck tradition. I decided I would not go to an

all-you-can-eat for my birthday dinner. I chose Vincent's Seafood Restaurante. Vincent's was as swanky a place as I had ever eaten at in Dallas.

Slight digression. My father never gave me the "sex talk" when I was a young man, but he did give me the "restaurant talk" about what restaurants to avoid because they will overcharge you. The list went something like this:

Avoid:

1. Any restaurant with linen tablecloths.

2. Any restaurant where the waiters wear jackets.

3. Any restaurant with an *e* at the end of the word "restaurante."

4. Any restaurant where they charge for refills of iced tea.

Vincent's had them all. But what made Mom almost choke on her saltine was when I ordered an appetizer. I could have been the first Tobolowsky in history to order an appetizer. The appetizer was bread at all-you-can-eat places. They gave it to you for free and kept it coming. At Vincent's I ordered a half dozen oysters. On the half shell.

As far as Mom was concerned, this was not the act of a rational mind. I'm sure she chalked it up to my being an actor or the corruption that comes from living in California. And she was probably right on both counts. They brought the oysters on a bed of rock salt. I offered Mom one. She looked at me as if I had handed her a bucket of snot. She declined.

I ate my oysters, dipped in red sauce, in silence. As we waited for our main course, Mom reached over and started grabbing the empty oyster shells off of my plate and stuffing them in her purse.

I almost choked on my Tabasco. The following conversation happened in a tense, rapid whisper:

"Mom, what are you doing?"

"I'm taking the oyster shells."

"Why?"

"I'm taking them home. If we are going to pay five dollars for what amounts to a plate of salt, I'm not going to waste the shells."

"What do you mean, 'waste the shells'? You can't use the shells. Nobody uses the shells. They have oyster liquid on them. How are you going to use the shells?"

"I can make a soap dish out of them."

"Soap dish? We don't need a soap dish. Nobody takes the shells home to make a soap dish."

"I can make buttons out of them."

"Buttons! Who makes buttons? You've never made a button in your life. Don't you need some kind of button-making machine? You just buy buttons at the dime store. Leave the shells. Mom, if you take the shells everyone will think you're crazy."

She returned the shells to my plate of salt, grudgingly.

Mom was the epitome of wackiness in a good-hearted way. My brother, Paul, told me about the time he had a one-hour layover at the Dallas airport. Mom drove out to see him. In the brief meeting, she brought him out to her car, tied a tablecloth around his neck, gave him a haircut, fed him his favorite dinner (pot roast), and pulled out the family cat for him to pet before he had to rush in and be on his way to Austin.

A second memory of Mom. It was twentysome-odd years later. I was lucky. I got a job shooting a movie in Dallas. I decided to bring our youngest son, William, with me so he could hang with his grandparents. William was five. Mom volunteered to do baby duty while I worked. At this stage of his life, William loved turtles. He loved turtles more than about anything, so Mom decided to take him to Turtle Creek where the chances of seeing a turtle were high.

When I got home from the shoot that evening, I walked into a lot of excitement. Mom ran up to me and said, "Stephen, we had such a good day! We were walking through the park along the creek. It was so beautiful and there were so many ducks and swans and— we found an egg!"

Mom led me around the corner. She had converted our breakfast area and part of our living room into a makeshift hatchery. She had pulled a little table from the garage. She found a small basket and filled it with newspaper and strips of soft cloth. She took Dad's reading lamp and had it tilted into the basket for warmth. I took a peek. Lo and behold, there was an egg.

William was watching the egg with fascination. He whispered that its mother had left it. It would die unless we gave it a home. Mom said that it seemed like the only right thing to do.

William instructed us that we had to turn the egg to help it hatch. Mom explained she had been turning the egg every hour. William nodded with authority. That was right. You had to turn the egg. We all took turns turning the egg that evening.

I was shooting the film for about a week more. Seven days. Seven days spent in egg turning, egg checking, egg speculating. Mom would get up throughout the night to turn the egg. I would lie awake at night certain that one morning we would wake up and find some kind of mallard on the breakfast table.

William talked about the egg constantly. He said we had to make certain that when the baby was born we didn't touch it because that would put "human smell" on it and no other birds would come near him.

I asked him, why in God's name did they take the egg in the first place? Taking the egg from the creek put "human smell" on it. And now we were stuck. If it hatched we would have a human-smelling bird that would be lonely all of its life or Mom and Dad would be stuck taking care of a wild bird in the backyard. Dad piped in quietly, "Or eating it." That didn't help. William was upset. Mom felt guilty.

I took Mom aside and told her that there was one solution. We had to get the egg back to the creek before it hatched so its mother could find it and take proper care of it (wink, wink, nudge, nudge).

Mom and William came with me to the creek to pinpoint the area where they discovered the egg. It was a busy day. There were lots of picnickers, lots of hand-holders, lots of bike riders. Very few birds.

Mom and William became unsure of the exact area where they

snatched the egg. William was now upset that if we just put it on the ground, the mother would never find it. It was tantamount to bird murder.

We drove home with the egg. It went back into the nest and for our final days in Dallas the routine continued. William felt sure that the egg moved. I don't think it did.

The day arrived when we had to go back to Los Angeles. William wanted the egg to go back with us. Mom hinted that it was probably the best thing to do. I called my wife, Ann, at home and told her we were bringing back a charge. She wanted to know if it was alive. "Sort of," I said.

When we got back to Los Angeles, Ann took over from Mom and built a makeshift incubator using my older son Robert's reading lamp aimed at a small basket filled with shredded cloth and newspaper. William explained about turning the egg and "human smell." Ann sighed and went to look up the gestation period of various ducks and geese to get an idea how long this period of our lives could last.

Time dragged on. After five weeks we were both sure that the egg was a goner, but we were unsure as to what to do. We decided to throw the egg away. If there was a crisis, we would tell William that we took the egg to the Los Angeles River where we saw a family of ducks, and we put the egg by the water and when we left the ducks were waddling toward the egg. In other words, we would lie.

But on the way to the trash bin, the egg was dislodged and it fell onto the concrete driveway. It cracked. And to our amazement—we discovered—it was a hard-boiled egg from someone's lunch.

For six weeks we had guarded, warmed, turned, protected, took field trips with, flew cross-country with, spent sleepless nights fretting over someone's lunch.

I called Mom with the news. She took it in stride. The time she spent protecting the dream of her grandchild was time well spent.

I have no idea why the thousands of days and troves of far more significant moments graciously recede before this memory of my mother, William, and the egg.

If I were a reader of dreams living in Talmudic times, I could venture a guess. I would say that both of these memories of Mom show the common thread of a woman who had a close relationship to the miraculous: someone unafraid of making buttons out of oysters and wild birds from picnic baskets. For my brother, Paul, she could turn the front seat of an Oldsmobile into a family home complete with a cat and a pot roast. She was an alchemist who maybe, on occasion, could spin common cloth into gold.

———

I AM ALWAYS amazed and confused when the government appoints a committee to get to the bottom of something. In the political world there is comfort in putting what we call "certainty" in the hands of someone else. It's understandable. Sometimes everything you know is wrong.

My son William attended a co-op preschool. It was outdoors in a fenced-off area of a city park and all of the parents took turns being teacher's assistants. In translation, that meant washing hands, taking to the potty, and keeping the little ones from hitting each other with folding chairs.

There was one five-year-old boy who had a regular routine. He would arrive at school. He would run into the toy shed and emerge five minutes later in a dress, feathered hat, and pearls. He would sling a purse over his shoulder and start pushing a baby carriage around. The teacher never said a thing about it. None of the kids said anything about it. They just kept running around throwing dirt at one another. None of us "teacher's assistants" said anything, either. We would just look at each other. And through that eye contact—in a millisecond—entire volumes were exchanged. And in that exchange came the precious commodity called certainty. We were certain we knew all about this little boy—his past, his present, and his probable future walking the runway during Fashion Week in New York.

One day the little fellow was in a corner of the yard trying on some new jewelry and a pair of heels that matched his purse, when his mother sat down on the bench next to me. She smiled and sighed. Her voice filled with emotion: "It's so dear. Look at him. It's amazing."

"Yes. Amazing," I said.

"He's our miracle child. See, we had a daughter. She died when she was eleven months old. It was the end of me. My husband and I were inconsolable. We thought we could never live through it. We always kept our daughter's room just as it was. Then I got pregnant again, and we had a boy. And when he was old enough to crawl, he went down the hallway and pushed open our daughter's door. He would spend hours in there playing, and laughing, and talking. He would go into her closet and drawers and pull out her clothes and try them on. I knew it was the spirit of my daughter telling us she was still with us. And whenever I see him at school putting on those dresses, I know she is here, too. She's with us every day. It's a miracle."

I took a breath. If you put me in a room for a hundred years with a typewriter and a million monkeys I would not have come up with that story.

And I'm not sure how much of a miracle it was. Whatever your read on it, be it a scenario for a Hallmark movie, or *The Twilight Zone*, or just another large file in a social worker's office—the important words here are *I'm not sure.* Certainty was gone. Everything I thought I knew was wrong.

We are bombarded constantly by supposed facts seducing us with that thing we like to call certainty. Don't get me wrong. I like certainty. But I'm starting to think it's not the bedrock we need to build our lives on. It's more like Fritos: a comfort food best taken in small doses while drinking a beer and watching the game.

The area that specializes in certainty is science. It's funny how much trust we put in science when its track record throughout history has been so bad. The problem is that science not only tries to describe the observable, like the tides and the height of mountains, but also the unobservable.

I read in a science magazine that human beings send out an invisible DNA message through our eyes containing thirty-three different sexual signals. This happens within a fraction of a second upon meeting potential mates. The message includes body characteristics, sexual preferences, and ranges of desire.

It's believable. This would explain why I almost never had a date in high school. It meant that it was impossible to hide from women that I possessed the "love handle" gene.

The article tried to explain the science behind "love at first sight," that it was not an emotional thing at all but a rather amazing form of genetic communication that established sexual compatibility. The essence of the article seemed to offer a bargain. Trade one invisible thing for another invisible thing, with certainty. Trade in love, and we'll give you genetics.

I have come to believe that in our lives we have to accept some form of the invisible—with certainty. Some are easy, like gravity. Cavemen accepted that if they dug a hole deep enough a mammoth would fall into it. And dinner is served.

Other things are not so easy. Since the whole truth is not always available to us, we have come to use an alternate system of perception: intuition. Intuition told me there was something wrong with the way my front door looked when I came back from a New Year's party. I opened it to find my house ransacked. It told me to take a kitty from a rescue-cat woman because of the look in its eye. And I was right. It proved to be an excellent kitty.

I never get phone calls from Judy. Never. She's my sister-in-law. I was on my way to exercise class when my leg started vibrating. I pulled out the phone and saw the digital ID: Judy's cell. In that millisecond my blood ran cold. That's when I became aware of the certainty that bad news travels fast. I answered the call. "Stephen, it's Judy, your mother's had a heart attack."

"I'll be on the next plane."

When I got to Dallas, Mom was in the ICU. She was asleep. I had brought my book and a portable radio, figuring it could be a long day. As I sat there with Dad, I remembered my last trip to Dallas.

Mom had been developing Alzheimer's disease over the past few years. I don't know enough about it to know what stage she had reached. She hadn't been able to read for a long time because she couldn't follow a story or remember the characters. In the evenings her memory traveled in a sixty-second loop. She would ask me if I wanted some grapes or some hot tea. And if the temperature in the house was too hot or too cold for me. And then she would ask me again. And again. And again. And I would get impatient and ask her politely, but not lovingly, to sit down. And as awful as that trip was a few months ago, sitting now, in this hospital room, I would have given anything to be back in our living room with her asking me about grapes and tea.

She didn't wake up that day. I read and listened to the radio and talked to Dad. My brother, Paul, came. We sat grimly. Paul is a doctor. He would look at the monitor providing readouts of her vitals: her heart, her blood pressure, her blood chemistry. He pointed out numbers. Science had reared its head. I was fixated on the screen now, too, looking for a positive change.

We went back to the house for a break before the evening watch. And even though there were three grown men walking around the living room, there was a palpable emptiness. Something invisible.

We went back to the hospital about nine in the evening. We were going to check in on Mom and then go out to eat. Paul and I were discussing Mexican versus Italian versus Cheap Italian, when a buzzer went off and nurses started running. They ran into Mom's room. We all understood something terrible was happening.

She had another heart attack. They kept us out of the room while they performed emergency procedures. I was certain at that point in time that we were not going to have dinner at all. After about an hour her doctor came and talked to us. He said she had stabilized and her heart was beating normally again. He would monitor her through the night. We should go home and get some rest. We would "keep our fingers crossed" that she would be better in the morning. The "fingers crossed" bit was a disturbing lack of certainty from a man of science.

The next morning we arrived at the hospital at about seven. As we got off the elevator, one of the nurses looked at me. In her look a thousand pieces of information were transferred through our eyes: "It was a bad night and it's going to be a bad day." In that instant I knew that this was the day my mother would die.

We rounded the corner and there was her doctor. He looked at us with what I call a "golfer's smile." Even when a golfer makes a putt, his smile is usually turned down in the corners like a partial frown. He knows there's a water hazard on the next hole. The doctor told us it was a bad night. We should go in and say our good-byes. She may only have a few minutes.

Minutes?

We walked in. She looked so small in the bed. Unconscious. The monitors showing a weakened heart along with a lot of other numbers that meant nothing to me but made my brother raise his eyebrows and look at me with terrifying certainty.

My sister was flying in from South Carolina where she worked at the university. Our hopes had been reduced. We just wanted Mom to live long enough for Barbie to get here. And in my heart, now, I would have given anything to sit in a hospital room yesterday reading Charles Dickens with Mom sleeping, thinking about eating Italian food and wishing I were back in our living room smiling and saying with kindness that the room was comfortable and the tea was good.

My cell phone rang. It was my sister. She was at the Dallas airport and on her way to the hospital. I told Paul, "Barbie's here. She got an earlier flight. She'll be at the hospital within the hour." And here is when I had my miracle. Mom's heart started beating again. Like it did yesterday. The doctor came rushing into the room. His face showed surprise. He wanted to make sure his equipment was working right.

It was true. My mother had stepped from the brink. After Barbie got there, we stood around Mom and held her and each other. And then, unexpectedly, we started laughing—laughing and telling Mom stories. Mom and the cat. Mom and the roast beef. Mom and the basketball player—endless and hilarious.

And while we were together, all together, laughing—Mom's heart stopped. Not all at once but over a couple of minutes. The laughter stopped. The monitors showed a flat line with an occasional, inconsequential blip. The doctors and nurses rushed in again.

I am not certain that my miraculous moment was a miracle at all, and that Mom stayed alive until we could all be together and left when she heard us laugh and knew we would be all right. And whether this could be a scenario for a Hallmark movie or a *Twilight Zone* or just another in a series of coincidences that make up a life, I am certain of something invisible in that room. Something powerful. Something faster than the speed of light that for a moment was in our midst and in our hearts.

6.

THE MIDDLE CHAPTERS

I CAME OUT to Los Angeles in the year of the bicentennial, 1976. It was the year of the tall ships. I had broken my big toe two months earlier on my last day as a graduate student at the University of Illinois. After weeks of wearing a gigantic cast, I was making baby steps back to the world of Man and was wearing what Mom called a "moon shoe" on my right foot.

It was a good news/bad news situation. The bad news: I was not fully functional. The good news: I learned to drive with my left foot. Because I was somewhat handicapped, my mother decided to help me make the long drive to L.A. That was also a good news/bad news situation.

The car was as full as a car could be. It was like something in the *Guinness Book of Records*. The trunk was packed. The backseat was stacked to the roof. The front seat was full. Even the driver had to sit with a clothes basket on his or her lap and a stack of magazines under his or her chin.

Mom and I developed a "buddy system." When we got to a rest stop, whoever was in the passenger seat would have to get out of the car, run around, and open the driver's door. They would unload the baskets and magazines so the driver could get out. After the rest stop whoever was driving would get back in the car and be buried under baskets and magazines before we took off again.

After four days of driving we reached Hollywood. We found an apartment building with a vacancy. Mom thought it looked clean primarily because it was painted white. My room had a Murphy bed that pulled out of the wall. I liked the basic concept of the Murphy bed. It was perfect for Hollywood. At its core, it was delusional. It allowed me to think I had a big living room during the day and a big bedroom at night. Mom cleaned the kitchen and bathroom. I put my twelve-inch black-and-white TV set on an orange crate from the alley. I plugged it in, there was the evening news, and wham—I had a home.

Mom and I went to the grocery store and bought provisions. I bought cereal, milk, bologna, bread, mustard, and pickles. Add beer and you have the four basic food groups.

Mom got a plane ticket to head back to Dallas. She hugged me and with a look of love and terror, issued her parting words: "Stephen, whatever you do, don't go into porno." And she left. And I was on my own in the City of Angels.

I was not naïve. I was twenty-five years old. However, I was living in an area that was dubbed West Hollywood. Every morning I had breakfast at a place called the French Market. The customers were all men. Many of the men wore leather pants, or leather vests, or cowboy outfits. One morning a man asked if he could sit with me. I assumed there was a shortage of tables. When I continued eating and reading my newspaper, the man stormed off. I had no idea why. One morning a waitress came up to me and asked what "we" did during the day. "Who is 'we'?" I asked.

She said, "You guys."

I said, "Which guys?"

She said, "Gay guys. What do you gay guys do during the day?"

Oh. My. Gosh. All the clues came together like the end of a Hitchcock movie—the muscle shirts, the exposed butt cheeks, the leather chaps. These were gay guys, not cowboys! My Texas upbringing had lulled me into a false sense of normalcy.

But there was nothing normal about California. The weatherman on TV mentioned that we were moving into "earthquake season." Earthquake season? Back home we called it August. Then came the fires, which from a distance at night were lovely in an Armageddon sort of way.

Then the floods came. I had some friends who had also moved out from Dallas who lived in the country. Topanga Canyon. They lived in a house where the sixties rock band Canned Heat used to live. Storms hit the area and Biblical floods now threatened what had been spared from the fires. They called me to see if I could lend a hand in saving what was left.

With all of the rain, the normally tiny Topanga Creek was now a torrent. You could see cars being swept out to the ocean. My friends' home had been sitting safely above the canyon. But the water had risen overnight and ripped away the entire foundation of their home, leaving the living room and second story above it teetering over a forty-foot cliff.

The only thing left of their bottom floor was some slats of hardwood flooring extending twenty feet into space over the gorge. It connected to a rain-soaked portion of the opposite wall. And teetering up against that distant wall was their stereo. And on that stereo was Fleetwood Mac's new album, *Rumours.*

Whenever I had visited them in happier times (like a week before) that album was playing nonstop while they passed around a joint and talked about college or dogs or sunsets. There was an unintended irony in my friends humming, "Don't stop thinking about tomorrow," in the middle of this destruction.

That evening they came up to me with a long, thick rope. "Stephen, glad you could come out. We've come up with a plan. We want to know if you can get the record player?"

I looked out over planks of wood. I could see and hear the rapids through the broken and missing floorboards.

"I don't know, Joe. It looks scary," I said.

Joe put his arm around my shoulder. "Don't worry, we'll tie this rope around you in case the floor collapses."

I looked unconvinced.

Joe, whose face is etched in a perpetual smile, continued, "Stephen, I was in the merchant marines and can tie a good knot. There's a big, strong tree over there. We'll tie the rope to it. You'll be secure. Trust me."

So that was Plan A.

"Why pick the biggest, heaviest guy for this job?" I asked. "Why not a small woman?"

A small woman answered, "Because I may not be strong enough to carry the stereo back." I learned then that feminism worked better on a college campus.

But she had a point, and after we shared an unusually large reefer, I agreed to get the stereo.

Joe tied a knot the size of a cantaloupe around my waist. I headed out across the boards. Here's where I had a teaching moment: Any endeavor has unintended consequences. Any ill-conceived endeavor has more.

As I walked onto the pieces of unsupported flooring, they started to bend downward with my weight. With each step the floor creaked and groaned and bowed down another few inches. A quick review of the remaining scraps of sophomore trigonometry still in my brain calculated that at this rate, even if the boards didn't break, the planks would be bent down at an eighty-degree angle by the time I reached the stereo. I would never be able to get back.

I had another teaching moment. With the poker motto "If you think it long, you think it wrong" as an inspiration, I coined, "If you think it short, you must abort." I stopped and made a decision. I came back. Joe undid the rope and went out himself. He rescued the album and the turntable. The speakers didn't make it.

I walked back to my car feeling a coward. I had chickened out. I started to drive home, and I felt a burning pain, not in my cheeks from shame, but in my middle, just below my belly button. I figured it was a bruise caused by the big knot. I got home and took a shower. The pain hit me again. A deep, prolonged burn. I went to bed and didn't think anything of it. Until the next morning when it hit me again.

I knew something was wrong. But what? Internal hemorrhage? That was my first thought. The location made me think of appendicitis or maybe colon cancer.

Health is a lot like horseback riding. I ride horses now. People ask me if I am a "good rider." The answer (for me and a lot of people who ride) is I'm good if the horse is going the same place I'm going. If the horse wants to go a different place, I'm not so good. It's the same thing with health. We all are convinced that we have good health, until we don't.

I needed a doctor, but I didn't know any. My dad was our family doctor. Medical care was something I never had thought about in my entire life. It never crossed my mind I'd get sick in Los Angeles.

How does someone find a doctor? Who was good, who was bad, what part of town did he work in, how would I pay for it? It was overwhelming. I tried to use the Yellow Pages but a lot of the doctor ads were in Korean.

I had a system. It was the same system Billy Hart taught me when we were in the Dangerous Animals Club and were hunting for tarantulas. I got in my car and drove in ever-widening concentric circles using my apartment as the midpoint. I figured I would stop at the first doctor's office I saw, and that at least would be the closest.

The office I found turned out to be an Urgent Care Facility in the heart of Hollywood, not far from the French Market. The doctor in charge that day was a man named Dr. Glitter. I waited for about an hour in a room full of cowboys and longshoremen. All of my breakfast companions.

When I got back in the examination room, I told Dr. Glitter everything. I had no idea what was or wasn't important information. I told him about the flood, and the stereo, and rescuing the Fleetwood Mac album from the turntable, and the big rope around my waist, the size of the knot, the length of the rope, and its distance from the tree.

To his credit, Dr. Glitter listened patiently, though he glazed over at my description of the increasing angle of the bending floorboards. Then I told him about the burning pain in my middle and the location below my belly button. He raised his eyebrows and with a touch of just a little too much Noël Coward for my taste, he asked me to "drop my drawers."

He felt around my groin. I was getting uncomfortable. Then he said, "Up on the table on your knees and elbows." I had never had a prostate exam in my life. No one prepared me. I was suspicious that I had stumbled into some gay satanic cult.

The only way I can describe the prostate exam was that it felt like someone was ripping out my insides with a red-hot pair of pliers. Dr. Glitter felt around and then mumbled, "Hmmm, I think we have a boggy prostate here."

I had no idea what he was talking about. He told me to get dressed and then he hit me with the hard facts. I had a prostate infection with epididymitis. I asked what that was. He said, "Inflammation of the balls." I was horrified.

In the sixth grade, I was wasting time looking through an encyclopedia in study hall, and I saw a picture of a group of African natives with huge, gigantic balls. They were holding a big snake over their heads and their balls almost touched the ground. Oh my God! Was that my future? Kiss my acting career good-bye. How would I ever shop for pants?

Dr. Glitter told me I would need antibiotics. He asked me if I had a "strong" jockey strap at home. I said I didn't know they came in strengths. He said go out and buy the strongest one I could find. The good doctor told me that exertion and vibration made epididymitis worse. So I should stay in bed, wrap my testes in ice, and prop them up on a pillow. If I had to go anywhere—put on the strong jockey strap and take the medicine. Then come back and see him in a couple of weeks.

I shuffled out of the office. I looked like I was trying to hold an orange with my butt cheeks, but in truth I was afraid to jounce too vigorously. I had to keep my balls from growing at all costs. As I made my way through the crowded waiting room, Dr. Glitter stuck his head out and called, "Remember, Mr. Tobolowsky, wrap those testes in ice and prop them up on a pillow!" Every conversation in the room stopped. Every magazine lowered about two inches. Every cowboy looked at me. I smiled and pretended he was talking to someone else.

When I got home my girlfriend, Beth, asked me what was wrong. I started to tell her. That's when I learned all relationships have limits. Our limit was discussions about scrotal swelling. My friends out in Topanga asked me what was wrong. I had difficulty explaining. The extratight jockey strap constricted my speech. Some maladies have no curb appeal.

Curb appeal for diseases only matters when you're healthy and listening to someone else's problems. Alcoholism has always had more curb appeal than overeating. A broken bone always has curb appeal. You just look a little silly with the cast. You are only temporarily out of commission, and you usually have a good story. A broken bone is in the same category as a dog bite or being in rehab.

Infected prostate. Swollen balls. Zero curb appeal.

The antibiotics patched me up quickly, but Dr. Glitter told me that I might have problems off and on the rest of my life. Apparently the testicle is a miraculous thing. There is something like two linear miles of tubing in each ball. Teeny, tiny tubing. The immature sperm starts at one end and it travels all the way to the other and on the long journey it matures. Like high school for sperm. Because the tubing is so tiny it is impossible for antibiotics to get everywhere a germ could hide, so recurrences are normal.

For the next several months, whenever I got that certain feeling in my gut, I would take an ice-cold can of Coke and stick it between my legs. It put the fire out and felt great, but it had the same effect on my friends as if I were a dog dragging my butt across the living room carpet. No curb appeal.

Time passed. We slid from earthquake season to fire season and neared flood season once again. The fire I had down below kept intruding into my life. There was no cure. I felt a little like Job. Some friends of mine from Texas came to town and I took them to the French Market for breakfast. Over omelets I started explaining the size of my scrotum and what a boggy prostate was.

While they listened to my horror story, out of the corner of my eye I began registering some changes in my fine old eatery. Lots of empty tables. That was odd. The place was always packed. Many of the regulars were gone. Some of the regulars who I could recognize were looking like they lost a lot of weight. Some young men wore bandages on their arms. One man at the counter had what looked like holes in his face. I had no idea what was happening. I hadn't put all the clues together. I didn't know it was a visitation from the Angel of Death.

In a city that prided itself on its disasters, no one had mentioned that something called GRID was on the loose. I heard it whispered about in the restaurant and on the street. In a few months, we heard the word "AIDS" for the first time. If I were to give Armageddon a face, it would not be the fires or the earthquakes, but one of the faces of these young men.

Just like me, they came out to Los Angeles to find something. And I guess they did. No one ever said Pandora's box had a warning label on it.

There is a Zen parable: A young married couple goes to the Master for a blessing. He looks at them and writes on a banner, "Grandfather dies, father dies, son dies." The couple is horrified. They curse the Master. How could you write such a terrible thing and call it a blessing? The Master looks at them calmly and answers that this was a blessing. This was the formula for a happy life. Grandfather dies, father dies, son dies. If the order is different you will have the greatest of sorrow.

Los Angeles had become a city of unintended consequences. A land of dying sons. My malady, besides having no curb appeal, had become trivial to boot. I was no longer the central victim in my own life.

My Zen story goes like this: During this year of horror and fear when no one knew what was going on, I went to a barbershop. There were three chairs. Two of the barbers were old Italian men who had been cutting hair their entire lives. The third chair opened up. The barber was a young, painfully thin gay man, probably in his late twenties.

I sat in his chair with some hesitation. He smiled and told me not to worry. I wouldn't catch anything. He started cutting my hair. He told me he had come out from Indiana. He wanted to be in show business all of his life. It hadn't worked out but fortunately he had been to beauty school and could work as a barber. Then he had gotten sick. His condition was fatal. His mother wanted him to come home, but he was going to stay in Los Angeles with his friends and work as long as he could.

For his mother, he decided to do something he had never done. He would write the story of his life and give it to her as a parting gift. He told me he had one practical problem. He knew how the story began, and how it would end, but he had no middle chapters.

The face of that young man haunted me for years. And like many things that have come into my life unexpectedly, it has often been unappreciated.

It took me years to realize that the boy from Indiana was a blessing. He taught me that there is always hope for a life well lived. You just have to tell your story. The middle chapters start on any afternoon when you decided not to give up. For me, they may have started that day.

7.

THE FLIGHT OF THE BUMBLEBEE

HOLLYWOOD HAS MANY gatekeepers but few gates. There are legions of people whose only purpose is to send you packing. Agents, assistant agents, receptionists, casting directors, assistant casting directors, retired casting directors, acting teachers, friends of acting teachers. They all seem created to tell you no.

Acting students often ask me, "How did you start your career?" This is a civilized way of asking a series of far more terrifying questions: "How do you get an agent?" "How do you get auditions?" "How did you get your first job?"

The answer is both depressing and liberating. Here it is: there is no way to get started. It's like scientists who say that according to the principles of physics, it is impossible for a bumblebee to fly. They can't do it.

Yet they do.

When I arrived in town I was so desperate to make inroads into the impenetrable, I tagged along with a couple of my friends, also unemployed actors. Our plan was to hang out with a friend of theirs who was a more experienced unemployed actor. This friend's cachet was that he had just been accepted into an acting class that was supposed to be "really good." What that meant was that some of the students in the class had worked professionally.

Through this friend we aimed to get the connections to pay some-one money to take an acting class where we could do scenes with someone who at one point in time had an agent. That was Plan A.

Every Thursday at eleven p.m. we would go over to the apartment of the grand dame of the "good" acting class. Her name was Giva. She was around seventy, had dyed red hair and false eyelashes. She had been a longtime member of the class. Her claim to fame was that several decades ago she had been an unemployed actress in New York. The New York thing was the selling point.

This was our way of networking. We would sit up for hours and drink red wine and listen to Giva talk about the business. She would give us tips as to how to succeed and how to get ahead. Occasionally, someone would gain her favor, and she would offer to put in a good word for him or her to get on the waiting list to get into the acting class.

But networking always comes with a price. At about one a.m. Giva would start to cry and talk about her husband, Lou, who had just died. They had been married for years and years and were insepa-rable. It broke my heart. She spoke of his kindness and generosity, his powerful intellect and his humor. Then I noticed after sharing her tales of love and loss for about an hour, the monologue would take an almost Sybil-like turn into what a self-centered bastard Lou had been. He was abusive and controlling. She never could please him. This part of the evening went on till about three a.m. or until the bag of Fritos was gone, and I had to excuse myself.

Every week was the same thing: show business advice until one; then the flood of tears and a deification of Lou until about two; fol-lowed by burning him at the stake until dawn. I was confused. Sym-pathy always requires a well-defined protagonist. My late nights with Giva left me with an uneasy feeling that my new world had no clear boundaries.

One week, Giva turned her attentions on me. She used me as an example of a "lost cause." She told our little group that she could never recommend me for the acting class. It would be a waste of time. She pointed out I could never succeed because I wasn't "a man's man." My voice needed to be deeper. My physique more powerful. My demeanor more dangerous.

Not only was I insulted, but it was clear my weeks of networking were a bust.

My first instinct was to take the low road. I asked her how she thought she could judge me. She had never seen me perform. I told her that I was a comedian. I didn't need to be a man's man.

A gigantic silence descended on the room. No one looked at me. I decided to keep speaking. Always a mistake. I told her that it was inconsiderate to go on and on about Lou every week. That there was no way we could participate. It was unpleasant to listen to her tear him down. Even worse, it was boring.

Again, silence. Giva mustered a tear and told me that I was an insensitive man. I told her she was right. I was. But no one had ever accused me of not being a real actor. And to prove it, one of the attributes of being a real actor is that you have to know when to get off the stage. I did. I left.

I always felt pretty bad about being mean to Giva. I knew I should have taken the high road. I was just going too fast and missed my exit. My only consolation was that in the middle of it all, I saw from a twinkle in her eye that I didn't really hurt her feelings. She had a strange little smile. The actress in her was thrilled to be center stage again.

That was the last evening I spent trying to get into the "good" acting class. My friends went back for a few more weeks. Giva still gave advice and talked for hours about Lou. It dawned on me that my experience with Giva was possibly a haiku of Hollywood: where you're headed is not nearly as important as the road you travel to get there.

Anyone serious about acting professionally has to tackle the problem of getting an agent. It's like getting a loan from a bank. If you need one, you can't get one. I sent out pictures and résumés to various agencies with no response. There was a rumor that an associate of the big talent agency in Dallas was heading out to L.A. to open up a West Coast office. What made this rumor particularly tasty was the secondary rumor that all Dallas talent in L.A. was "automatically in." I couldn't believe my good fortune. Could it be possible that this impossible step was already a done deal?

No. It was not possible.

Kelley Green arrived in Los Angeles and set up meetings with all of her "Dallas people." The meetings had to be scheduled around her regular job. During the week she sold rain gear on commission at the May Company, a local department store.

It wasn't so much that I minded having an agent whose full-time job was selling umbrellas. I was more disturbed at having an agent who thought selling rain gear in a desert was a good idea. I didn't feel Kelley was the right choice for me. Against my friends' advice, I turned Kelley down and once again faced the wilderness.

I bought an actors' newspaper that had a list of agents. I went down the list until a name jumped out at me: Carroll Farrell. It rhymed. I liked it. It sounded showbizzy. I called up for an appointment. The secretary called me back and said Ms. Farrell would see me. My first returned call! I wanted to open a bottle of champagne.

I went in with my 8 × 10 photo. It was taken in Dallas before I left. It was moody. I wore a black turtleneck against a black background. I looked like a severed head in a medical textbook. I typed out my pathetic résumé that included two college productions of *A Midsummer Night's Dream*, two productions of *The Importance of Being Earnest*, some anti–Vietnam War plays, and a couple of student films that would never be seen by anyone.

I sat in her waiting room about to pass out from stress. A lot rode on this meeting. She was in her office interviewing a working soap opera actor who was seeking representation. The walls were so thin I could hear every word. It was brutal. She was abasing him for not having any real professional experience. He protested that for the last two years he was a regular character on a soap opera. That wasn't acting, she told him. My puny résumé shrank in my hand.

He left the room flustered and battered. Ms. Farrell called me into the room. She was not what I expected. She had a bouffant hairdo and wore a one-piece knitted jumpsuit. I sat down and she looked me over. She reached for my résumé and photo. Without changing her expression, she muttered, "You'll need new pictures." She looked over my résumé and put it down. I started to tell her I also had done a season of summer stock in New York. She interrupted me. "That doesn't matter." She continued to look at me. "What does matter is your name. I can never sell someone with a name like yours. Stephen Tobolowsky. Never. You'll have to change it."

I thought about my father and grandfather. I thought about the generations of my family in Russia and Poland lost to any written record by wars and persecution. And then I said, "What name could you sell me as?" She considered it for a moment and then answered, "Steve Adams. I could sell you if you changed your name to Steve Adams." I said, "Great. Why don't you tell people you represent an actor named Steve Adams. If they hire me, I'll change my name."

I called home that night and told Mom and Dad I had met an agent who wanted to sign me, but I might have to change my name. With almost no hesitation at all both Mom and Dad said, "Whatever it takes." I was shocked.

I had some résumés made up that said "STEVE ADAMS." I dropped them by to show Carroll the next day. She was on the phone. She multitasked and in midconversation she nodded her approval of my name change. I left. About two days later, I got a phone call. Carroll needed to see me right away. She had a job for me. I rushed over to her office. She asked me if I played basketball. I said, "Yes!" I told her I had even played on a team when I was eleven. I was a forward for the Carpenter Crusaders and had a scoring average of four points per season. I remembered crying a lot and getting knocked into the stands. I recalled being scolded by my coach for not wearing an athletic cup. Even though we never won a game, now I was thrilled. When you are an actor, everything is on the résumé. Your life is your palette. She asked me how tall I was. "Six foot three," I said.

She looked me over and said, "Can you be six foot six?"

Pause.

I told her, "Yes. In three-inch heels."

Carroll looked disappointed and said, "Then I don't think this is going to work."

Carroll was right. It wasn't. It was important to have an agent that appreciated the traditional laws of physics.

But Hollywood was a place where the traditional laws of physics didn't necessarily apply. One of the apartments I looked at during this period had an odd feeling to it. I was huge. I could barely get through the door. I felt like the Giant from "Jack and the Beanstalk" when I sat at the kitchen table. The landlord told me it was built to "Western proportions." I had no idea what he meant. He told me in the old days of the silent Western two-reelers, they used to build all of their sets to seven-eighths of what their real size should have been, making the stars look bigger than they really were.

It was the opposite of telescopes. In astronomy, the great telescopes are rated not by how big they make something look but by how much illumination they allow. That was not the rule of Hollywood. Was I ready to commit my life to a world that made up its rules as it went along? Maybe somewhere I would find a like-minded soul, an agent looking for an actor.

I got my second returned call. It was from an agent who said he liked that I had theater training. *A Midsummer Night's Dream* was one of his favorite plays. He asked me to come by his office Monday at noon. I did. He wasn't there. The door was locked. I went home. I called and asked him if I got the time wrong. He called me back and said no. He was at lunch and just forgot. He suggested I come back in at the end of the week. I did. He wasn't there. The door was locked. I went home. I called him and asked if he forgot again. He returned the call a few days later. He apologized and said something had come up.

He asked me to come back that afternoon. I asked if he was going to be there. If he wasn't, I was going to have to hunt him down and kill him. He laughed, and said he would be waiting for me. I went back that afternoon. The office door was open.

He said he didn't want to take me as a client unless I auditioned for him. I told him I was prepared. I had a modern monologue and a Shakespeare. I could do them right there, right now. He said no.

He was something of a writer and wanted me to do some of his material. He handed it to me. It was some speech like you'd find in a Clint Eastwood Western where they couldn't afford Clint Eastwood. It featured all the typical clichés like "the hot sun beating on your back," and "the stench of being in this Mexican jail," and "eating bugs for breakfast," and "gettin' lynched." It was bad, but I was unsure of the boundaries of acceptability of my new world.

I told him I would learn it and come back. He said no. He wanted me to come to his house Friday night and perform it.

Oh dear.

I had seen *The Graduate*. I didn't know what to do. If I don't show up and he's legit, I miss out on getting an agent. If I show up and he's not legit, I take the chance of being drugged, raped, and sold for body parts. There was no contest. I needed an agent.

He told me to come by at eight p.m. I got dressed in my little sports coat and tie, and headed off with my Thomas Guide map book of the Los Angeles area. He lived up in the Hollywood Hills. I made my way through the labyrinth of alleys and one-lane byways around the Hollywood Bowl. I found the address and parked. I took a deep breath and walked up to a huge wooden door and knocked. A maid answered and showed me inside and, surprise of surprises, there was a party going on! There were about forty people all smartly dressed eating finger food and drinking cocktails.

I saw the agent on the far side of the room in a creamy silk shirt talking and laughing with one of his compatriots. He saw me and put his food down and shouted out to the room: "Everyone! Hey! Everybody! Quiet down now, we have a special treat tonight. We have a little extra entertainment. This young actor came to my office a couple weeks ago wanting me to be his agent." There was a smattering of laughter and applause. He quieted everyone down and continued, "Tonight he is going to audition for all of us. So if everyone will grab a seat let's watch, ah . . ." (He didn't have my name quite memorized yet.) "Sorry, what was your name?"

"Stephen . . . Stephen"—(I didn't know if I should say "Adams"— screw it)—"Tobolowsky."

"Stephen."

Everybody was a little shocked. I could see one woman looking as though this would be a lot of fun, then looking as though this was kind of weird, and then looking as though she would rather be anywhere else. I waited for everyone to get quiet. If nothing else, we would share the moment. If people kept eating shrimp, I stared at them. Everyone stopped. There was silence. I was thinking all I had left in this exchange was my dignity. If this guy wanted me to do a speech about bugs in the food at his party, that's what I would do. I delivered the speech to one woman in the front row. I never broke eye contact. I finished. I bowed. I left the house.

I drove home. I never called the agent again. He never called me. I ended up running into him a dozen times over the next twenty years. I was always polite. I never spoke of the party or the audition. My evenings with Giva taught me to hold my tongue.

The lessons of Hollywood are never what you think. That's because Hollywood has never been a part of civilization. It has always been an antidote to civilization. It has been a refuge and an escape. It manufactures ways to kill time, and consequently it's a war zone. And in a war, sometimes, discretion is the better part of valor.

8.

THE PRICE OF NOTHING

I WAS ONE of those kids whose entire life was supposed to happen in the future. Everything that was happening now was in preparation for it. I had to do well in grade school to get into the high academic class in high school. I had to do well in high school to get into a good college. I had to do well in college to get a good job. So in 1973, I had finished four years of college, and was qualified to do nothing except maybe give back rubs.

I had followed the plan faithfully, but I was in my midtwenties and already running out of options. When you aim at something so remote as being a professional actor, it's easy to feel the panic of failure early and often. I started looking through the help wanted ads in the *Dallas Morning News*. I had to find real work to buy myself time.

I managed to land a one-day job. I got twenty-five dollars an hour on Election Day holding up a sign for a man running for the U.S. House of Representatives. The man's name was Harold Column. I had no idea who he was or what he stood for. All I knew was that the poster had his name, Harold Column, in blue and white along with a picture of a column. It was symbolic of something, I'm sure. It could have meant he was strong, or supportive, or a ruin. I had no idea which.

I started pacing back and forth at my required one thousand feet from the polling place when an intelligent-looking young man came up to me and said, "Okay. I'll give you five minutes. Why should I vote for your guy?"

My brain whirred like the chamber of a six-shooter with no bullets. All I could think to do was to act like politicians I had seen on TV. My face pulled into an Ivy League smirk, I nodded my head knowingly and said, "Well, the rumors of corruption are enough for me to want a clean slate."

The young man said, "What corruption?"

"You know. The financial thing. The misappropriation of funds."

"I haven't heard anything about that. Who reported it?"

"It was in the *New York Times*. I think." I felt myself breaking out in flop sweat. I could no longer sustain the ruse. I broke down and said, "I have no idea what I'm talking about. Don't listen to me. Vote for whomever you want." About fifteen minutes later the campaign manager for Harold Column came over and took my sign away from me. My work as a low-level political operative had ended.

After that I taught drama at the synagogue down the street. I put together a talent show for the dozen ten-year-olds in my class. I gave each child a little monologue. It was cute. But then came something that blindsided me: the Attack of the Mothers. No one warned me. They ragged me up one side and down the next. Their child was not doing enough. Their child could also sing. Their child did impressions. Rather than being the voice of reason, I just added acts to the show. The performance expanded from an already uncomfortable ninety minutes to over four hours of unrelenting performances by untalented children. They did Richard Nixon impressions, lip-synched to Sonny and Cher songs; they did oral interpretations from *The Diary of Anne Frank*. There were only two positives from that evening: One, I left early. And two, the parents had to stay. It was an Instant Karma moment. The next week I was fired. Another Instant Karma moment.

After that I got a job reading to a blind woman two hours a day, three times a week. She was in her eighties. She was one of the richest women in Dallas. We read Nobel Prize–winning authors from

Winston Churchill to John Steinbeck. It was a great experience. About three months into it, she wanted a change of pace from *The Grapes of Wrath* and *Siddhartha*. She pulled out a rough draft of a book she was writing. It was an autobiography of sorts. I opened the typed manuscript to page one. I was shaking by the end of the first paragraph. It was the dirtiest book I had ever read. There are not enough Xs in Hollywood's rating system to do this book justice. It was filled with so much graphic sex and violence, it could have been written by Jean Genet's evil twin. The whippings, the electrocutions, the group sex—and that was in the first ten pages. The "book" was over one hundred and eighty pages long.

I kept plugging away at it. She sat there demurely and then would ask what I thought of it. I would say, "Pretty scary. Pretty scary stuff." And it was. But on the bright side, it made me see God's point of view as to why he wanted to destroy mankind.

I felt like none of these jobs were moving closer to any real goal, except maybe alcoholism. I needed to focus on acting jobs. That's what I wanted to do, and I should hold out until I got a shot. I didn't have to wait long. I was offered a job. It wasn't to be in a play or a commercial. It was to be a member of a sketch comedy group and perform at the Hyatt House in Dallas. It all sounded good until we learned we would be paid in food.

It's tough when an employer offers to pay you in food or beer. You always feel like you have to be a glutton to get your money's worth. They brought in Chinese food at the beginning of rehearsal. I would eat two heaping plates of whatever was in the cartons. I had no idea. It's one of the definitional problems with Chinese food. There is a certain lack of clarity about what you're eating.

The comedy troupe worked on a series of skits written by our director, Don, and his wife, Judith. They included a bit about a conference where advertising icons are real people—so the Marlboro Man puts the moves on Virginia Slim. The Michelin Man wants to eat more doughnuts. There was another hilarious bit of fluff on how a rich man goes to the bathroom. None of it would qualify as "A" material, even at the Grand Ole Opry.

When we moved the show to the Hyatt, I witnessed something incredible. Because of the fast turnaround in the scenes, all of the actors would have to do what they call "underdress." This is kind of a stage magic trick where you wear the costume for a future scene under the costume you are currently wearing. In a fast change, you just strip off the outer garments and reveal the next costume. It works great as long as you aren't wearing anything unusual.

One of our actors was Jack, a former linebacker for the Chicago Bears. He played all of our businessmen and presidents and/or rich men going to the bathroom. He played the president of a company right before he played the Marlboro Man, so they wanted him to underdress. Underneath his blue wool business suit and wool turtleneck, he wore blue jeans with real leather chaps, a red cowboy shirt, a leather vest with fringe, and a bandana.

The first night in front of the audience was also the first night we had all of the costume pieces. Jack looked like a slice of beef Wellington. Under the weight of the eight layers of clothing, he began to sweat during the boardroom skit. First his forehead. Then his face. Within five minutes he looked like Charles Barkley in the fourth quarter at the free throw line. Sweat poured off his nose. I could tell it was affecting his mind. His eyes rolled around in his head and then they would dart around the room. Sweat puddled on the table in front of him. He snapped. He stood up from the table and roared, "I CAN'T TAKE IT ANYMORE!" And he started ripping off his clothes.

The audience had no idea what was happening. They gasped as he fumbled for his belt buckle and started to unzip his pants. They were confused when he pulled down his suit pants revealing another pair of pants and leather chaps underneath.

He started undoing the cowboy pants. Now the audience thought it was so horrible it had to be part of the show. They laughed. Jack yelled at them, "Motherfucker. I'm dyin' up here!" They laughed harder. He pulled his cowboy pants down revealing his boxers. He kicked his legs furiously to get the cowboy pants off but they were tucked into his boots. He started raging around the stage throwing his shirt and vest off. He yelled, "Go ahead and laugh! In case you haven't noticed I'M A BIG MAN! I HAPPEN TO SWEAT A LOT!" The audience roared. I stood on the side of the stage transfixed by the disaster. Jack ended up bare-chested in boxers still wearing the leather chaps. The cowboy pants were dragging on his ankles caught in his cowboy boots. The audience began applauding as he shuffled around the stage looking for an exit.

The performance of our "revue" ended here. There was no coming back from this. We took a curtain call and counted ourselves lucky that Jack didn't hurt anyone. That was the end of our free Chinese food.

I sympathized with Jack. I felt the same about my life in Dallas. The fit was too tight. Many currents pulled at me at the time: life after college, life with my girlfriend, Beth, decreasing options on the horizon. After the failed nightclub act, I decided to pick up my many different costumes I had scattered on the ground and pack my bags. I had to leave my hometown. I didn't know where I would go or what awaited me. In Dallas, I had done all I could do to define the bottom. And that's not such a bad thing. The bottom is always a good place to start.

My MOTHER PICKED out my first apartment in Los Angeles. I've said it was a single room with a Murphy bed that pulled out of the wall. It had several things going for it. It was in Los Angeles. It looked clean. It was furnished. And it was cheap. The rent was $165 a month. I repeat, $165 a month! Cheap was good. I didn't have a job or any prospects for jobs and needed my meager savings to last.

I only stayed in this apartment six weeks. I would have stayed longer if my room wasn't invaded by a gigantic swarm of ants about a yard wide and marching steadily under the painted-open crack of my kitchen window.

I talked to my landlady. She said she would talk to the "bug man." Los Angeles has lots of people that handle vermin who are known as "man": bug man, rat man, mold man. They are low-level superheroes. She reported back that the bug man told her he had just sprayed the area. It probably caused some "displacement" of the colony. Apparently, into my apartment.

The next day, the ants were gone. But the following morning they returned. Millions of them. I figured they just went back to pack. They told their friends that they found a cheap place with a pool. Some even made it to my bed. I was starting to feel like Charlton Heston in *The Naked Jungle*. I could only imagine the phone call the landlady would have to make to Mom and Dad: they broke into my apartment and found a skeleton holding a beer in front of the TV set. They're awaiting results of the tests, but they fear the worst.

I had to move.

I found another apartment about three blocks away. It was bigger and more expensive. It was $220 a month, unfurnished. "Unfurnished" is the word that separates man from the beasts. But I was desperate. I could sleep on the floor. I took it. I looked at ads in the neighborhood newspaper and bought a kitchen table and chairs for ten dollars. A sofa for twenty-five dollars. Within two hours, I was furnished.

I went to the store and loaded up on more cereal, milk, bologna, and pickles. Paper towels and toilet paper—and an apple pie. The larder was full. I felt empowered. That night I watched the late movie on my sofa, eating pie. I felt like a hero in Greek mythology who had slayed his first monster. It was almost midnight. I looked out of my living room window and imagined myself a lord of all I surveyed. For the first time in my life, I had a view.

That's when I found out my new apartment came with a naked man. He was about two hundred feet away across the street in another apartment building. I didn't see all of the naked man, just enough to know he was naked—and that he was a man. His kitchen faced my living room. It was always dark in his apartment but whenever he opened his refrigerator, the light illuminated him from nipples to knees.

Over the next few weeks he became a permanent character in the little movie I called *What I See Out My Window at Night.* The light would come on across the way—there was Naked Man. I tried to think of names for him but nothing suited him better than Naked Man. Friends would come over and ask if Naked Man had been in the kitchen yet. We would often sit around pretending to watch the late movie, waiting for Naked Man to open the fridge and grab some yogurt.

For weeks all I knew about Naked Man was that he snacked at night. Then one morning at dawn I heard Naked Man having sex in his apartment. It was unmistakable. I heard him. I heard her. Then in the middle of sexual huffing and puffing, I heard a dog start barking in their bedroom. It sounded like a Lab. Naked Man yelled, "Get outta here. Go away. Git!" The dog continued barking. Naked Man yelled, "Shut up! Shut up! Bad dog! Bad dog!" The woman was polite and continued to groan through it all. But when the dog kept barking she yelled, "Shut up! Get him outta here!" And they say romance is dead. In a Zen way, I think the dog brought the two of them closer together.

The pressure of the higher rent was working on my mind. It even robbed me of the pleasure of enjoying *The Life and Times of Naked Man.* On television they had a segment on *60 Minutes* on "The Price of Nothing." This is the index of how much it costs just to breathe in a certain city and use nothing. If you got an apartment and turned on the utilities but never used them, you would still have to pay the "price of nothing." In Los Angeles, "nothing" costs more than in almost any city in the United States. My dream of being an actor was on a very short leash.

Then, as if in answer to a prayer, I was reading one of the actor newsletters and there was an audition for an Equity job. Equity is the actors' union, so it meant a real job—a paying job. It was for a children's theater group called Twelfth Night Repertory Company. I thought, "Great. I worked with children in Dallas. I liked the play *Twelfth Night.* Let's do it." The requirements for being in the company were high. You had to play two musical instruments, which I did. I played the piano and guitar.

Twelfth Night required that you had to be expert at improvisation. Hey, I furnished my apartment for thirty-five dollars in two hours. Improvisation doesn't get any better than that. You also had to speak a foreign language—I took German for two years because Claire Richards, a girl I had a crush on since the second grade, took German. I had even committed two German phrases to memory. *Man kann ihn immer an seiner Stimme erkennen. Ich müss mir eine neue Jacke kaufen.* Which means "One can always recognize him by his voice" and "I must buy a new jacket." I learned these phrases not because I thought I would ever need them in a real-world situation, but because when you say them together fast it sounds like you can speak German—which was exactly what I would need to do for the people at Twelfth Night Repertory Company.

The auditions were held at an address in the San Fernando Valley. They told me to come prepared to play instruments, sing, dance, and improvise. Wow.

Driving through a residential area, I realized the audition would take place at someone's home, in someone's garage. Walking up to the garage, I had clarity. I wanted this job more than I had ever wanted anything in my entire life.

A youngish man and woman sat at a table in the driveway and looked at my résumé. He raised his eyebrows:

"You speak German?"

I hit him with, *"Man kann ihn immer an seiner Stimme erkennen ich müss mir eine neue Jacke kaufen."*

He nodded. "Good. Good."

She asked, "At what level do you play guitar and piano?"

"On the piano I play Beethoven and Mozart, mainly classical, a little rock and roll. Guitar—just rock chords. I was a backup guitarist."

The man asked, "Do you play any jazz?"

"No, not really. But I can learn."

He smiled at that answer. Lesson one: never underestimate the power of your willingness to learn.

They called out about eight other people who had come to

audition. The man and woman told us to get at one end of the garage. We lined up. She said, "I want to see you move. You are going to go from one end of the garage to the other, but we will tell you how. First, you're cats!" I had pet cats my whole life, so this was easy. I even stopped halfway across to cough up a fur ball. This went over big. We kept walking back and forth. They switched gears. "Now you're five-year-olds!" "Now you're walking through peanut butter." "Now you're on Jupiter!"

In college I was in an improv group where we did things like this all the time. We walked through peanut butter. We walked like we were five-year-olds. We never walked on Jupiter, but we did walk like we were on the bottom of the ocean, which I figured was a lot like walking on Jupiter.

We went inside the house to the piano. They asked me to play. I started with a little "Moonlight Sonata" and then shifted to the beginning of Grieg's Piano Concerto in A Minor, then shifted to a French Chopinlike waltz. I lingered on the piano and puttered around with some rock and roll chords so there was no doubt I could play.

They explained to all of us that there were only two positions available. If we didn't get in this time, we shouldn't fret. There may be other opportunities in a few months.

A few months! No way. I was going to get one of the two slots. I knew it. Between the piano and coughing up the fur ball, I had sealed the deal. I went home confidently uncertain about my future with Twelfth Night Repertory Company.

Two days later I got the call. I recognized the woman's voice. She told me I did great on the audition, but I didn't get the job. I had a small stroke at that moment. I lost the power of speech. I just hummed and grunted that I understood and I was happy to have the chance to audition. She continued that everyone was impressed by what I did and if a spot opened up, she would call. I hung up the phone and stared into space.

The evening sun started to set. I couldn't even get up to turn on a light. Eventually, I went to take a shower to wash off the stench of failure. I came out drying myself and walked into the living room. I turned on the set. The Channel 2 news burst forth, bathing me in the light of the TV. At that moment, I had that eerie feeling on the back of my neck. I whirled around and looked out the window and saw Naked Man standing by his open fridge looking toward my apartment! Distracted by despair, I had become Naked Man's Naked Man! I dove onto the couch, afraid to get up for what seemed like hours.

I had failed. This was my best shot at a real job. I tried to mix things up the next day to help me forget. I ate bologna for breakfast and cereal for lunch. I was watching cartoons on PBS when the phone rang. It was the woman from Twelfth Night again. She said, "Stephen, I told you I'd call back. I didn't think it would be this soon. I wanted to see if this interested you. As you know, we have filled the spots on our English-speaking cast, but we are thinking of starting an all-Spanish-speaking company doing Mexican folk-tales in the schools. You would play the piano and guitar and play some parts in the show. Do you think you could do that? I know you said that your second language was German."

"Yes. I took German in school, but I grew up hearing Spanish my whole life. I'm from Texas. We ate at El Fenix all the time. I've always wanted to learn Spanish. I could do it. I could learn the show phonetically and take Spanish at the same time."

"Really?"

"Absolutely. It would be like learning Shakespeare. This is a job where you get paid, right?"

"Yes. You'll start out at $216 a week. And possibly more depending on the number of shows you do."

"I'll do it. I'll take it. When do we start?"

"Right away. You have four weeks before your first show. Do you want to think about it and call me in the morning?"

"No. Nothing to think about. This is exactly the kind of thing I do. I love children. I love to play music. Sign me up."

"Well, I appreciate the enthusiasm. The job is yours."

"Thank you. Thank you."

I hung up the phone and almost passed out from joy. I had done it. I got a job! In acting! That paid money! Yes, it was in a foreign language but that would just be part of the challenge. I called Mom and Dad to share the good news.

"Well, honey, how long do you have to learn Spanish?" Mom asked.

"Couple of weeks."

"Can you do that?"

"Well, that Dutch rock group Shocking Blue learned English phonetically and had a huge hit with 'Venus.' It can be done. I'm sure the words will be simple. The show is for children."

"Well. All right."

I could pay my rent. I could buy things for the apartment: a cup to hold my toothbrush, deli sandwiches, more pie, a color TV. I was on the verge of becoming a consumer.

I headed out to the local library to start learning Spanish. First book I saw: *Berlitz: Learn Spanish in 90 Days.* That wasn't going to cut it. I saw another book, *Spanish in a Month!.* I was thinking, at least we were moving in the right direction. I kept scanning book titles until I got to: *Learn Spanish in One Hour.* Bingo. The mother lode! This book is exactly what I need. I would walk into rehearsal the next day with the language learned!

The book was not a real working template for learning a foreign language. There was no grammar. There were no verbs. There were few nouns. It was primarily a book of words that are the same in Spanish and English such as *federal, national, cafeteria,* and *taco.*

I would have to learn this play by rote. But we had time and I had discipline. We worked on the show for several hours a day for three weeks straight. It was all coming together. I played a bad guy in a sombrero and a mustache. I played guitar and shook maracas when needed. I used hand puppets with comic effect singing songs. I would then run over to the piano and start playing a cha-cha. The kids would love it.

It was the day of our first school performance. We had two shows in Indio, California. The first show was a snap. Not a single mistake.

We were high-fiving backstage while out front they moved the fourth, fifth, and sixth graders out and moved the first, second, and third graders in. I put the sombrero back on and rushed out to play a little dramatic rumba music on the piano. The kids were booing me, and I was making faces at them like "I'm gonna get you. I'm gonna get you . . ." They laughed. Everyone was having a good time. Then the play started.

Our boss, a beautiful Peruvian actress named Jenny Gago, played the heroine of the piece. She was dressed up like a little girl. She was lost and about to be kidnapped by bandits (me). In the play, she comes to my door. I bow to her and with a wink to the audience say *"Pasa, jovincita."* Which means "Come in, little girl." And all of the kids yell at her not to come in with me. It was great.

Whether it was the adrenaline or exhaustion I can't say, but when the little girl came up to me, my mind went blank. I tried to remember my Spanish, but it swirled in my head like alphabet soup. Instead of saying, *"Pasa, jovincita"* ("Come in, little girl"), I said, *"Peto, jovincita,"* which means "Fart, little girl." The audience erupted. The teachers ran back and forth to quell the chaos. Jenny looked at me in horror. I still had no idea that I had said anything wrong. I stood grinning with the big sombrero, twirling my mustache. The play continued. At the next juncture, I was supposed to say, *"¿Tienes algunas preguntas?"* which means "Do you have any questions?" My mind went blank. I muttered a combination of Spanish-sounding words that almost sounded like that. The audience once again exploded in shouts and cries. I was told later I said to the little girl to "Sit on it and squeeze." Through the laughter and screams, Jenny stared at me. I asked her what was wrong. She just whispered, "You're fired."

It was the only time I had ever heard of an actor being fired onstage during a play. Afterwards, she asked why I did it. I told her I had no idea what I did.

That was the end of my performing in Spanish with Twelfth Night Repertory Company. It was the end of my job. However, a man in the audience saw my single performance in Indio. He was a TV producer for SIN, the Spanish-language network. He tracked me down and asked me if I would do a commercial for him, in Spanish. Which I did. I made $500 for the day playing the dumb gringo who can't speak Spanish. The commercial was so successful he hired me to do two more, in Spanish.

I was not done with Twelfth Night Rep, either. They called me a month later and said they were willing to let bygones be bygones. They asked me if I wanted a job in the English-speaking company. I accepted. Jenny Gago was still my boss. She forgave me, and for three years, we performed all over the state. The governor at the time, Jerry Brown, declared us the official theater company of California. Our company grew from eight people to over eighty people. Some of the alumni were none other than Mare Winningham and Brian Stokes Mitchell. It still amuses me to think of Brian Stokes Mitchell acting with a sock puppet.

It wasn't long after I got the job in the English-speaking company that I decided to move again. I bid farewell to Naked Man and left the apartment and the used furniture behind. I rented a house. Two bedrooms, a kitchen, a swing on the front porch, and a backyard. I was a working actor. I was making $260 a week. A consumer at last. A success. But I had the strangest feeling I couldn't shake. I didn't know where it came from and I didn't know where it was leading me, but its meaning was clear. It was not the time to be blinded by good fortune. The price of nothing was getting higher every day.

9.

ONCE IN A LIFETIME

THERE IS A story my brother told me from when he was an intern at Boston City Hospital. It was about a woman who came into the emergency room laughing, saying, "This is my lucky day." She had been in a car accident—but right in front of the hospital. So she just got out of her car and walked right in. How lucky can you get? She was put in a bed in the emergency room and was laughing and joking with interns and residents. She had a vivacious personality. She was telling all the doctors and nurses to do what they had to do so she could "get the hell out of there."

One of the interns left her room and went to the doctor in charge. The intern was shaken and asked his superior what to do. He just checked the vitals of the woman who was in the car accident, the same woman who was carrying on down the hall, and she was—actually—dead.

The doctor in charge grabbed the clipboard and looked at all of the numbers. There had to be a mistake. He went back to see the woman who was still laughing about her fortunate misfortune. She asked him when she was going to get back home. The doctor said, "Soon." He just had to double-check some things. He ran another series of tests and came back out to the intern.

The impact of the accident had destroyed every organ in her body. She was, for all practical purposes, dead. But her body didn't know it yet. Her vivaciousness was a product of shock, not joy. The best they could do was to keep her quiet. The doctors didn't tell her about her condition. They just asked her to call her husband and tell him where she was.

The intern gave her a sedative and sat with her and talked. She fell asleep and died two hours later.

I recently asked my brother for more details on the story. He told me he had never heard it before and that it certainly didn't happen to him. He said I was mistaken.

How was that possible? I remember the night when I heard it in Newton Lower Falls, Massachusetts. The story had haunted me for years with a sort of primal power and now the prospect had arisen that the whole thing was not true. Did I just make it up?

Truthfully, I've gotten no comfort from the inconclusive origin of this story. It just moved in my brain from the "medical oddity" area to the "urban legend" area, which resides in the same subdivision called "crazy adjacent."

I'm wondering if my lack of relief is because I know the story is true. Not that a woman walked into a hospital laughing saying it was her lucky day, but that it is possible that you can be dead and not know it.

I'll go further. I know it happens all the time. And not just obvious cases like my friend, actress and marathoner Kitty Swink. She felt sick one morning before a run and dropped in to see a doctor and found out that she had late-stage pancreatic cancer. She went into emergency surgery that day and survived.

It happens in less dramatic ways every day with relationships. My girlfriend, Beth, and I had been together for fourteen years but something had not been right for a while. Something indefinable. There was a distance growing between us. Like other accident victims who repeatedly say, "It all seemed to happen in slow motion," our relationship was fatally adrift. We never knew it.

I don't think it was our fault. A lot of times we have trouble recognizing the fatal or near-fatal collisions in our lives as they often come in disguise. One of my collisions came in the guise of a party Beth and I threw at our home in the Hollywood Hills one New Year's Eve.

The invitation said our party went from "Nine p.m. until—?" There is almost nothing more inviting than a "?". But as I look back, one of the things I have the most trouble believing was that the party started at nine p.m. Nine p.m. is bedtime. Ever since I've had kids, if I'm not in bed at nine p.m. watching reruns of *Law & Order*, it means I've been arrested or I'm doing a night shoot. But this was back in the 1980s, the decade that made self-destruction a popular form of recreation.

I had some argument with Beth right before the party started. I made a martini to calm myself down. It worked so well I made another one and chased it with a reefer. One of the first guests to arrive was a rock and roll friend of mine. He came dressed as a surgeon holding a plate of cocaine. I did a line. That had the effect of falling thirty feet into a vat of coffee. Then another rock and roll friend came in with tabs of acid. I put one on my tongue. The elapsed time from the first martini to the last tab of acid was about twenty minutes. I had my first misgivings that I had overmedicated.

Two hours later I was naked, wearing a red derby. Our house was overflowing with other overmedicated people. Outside, the hot tub was cranking at about 105 degrees. Girls were taking off their clothes and jumping in.

As a rule, once girls start to take off their clothes, events change. You can count on it like the tides. This party was no different. The men moved their beer drinking en masse toward the hot tub area like they were iron filings being pulled by a magnet making a beard for Wooly Willy.

My friend Budge got an idea. That was never a good thing. He was an actor, but he also made money as a writer. In porn. And not just any porn. He wrote movies for none other than Marilyn Chambers. He wrote under the pseudonym Manny Haten. I looked him up on IMDb. One of his many works was *Insatiable II*. Still available on video.

He made some phone calls to about half a dozen of his porno friends. They were shooting *Wet and Wild Nurses* in the vicinity. He told them to drop on by. That did it. Just like taking too many carbon rods out of a nuclear reactor, there is a tipping point where you reach critical mass. The porno people were it. And I have to take my hat off to them. They were highly sociable. They took almost no time in making themselves right at home. They came in, grabbed a couple of light beers, grabbed some chips and salsa, and then started having sex with everyone.

Ordinary men and women who had been drinking Bloody Marys and talking about how tough it was to get auditions dropped their paper plates, stripped, and started having sex in the backyard. Or on the living room couch, or in the back bedrooms, or in the Jacuzzi. Just the fumes from the hot tub could make women pregnant downwind.

It was like something you would imagine during the last days of the Roman Empire. Any second you expected Caesar to walk through the front door.

Caesar never made it. Instead, it was Sir Ian McKellen. Yes, Sir Ian heard there was something interesting going on. I have no idea how. I have a kind of psychic theory mixed with *Star Wars* that when there is a rift in the moral universe it sends out a sort of Bat Signal for all the curious. It says, "Come one, come all—something like this may only happen once in a lifetime."

Rickie Lee Jones came over. Before jumping in the hot tub, she sang "Under the Boardwalk" a cappella in the living room. That remains one of the most beautiful musical performances I have ever heard.

Karla Bonoff, Bonnie Oda Homsey (one of the lead dancers of the Martha Graham Dance Company), and blues singer Bonnie Bramlett all dropped in to see what the commotion was about.

This was it. This was the Hollywood party I'd heard about my whole life! And it was at my house! And I was the host! Despite being naked and wearing a red derby, despite standing on ground zero of a hands-on display of the seven deadly sins, despite being high on acid, cocaine, marijuana, beer, and martinis, I never did anything. I was too busy loading the dishwasher, putting out bowls of chips, refilling dip, opening beers for people, getting desserts on plates, cleaning vomit off the walls, and sweeping up broken glass. Debauchery requires maintenance.

A friend of mine, Mary, said she would help me put out more food. She mistakenly filled a bowl on the table with my dog's gourmet liver treats. By the time I discovered the error, half of them were gone. No one complained.

Rickie Lee asked me to make a toast. I had no idea what to say but then I raised a glass and yelled out, "Here's to dumb luck!" The crowd cheered and raised their glasses. And I guess it worked. No one died that night.

The party lasted thirty-three hours. At the end there were a dozen naked bodies on my living room floor. It was dawn of a different day. I was cooking eggs and salmon. There were open bottles of champagne everywhere. I went outside and slipped into the pool. It was cold and quiet. I ducked down into the water so that just my eyes were above the surface. I held my breath and stayed silent for as long as I could. Then, flapping down onto the roof of the house about thirty feet away came a great horned owl with a wingspan of about six feet. It was amazing. He must have heard about the party, too.

I felt invigorated by the water and the owl. I put my red derby back on. I finished cooking breakfast for the remaining revelers and noticed a cluster of shiny metallic Mylar-covered helium balloons floating in the corner of the living room. I thought I would greet the new day with a private moment. I opened my front door, saw the rising sun, and said a little prayer.

I think I prayed for peace of mind. I may have prayed to get my life back or to find love again. And if that was too much to ask, I prayed to at least find my connection with Beth again. I released the balloons. They drifted up, up into the sky. And then they veered into a transformer on a telephone pole. There was an enormous electrical explosion. All of the power in the area went out. I ran inside and closed the door, hoping neighbors didn't see the naked guy with the red derby and the shiny balloons.

I made my way down the hallway to my bedroom. I lay down and closed my eyes. My mind was spinning endlessly from the combination of the drugs and being awake so long. As my breathing slowed and as I felt myself start to drift away, the last thing I remembered was what I whispered a few moments ago to the rising sun. And I was afraid. I was afraid that not all prayers are answered, or that maybe they are, but not in the ways we expect or in a language we understand.

AT A CERTAIN point, Beth and I had inflicted enough misery on each other that if a meteor fell from outer space and took us both out, the average happiness of Planet Earth would have gone up two percentage points.

We broke up. I moved to another place about a mile away, and Beth went back to see her family in Jackson, Mississippi.

Curiously, at the same time that my personal life hit historic lows, I got a gigantic career break. My agent set up a meeting with Alan Parker for the film *Mississippi Burning*. I was being considered for the part of Clayton Townley, the head of the Ku Klux Klan. I went in and met with casting great Howard Feuer and Alan Parker in Century City. I was not nervous at all. Probably because I was miserable. Misery is nature's form of Prozac.

My calmness could also have been a product of a simple artistic truth: I had an idea. I *knew* who Clayton Townley was. Lots of people think acting is about emotions. Can you cry? Can you laugh? Can you scream? Well, guess what, you can. We are all human beings. We are emotional creatures 24/7. But do we know what we're doing? That requires an idea. Most of the time actors just throw themselves at a part in what I call the Linguini Method. Throw it against a wall and see what sticks.

I thought about Clayton Townley and one notion came back over and over again. He didn't think he was a villain. He thought he was a hero for the white race. An advocate. I would not play the man as if he were one chromosome short of being a human, the way most of the villains in action films are portrayed.

I walked in and shook hands with Alan. I was thrilled to meet him. He was always one of my favorite directors. Completely unpredictable. From *Bugsy Malone*, to *Fame*, to *Midnight Express*, whatever he touched became visual gold. I was surprised I wasn't starstruck. Alan looked me over once and smirked, "Clayton Townley. How do you see the man?"

"Abraham Lincoln."

"Beg your pardon?" Alan said.

"He sees himself as Abraham Lincoln, saving a nation," I said. "I intend to play him as a hero."

Alan lifted his eyebrows and nodded. "Let's read some."

I read a couple of scenes looking out at a golf course across the street. I never looked at Howard or Alan.

My agent called up and said it went well. I was going to have a callback. Great news. I went back a week later and did the same performance. Alan called me back a third time. Now I was getting nervous. In the waiting room before the audition, the secretary smiled at me. She said they liked me a lot. She said that a lot of the other actors reading for the part were trying to be scary. I seemed to be scary naturally. I thanked her.

I read a third time and still felt good. I heard nothing. After a couple of weeks I got a call that upped the anxiety level. Alan wanted me to read a fourth time. In Mississippi. Jackson, Mississippi. They would fly me out for the day, put me up at the Holiday Inn. I would read for Alan one more time, and then fly back to Los Angeles.

As much as I was thinking about the movie, I wondered if Beth was still there visiting family. Would I call her? Would I not? Would it be just my luck she would be hanging out at the Holiday Inn? The suspense made me crazy.

I flew out to Jackson. My audition was at one p.m. so they could get me back on the four thirty p.m. flight. I walked down to a nearly empty room on the first floor. All of the lights were off except one. There was just a desk lamp focused toward a chair where Alan asked me to sit. He was sitting in the dark across the room holding a video camera. I just heard his voice.

The audition started. Alan switched on his camera and said, "So. I had dinner with your ex last night. Beth."

I was unprepared. I just smiled and said, "Oh. That's nice."

"She is really something."

I said, "Yes. She can be very amusing."

Alan continued, "Why did you two break up?"

I answered flatly, "We had a disagreement as to what constituted a joke."

There was a silence and then Alan laughed warmly and said, "Very good. Very good, indeed."

I read through the scenes once more and went back to my room. I heard a day later that I got the part. I am not sure, but I think my reply to Alan's dinner with Beth tipped the scales in my favor.

I was hired for two weeks at $3,000 a week. This money was enormous. It meant in one week I could pay two months' rent and have money left over to see a movie and buy a giant tub of popcorn.

One of the scenes I was in was a huge outdoor torchlight rally. They brought in twenty-five hundred extras to be in the audience. It was rumored that one-third of them were using their Klan cards as ID to work in the scene.

When a scene takes place at night you can be sure that you will be shooting until dawn. As springtime in Mississippi was so uncertain, they asked me if I could hang out until they had a go-ahead from the weatherman. They just needed assurance that we would have a twenty-four-hour period with no rain. My two weeks of employment stretched into ten. I was paid for each week I stayed in Mississippi waiting for the green light. I felt like someone just dumped a truckload of money on my head.

Even though I wasn't working I was "invited" to come to the set. In this movie, the "set" could have been a two-hour drive to a remote town in Mississippi, Georgia, or Alabama. But I said yes. In life it's good to say yes. Unless you were at my last party.

I was in my trailer waiting to watch them shoot a scene with Gene Hackman when I had a knock on my door. I opened it to find Alan Parker at the foot of my steps. He had heard I was interested in directing, and wondered if I wanted to follow him around and watch him do what he does.

"Sure. Great," I said.

Since this was near the beginning of my career, I thought directors always invited neophytes to follow them around. Alan first took me over to film editing where we watched his editor Gerry piece together some of yesterday's work. I asked Alan why he wasn't supervising the edit. Alan looked at me with mild irritation. "Because it's Gerry. He's the best there is and he knows what I want. That's why I use him."

We went to see John Willett over in the art department. John told Alan he had made up a new batch of OMD. "What is OMD?" I asked.

Alan smiled and said, "Shall we tell him our secret?"

John laughed and said, "Sure."

Alan got a naughty look on his face and whispered, "It stands for Old Man's Dick. It is a mix of purple, yellow, and brown. We make a wash of it and paint it on every prop, every surface of the set, every chair, every table, every door. We make a dye out of it and dip every piece of clothing in it. It's everywhere."

"Why?"

Alan smiled. "You'll see tonight. Come to the dailies."

I went with Alan that night to the screening of the work from the previous day. I couldn't wait to see what OMD did to our movie. I watched the dailies but I couldn't see anything. There was no sign of the dye or the color at all. The scene featured a black man walking down the street. Some white men taunted him. I thought I noticed something, but I wasn't sure.

Afterward Alan asked me what I saw. "I didn't see the OMD," I said.

"I didn't ask what you *didn't* see—I asked what you *saw*."

I thought for a moment and then said, "The skin. I saw the black man's skin."

Alan's face turned a lovely red and he said, "Right. The OMD is on everything except human skin. When the human eye senses sameness, it tends to discount it, and it makes what is different jump out. This movie is about the color of a man's skin. With OMD we fool the brain into focusing on skin tone. Wait till you see it on the big screen."

I continued over the next weeks to follow Alan around into sound editing, into camera rehearsals, discussions over lenses. One day the routine changed. I sat in on a meeting about the next day's work. Alan stopped almost midsentence and said, "Stephen, how would you shoot this scene?" I had the cameramen, the director of photography, and head gaffer (the man who does the lighting) looking at me with a certain amount of confusion. I stammered and offered a shooting plan. Alan said, "That would work, but it's not very good. We're doing this." And then he would list a series of shots that I never would have imagined.

For the next month Alan taught me some of the basics of film-making. He constantly threw pop quizzes at me. Quizzes I never passed. He would shake his head and say, "Well, do you understand now?" I would nod. "Yes. I think." He would laugh and we would be on to the next.

At last, we got the go-ahead to shoot the big Klan rally. Alan was having a drink in the bar with all of the actors. He looked at me and said, "Now it's your turn. Don't fuck it up." Alan looked at me seriously, but I couldn't help smiling.

I didn't know what to make of my ten weeks being schooled by Alan Parker. At the time I thought he was being a good guy. Maybe an idiosyncratic guy. I don't know. But here was a man who was not my friend, not my family, not someone who owed me money, and he was giving me the benefit of everything he had learned. A lifetime of experience. And even more precious, he gave me his time.

Harold Ramis, on the set of *Groundhog Day*, told me that making it in show business was impossible. Everyone who has made it has to have at least four heroes. Alan Parker is one of my four. I tried to thank him once a few years ago when I saw him in Westwood. He looked vaguely irritated and said, "I don't know what you're talking about. Stop it. It was nothing."

It was everything.

10.

A WAGER WITH FREDDIE

I VISITED WITH some friends from high school when I was back in Texas last summer. They asked me what it's like to work in Hollywood. They didn't realize that they were asking a trick question. The trick is that a lot of what we know as *Hollywood* is not shot in Hollywood anymore. The governing factor is usually money. Hollywood can be anywhere in the world where production is cheap.

One of the centers of cheap production for the last two decades has been Canada, more specifically, Vancouver. Vancouver is a wonderful city filled with bighearted people and highly alcoholic beers. Even if you have never been there, you've probably seen it without knowing it. Any movie that takes place in a typical American town but with lots of Indian restaurants in the background is Vancouver. Any movie that takes place in Texas, but with mountains, is probably Vancouver. And any movie whose story features an alien, zombie, space zombie, vampire, ghost, walking dead, or living dead was probably shot in Vancouver. I don't know how Vancouver became the sci-fi/monster capital of the film world, but it is.

My guess would be that it began with the enormous popularity of

The X-Files. Many series followed: *The Lone Gunmen, The Outer Limits, Millennium, Poltergeist, The Dead Zone,* and the list goes on. If you ran into a fellow actor in Vancouver, it was always a good news/bad news situation. The good news was they were working. The bad news was they were probably working with a mummy.

The first commandment of Hollywood states that as long as the viewing public wants these films and they're cheap to make, they will be made. I know many people get cognitive dissonance when they try to put the notion of a science fiction movie together with "cheap." They're thinking of James Cameron or Steven Spielberg. The principle of entropy applies to everything in the universe. Science fiction movies are no different. There is a big trickle-down from the heights of *Avatar.* And most of that trickle happens in Vancouver.

There are lots of ways a science fiction film can be made on the cheap. First, you can save a lot of money on sets by having several scenes take place in a "laboratory." This technique is a big cost-cutter. A laboratory is just an empty room, anywhere. Put a Bunsen burner and boiling beakers in it and you have a chem lab. Add a body on a slab and you have a medical lab. Throw down some old computer monitors, black desk phones, and a map of the world, and you have a Defense Department lab. Add a map of the solar system, and you have a UFO-conspiracy lab. If the room is concrete, you have an underground lab. In Vancouver they let you shoot in the sewers so you get an underground lab with lots of gauges on the walls and running water.

One of the fringe benefits of shooting in a lab is that you can save on costumes by utilizing the "lab technician." Translated from producer-speak, this means an extra in a lab coat. Give them a clipboard, and they become an engineer.

By definition, a science fiction movie should not make sense. You don't need a script. It's nice if you have one. It's very nice if you have a good one—but it's not essential. Jeff Goldblum can turn into a fly or Roland Emmerich can trot out space people, or the Mayan calendar, or weather to destroy the world over and over again, and we all have a good laugh and go out afterward for cheeseburgers.

Rather than a real script, writers use a formula of something that worked before. You can roll your own. I'll give you five seconds to fill in the blank. The earth is invaded by _____.

I say horses.

Plot: A small town is invaded by horses that have been infected by a virus that came to Earth on a meteorite. At night, the horses change into beautiful, sexy women who go to nightclubs to find prey. They flirt with young men—get them drunk—then take them out to the stables to have sex. In the morning the young men are found dead with a saddle on their back. Curtain.

Title: *The Lost Rider.*

Setting: A veterinary lab in Vancouver.

The movie I was in was called *The Traveler.* But due to some random misfortune in timing, Bill Paxton was starring in another movie called *Traveller* to be released the same month. Our producers changed the name of our film to *The Visitor*, which was not scary. *The Visitor* sounded like it could be a domestic comedy about Gramps moving in over the summer or a coming-of-age comedy about a girl's first period. So they changed the name again to *Night Visitors*, which was not particularly sci-fi, either. If you add the word "Naughty," it sounds like a skin flick.

The plot of our movie was as follows: A spaceship crash-lands somewhere in the American desert (which looks an awful lot like a Vancouver suburb). I play a power-mad, megalomaniac colonel. I am put in charge of recovering the alien from the spaceship. My soldiers find the creature and take him to our secret lab, which looks a lot like the main hub of a Canadian sewer system. But then, in a strange breach of military etiquette, I begin a ruthless campaign of kidnapping and murder to eliminate anyone who knows about the spaceship and the little spaceman. I even take out some of my own men. Why? Why not. Not sure.

I asked the writer and director why it was such a big deal that people found out about the alien landing on Earth. They both looked at me like I asked the dumbest question since "Who gave the green light for this film?" The writer said, "Are you kidding? If news got out about the alien, there would be a worldwide panic. Who knows what kind of truth he would reveal to us."

I was so far off the track on so many levels. From my experience watching movies like this, aliens never know any truth beyond what's in the Boy Scout oath. Second, I always imagined it would be kind of fun if we knew an alien landed. If we made friends with them, we would probably get to ride in the ship. We could borrow some of their technology to develop a cell phone that worked.

The script had large helpings of the usual ingredients: women and children in jeopardy, angry men with guns, and an innocent, uncomprehending alien. Just like in real life. Clichés and idiotic nonscience peppered the dialogue. The script would have been depressing if it weren't so derivative. It gave me comfort to know this wasn't someone's original vision. It was a sausage made up of bits and pieces of every alien movie I had seen over the last forty years.

One of the main ingredients of this kind of film is something referred to as "suspense," usually leading up to a dissatisfying climax. There are several possible ways to establish suspense. In this movie, the chosen route is not to show the creature until the final scenes. Most of the movie was a tease. An alien tease.

As filmgoers, we know the visual shorthand used in these types of movies all too well: the sounds of a falling flower vase in another room, odd shadows moving across walls or under closed doors, slime on floors or doorknobs. It means an alien is nearby, but we missed him. Soon, we get the gnawing feeling that someone is setting up the camera in the wrong room on purpose. The central dramatic element becomes "will we see it?" The filmmakers confuse "suspense" with "frustration" that builds throughout the film until you feel like you're talking to an IRS agent at an audit, or playing golf.

Our producers claimed that they wanted to keep the suspense of the film in the "Hitchcockian tradition." Translation: the audience's psychological horror of imagining what the alien looked like was greater than seeing him.

When I saw our alien on the set, I agreed with the producers. It was better not having seen him for the first 95 percent of the film. Not so much out of being true to the "Hitchcockian tradition," but more in clinging to the "Shakespearean tradition" of "assuming a virtue if you have it not."

The alien came out of the makeup trailer looking like a green teenager covered in calamari. It did not inspire fear, only hunger. I kept looking at him and wishing I had a squeeze of lemon and some cocktail sauce.

Of course, the main reason why the alien was not seen throughout the movie was cost. Good aliens are hard to find. When you have a good alien like Ridley Scott did in *Alien*, you have a franchise.

When the day's shoot was done, we all got in vans and headed for our home away from home. All of the actors from the States working on other sci-fi movies were put up at the Sutton Place Hotel, a.k.a. Hollywood North, a.k.a. the Gray Palace. After a long day of menacing women and children, I would sit down in the Gerard Lounge, the hotel's wonderful bar. Relaxing amidst its paneled walls, burning fireplace, and prominent moose head, I was able to muse on how big an entire moose would be. I heard that the Canadian government has since cracked down on the Sutton Place and made them remove the moose head because it represented animal cruelty. A day late and a dollar short if you ask me.

On any given night you could have one of those highly alcoholic beers or a glass of what was described as "Canadian wine" and talk over the day's work with friends. You could mingle with the locals who knew this place was an "actor's bar" and hung out here in hopes of "getting lucky."

Packs of young, attractive Canadian actresses hung around the Gerard Lounge in hopes of getting discovered by a producer. There were apocryphal stories about the local actress who hung out at the bar and was cast as Queen of the Space Vampires. I always suspected a producer started those stories.

The next week we had to shoot one of the climactic scenes of our movie. Here, we experienced another common feature of low-budget science fiction productions: the last-minute rewrite.

The scene involved the confrontation between me and the heroine of the movie (played by Faith Ford). She steals the alien from me and hides it in a box. I retaliate by kidnapping her little boy. This scene was the exchange, the final showdown. Of course, my real plan was to take the alien and kill them all.

As originally scripted the action took place at night, in a deserted warehouse district with snipers in helicopters ready to take out our leading lady. Faith pointed out to the director and producers that it made no sense for her character to go to a deserted warehouse area at night to meet me. Her character was "smart." She would pick a safe exchange location. After all, she had the alien so she could dictate terms. Logic demanded the exchange take place during the day and in a crowd. Not only did that argument make sense, but it also meant they could cut the helicopters, which cost too much anyway.

When I discovered we were shooting the final scene at the Vancouver Art Museum during the day, I was confused. I went to the director and asked why we changed the scene's location. He explained the logic of not having the scene occur at night in a deserted place. I said it made perfect sense. But the previous 95 percent of the movie (that was already shot) was based on the logic that the alien had to be kept a secret. I killed anyone who found out about the alien. The reason for kidnapping Faith's son was to keep the alien a secret. If we exchanged hostages at the Vancouver Art Museum and in broad daylight, how could I keep hundreds of extras from seeing the alien? I would have to kill them all.

The director looked like he wanted to go back home to Argentina. He asked what I would suggest. "I would suggest a rewrite three months ago, but this isn't a time travel movie," I said.

He looked at me wearily. "So . . ."

"So . . . we have to do the only thing we can do at this point. We keep the alien in the box."

"Then how do you know the alien is in the box without opening the box and showing it to everyone?" he asked.

From years of watching Saturday matinees at the Texas Theatre, I had the answer. "We have to rely on the history of other alien movies. We have to use an 'alien detector.'"

"What?"

"Yes. We will need some piece of phony equipment, like a Geiger counter, that can tell if an alien is in the area. I'll pass it over the closed box. Read the display. It reads positive for aliens. Bingo. We move forward. No one will know."

The director thought for a second. He liked it. The search started for an alien detector. One of the guys in the sound department offered us a decibel reader. It was a handheld piece of equipment with a graduated scale and a moving pointer on the front. At one end of the scale it had a C and at the other end it had an A. I thought, "This is perfect!" The A at one end could stand for "Alien" and what made this even better was that there was a button on the side of the device and when I pressed it, the pointer would jump to the letter A. This way the cameraman could get a close-up shot of the device working. The director wanted to know what to do about the C at the other end of the dial. Was it confusing? Should they black it out? What does the C stand for?

I thought for a second and said, "Crustaceans." The C stands for 'Crustaceans.' Don't worry. It'll be okay."

And it was. We shot the scene with the alien detector. It remains in the final cut of the movie. No one mentioned it at the network, in the reviews, or in the letters to *TV Guide*. As I recall, the alien remains in the box the entire film, never to be seen. As in all science fiction we ended up following the "Chekhovian tradition": "In two hundred years, who will know the difference?"

That night I celebrated in the Gerard Lounge. I had drinks with the producers and the cast. It was the happy meeting of triumph and disbelief. We had navigated the uncertain bridge of reality and crossed over into an even more uncertain world where everything was possible.

I WAS IN Vancouver shooting the movie formerly known as *The Traveler*, formerly known as *The Visitor*, currently known as *Night Visitors*, and I had a day off. Days off in Vancouver can be wonderful. You can go to Stanley Park or Granville Island and explore. You can eat fudge by the pound at the candy store across from the hotel or just sit outside and sip a cappuccino at one of the three hundred Starbucks in the city.

I walked in the park by the seawall until it looked like rain and then I headed back. I went up to my room and turned on the TV. The television at the Sutton Place had three regular channels. I flipped on channel one. There I was on *Seinfeld*. I changed the channel. There I was again in an old TV movie, *The Marla Hanson Story*. I changed the channel again, and *bam*! There I was in *Thelma & Louise*, sitting in a helicopter with Harvey Keitel. It was supernatural.

There were lots of ways to interpret this omen. I could have been proud to be all over Canadian television, but that's not what I felt. I was working on a science fiction movie. Perhaps I had died at the fudge store earlier this morning and went into some sort of hell where I was doomed to watch myself forever. No, that wasn't it, either. What fascinated me was that each role on TV displayed me in a different state of baldness. It was like strapping into an unflattering time machine. Dorian Gray in reverse. The bottom line was I couldn't afford to age any more. I turned off the set and went down to the bar to kill some time before the television killed me.

It was early. The Gerard Lounge was pretty empty. Deb, the bartender, had been there for years. (Ann and I met Deb in this bar when we were dating.) I decided to sit at the bar, study my script, and chat with her. I started reading scenes for tomorrow when an older man sat down a couple of stools away from me. He eyed me, then opened his newspaper and began to read. There was the Zen sound of reading while drinking alcoholic beverages for a couple of minutes. Then, the man spoke to me.

"You an extra?"

"Beg your pardon?" I said.

"I see you're reading a script. I wondered if you were an extra."

"No. I'm an actor."

"Extras always say they're actors."

"Maybe. But they don't give extras scripts."

"So, you say you're an actor. Do you have lines?"

"Yes. I have a lot of lines."

"You don't look like an actor. You're bald."

"You can go upstairs right now and turn on your TV and see me with hair."

"Yeah?"

"Yeah. On three different channels."

"What do you play in the movie?"

"The bad guy. The main bad guy. I murder people."

I was thinking about murdering this strange man, and I had only been talking to him for forty seconds. In acting class, students always ask, "How would you play a murderer like Othello or Macbeth?" Easy. Imagine you're Othello and Desdemona comes into the bedroom and asks you if you're an extra.

I can't think of any other profession publicly hammered to the extent that acting is on a regular basis. I would never go up to someone and say, "So you say you're a waiter? What restaurant do you work at? Nice place, or just a McDonald's? If it's a McDonald's, then you're not really a waiter. Do you do dinner or just lunch? Do you have a jacket with your name on it? Oh, you *don't* have a *full* bar—just wine, okay, okay. I get it."

This fellow at the bar was riling me. But I thought that I was in this country for two more weeks. I didn't want to be arrested by a Mountie. It would be humiliating. I introduced myself.

"Good evening. I'm Stephen. Stephen Tobolowsky."

"Never heard of you."

"Well, what's your name, because I'm sure I've never heard of you, either?"

He offered his hand. "Freddie."

He didn't look like a Freddie but why would he lie about something like that? "Nice to meet you, Freddie. What do you do?"

"I'm a gambler."

"Really?"

"Yes."

"A professional gambler?"

"It's what I do. And if you play me, I'll break you. I mean it. I'll break you."

"Well, then I won't play you. I don't gamble, Freddie."

"That's what they all say. Then they take me on. And I have no mercy. I'm not kidding. I've broken men. They've cried. I took away their homes, their cars, their bank accounts, and they cried. They say, 'Please don't. Please don't. It's all I've got. I have a wife and family.' I just looked at them. I didn't care. I didn't even feel sorry for them."

"Well, that sounds a little hard, Freddie."

"If it's *all* he's got, he shouldn't have played me."

"You're right. You're right about that. That's why I don't gamble." I knew at this point I was involved with a crazy person, a drunk, or Satan. I didn't like my options.

"Afraid to lose?" Freddie muttered.

"What?"

"Are you afraid to lose? Is that why you don't gamble?"

"No. I don't gamble because I don't get pleasure in winning. I get tense when I win. I hate it when I lose, so what's the point?"

Freddie straightened on his seat. "The point is I'm a fuckin' millionaire. That's the point. I can buy this hotel. I can buy this whole fuckin' block. I can buy and sell you a dozen times over."

"Of course you can. That's easy. I'm an actor. I'm working on a space movie now where we never see the alien. What does that make me?"

"What?"

"Exactly. I can be bought, Freddie. That's kind of my job description. Stephen Tobolowsky. He. Can. Be. Bought."

Unaccustomed to verbal aikido, Freddie just stared at me. He pulled out a folded dollar bill. "You want to play Liar's Poker?"

"No! Are you kidding? Put that thing away. That's probably your goofy Liar's Poker dollar with six zeros on it. Put it away. I don't want you to break me. I don't want you to make me cry. I don't want to be another corpse on your doorstep, Freddie. I'm doing you a favor."

Freddie put the dollar back in his wallet. "Margo begged me to stop."

"Margo?"

"My wife. She begged me to stop."

"You should listen to her. Especially if you're already a millionaire. Maybe enough is enough. Do you have any children?"

"I have a son. He's studying to be a screenwriter at USC."

"A screenwriter? We could have used him on this movie. Well, God bless him. I hope he does well."

Freddie grew pale. "What does God have to do with it? God has nothing to do with it. Fuck that. I paid for his school. Not God. My son does the work and gets the grades, not God."

"Freddie, it's just an expression. I was only wishing your son well."

"Then keep your stinking God out of it."

My cheeks flushed. Freddie noted my shaken composure with another sip of scotch.

I've heard gamblers always look for the "tell" in their opponents. The little subconscious gesture that always tells the truth, the sign that betrays your bluffs and reveals what you hold dear. Freddie had been looking for mine, and he may have found it. The glue that holds a person together is either values or vanity. It is always detectable when we least expect it.

Two women in their midtwenties walked past us and took a table near the end of the bar. It caused Freddie to stop midsip. He watched them as they took their seats and scoped out the room. Freddie eyed them. He sipped on his scotch. He grinned and spoke to me with a certain air of conspiracy. "Hmm. They're cute."

"They're twenty-five years old, Freddie. They're supposed to be cute. That's their job."

"Should we buy them some drinks and go over there?"

"What?"

"Should we buy them drinks?"

I was unprepared for this turn. I don't know why. This man who had been trying to dismantle me all afternoon wanted to hit on these girls. And he wanted me to be his wingman.

"Freddie, we're married. What would Margo say? And they're young enough to be your granddaughters. Your granddaughters! What would you talk to them about? School? What cell phone plan they have? Try to get them to play Liar's Poker with you and break them? I'm sure if you went over there, you would make them cry. I guarantee it. I'll go further, if you bought them drinks and went over there, you would ruin their evening."

"You think?"

"One hundred percent positive. Absolutely. No question."

"Really?"

"Really. I'll bet you." The words were out of my mouth before I knew what I had said.

Freddie went silent. He stared into me. "What do you want to bet?"

"Well, you know how I feel about gambling—we'll have to make it interesting . . ."

Freddie's complexion started to transform. "Name it."

"I bet that I can prove to you that God exists. Right here. Right now. In fifteen minutes."

Freddie was glowing. "And if you lose?"

"If I lose I'll buy drinks for the girls and go over to the table with you."

Freddie was almost jumping off his stool. "And if you win?"

"If I win, we don't go over."

"What do you want from me?"

"Just the look on your face will be enough. I'm sure of that."

Freddie considered the wager. He looked at me again. He offered his hand. "You're on." He looked at his watch. "Fifteen minutes. Starting now."

I looked into Freddie's eyes and sensed a line of attack. "Freddie, what was the time in your life you were most desperate, in the greatest despair?"

Freddie smiled, his face softened. "I was twenty-seven years old. I was a geologist surveying one of the ice sheets of Greenland. It was winter. That means night. No sun. We were sent out in groups of four. We had small lanterns dangling from our backpacks so you could see the rest of the party in the dark. We had been out for hours. We were exhausted. We were walking back to base camp. A blizzard was coming in fast. It was over 100 degrees below zero. The wind made it hard to walk. I had fallen behind the rest of the group, but I could still see the three lanterns ahead of me swaying in the distance. With the roaring wind and the darkness I couldn't see where I was going. I lost my concentration, and I stepped into a hole in the ice. A crevasse. I fell into a fissure two thousand feet deep. But I was lucky. I landed on an ice shelf three feet wide— thirty feet down from the surface. Another foot out from the wall and I would have fallen half a mile. I landed on my backpack. I tried to get up. I couldn't. I was hurt. I didn't know if I had broken my spine, my pelvis, an ankle. I just knew I couldn't feel my legs. I couldn't move. It was quiet down in the ice. I could hear the wind roaring up top. We were given whistles for emergencies. I got mine out and blew it. And blew. It echoed in the glacier, but I knew in the blizzard they would never hear me. So I'm thinking if I tried to stand up and my leg gave way, or if I slipped on the ice, I'd be dead. If I tried to climb out and fell, I would never land on that shelf again. All I could do was lie there, looking up at the black sky, and die. And I know what you're going to say. That while I was lying there, I prayed to God. 'Oh please, please, God, please, help me!' I did not."

"No, I wasn't going to say that at all. I was going to say, 'Wow.' That sounds bad, Freddie. That is a bad situation. I was sitting here wondering how you got out. I can't believe you're sitting here. How did you survive?"

"And I know where you're going with this, too, and it had nothing to do with God. It was my partners. They saved me. They got back to base camp. And after about twenty minutes, they realized I wasn't coming back. They got dressed again and went out and found me. They pulled me out. They saved my life. Not God."

"Why?"

"Why what?"

"Why did they save you? You weren't family. I'm sure it wasn't your endearing personality. Why?"

Freddie raised his eyebrows. He sipped his drink. No answer. I pressed on. "I'm looking at it from their perspective, Freddie. They come back. They're wet and freezing, too. They get back to safety, to the fire. They undress, and even have a hot toddy and are getting ready to unload on the day. Then they realize you're not there. What do they do? They make a decision—a decision not based on logic—certainly not based on self-preservation or survival. They put their drinks down, curse you a little, and then they suit up and head back out into the storm. They left safety and comfort for you. They did it for selfish reasons. They knew if they left you to die it would haunt them forever. They knew that they had to do everything in their power to save your life. Not because it was you, but because it was life. In that instant they knew on a molecular level that life is holy. Yes, it was your friends that saved you. But they did it because they felt the invisible connection that holds us all together. And I would say that invisible cord is God. Without God there is no holy. And without holy, there is no you. You died on the ledge."

Freddie looked at me. I felt as though we sat there for five minutes, even though I'm sure it was only five seconds. And then he smiled. "Pretty good. Pretty good. Okay. I'll give you that one."

I was right. The look on his face was enough.

I don't know that Freddie bought everything I said, but I do think he was amused by my effort. Maybe that was Freddie's "tell." He would always have a weakness for someone who made an effort. Someone who suited up and went back out to face the storm. We ordered another round of drinks. Freddie paid.

He took a sip of his scotch and looked over at the girls again. "Do you really think it would be a mistake to buy them some drinks and go over there?"

"Freddie, I thought you said you were a gambler. And the way I learned it, the first rule of gambling is that if you're afraid to lose, you can't afford to play."

11.

LISTEN TO THE DOG

IT WAS CHRISTMAS Eve in Topanga. 1979. It was a party of about twelve friends. We had a turkey dinner with all the trimmings: apple pie, bottles of wine, homemade jalapeño jam. We were sitting around by the fire drinking buckets of cowboy coffee listening to *Blood on the Tracks* when Joe came out from the kitchen, smiling.

"Attention, everyone. I have an announcement to make."

We paused in our merriment.

"My Christmas gift to you all has come a little early. To brighten up your holiday I've put LSD in all of your coffees."

I stared into my now empty mug. Different phrases popped into my mind, like "Kill him, kill him, kill him now," "With friends like that you don't need enemies," and "Why are the lights on the Christmas tree moving around the room?"

You have to understand that I have never been an advocate for drugs, even in college, even in the late sixties. I never understood them. I avoided them. People who did drugs in those days didn't bathe regularly. They missed a lot of classes. They wore odd clothing combinations like T-shirts with top hats, and they listened to lots of FM radio. It all scared me.

I later learned that the main reason people took up drugs in grad school was to watch something called *Monty Python's Flying Circus*. I had no idea. So I broke down. In 1975, at the University of Illinois, I succumbed to peer pressure and smoked something called "hash" and watched the program. The show was quite humorous in its own right. Mercifully the "hash" had no effect on me at all. That time.

It had no effect the next week, either.

The third week it had an effect.

My friend's version was I was watching the show, smoking hash, and I passed out. My version was that the couch I was sitting on turned into a large, toothless mouth covered with cat hair. It swallowed me whole and I slid down an upholstered esophagus lined with chips and beer, and landed in the stomach of hell.

My first high. After this first experience, I was reluctant to use drugs again. This disappointed many of my friends. I never knew which part of the drug experience they wanted me to revisit: the nausea, the cat hair, or the loss of consciousness. The First Rule of drug use: *There is no experience bad enough, no decision boneheaded enough that it cannot be revisited—often.*

I counted myself one of the lucky ones. The only long-term effect of those Saturday evenings with the hash pipe was that I did start listening to more FM radio.

But I digress. 'Twas the night before Christmas. I had drunk a mug of LSD and the lights on the Christmas tree had started walking around the room. They were changing colors. My heart pounded in my ears louder and louder. I was furious that I had been ambushed over the holidays and I wasn't even visiting my parents.

My pal Joe, who put the acid in the coffee, told me I should calm down and "go with the flow," otherwise, my negative emotions could make the next few hours unpleasant. This pep talk spawned a truckload of negative emotions. It was way too much flow. That was about the time I realized that my brain was too big for my skull and my eyes could pop out of the front of my face.

I mentioned this to our hostess, who was staring at a row of jelly jars in her kitchen. She stopped and turned to me and said, "Cool. You're starting to rush."

"Rush?"

"Yeah. The blood really starts flowing. It can get pretty intense."

"Intense?"

"Yeah."

"Is that intense *good*, like sex, or intense *bad*, like stepping on a tack?"

She pondered the question, weighing many unseen variables. "It's, just, well . . . it's just . . . intense."

Rule Number Two of taking drugs: *There is no utterance pointless or meaningless enough that it cannot be construed as folk wisdom.*

I was "rushing." It was intense. And in this case it was intense *bad*. My skin was on fire. I thought I was going to have a stroke. My hostess advised that I needed to get in a cool, dark place for a while—like I was a jar of jam—or a crock of pickles. Act like a salamander.

That sounded good to me. I told her I always liked salamanders. They came in a variety of colors and had cool toes. I could do that. I started crawling on the floor on my hands and knees.

My hostess left her jars long enough to lead me down the hallway to the guest bathroom at the back of her house. This bathroom had ceramic tiles. It would be cool and dark. She told me I should lie down in the coolest and darkest place in the room, which was around the base of the toilet.

She soaked a blue towel in cold water and wrapped it around my head like a turban. I curled around the base of the toilet looking like Sabu, the Indian boy. She turned out the lights and told me to rest for a few minutes. She closed the door.

Utter and complete blackness.

If Einstein ever wanted a real-world scenario to prove his theory of relativity, I would offer this premise: take a man, wrap his head in a wet, blue towel, and have him hug the base of a stranger's toilet in the dark. I promise you: for him, Time. Will. Stop. The only way I knew I was still alive was that I had a reenergized sense of self-hatred.

I don't know how long I was in the bathroom. I crawled out, eventually. The rushes were gone, and I needed some fresh air. Turban still in place, I crawled back down the hallway. I hung a right at the kitchen, bypassed the laughter coming from the living room, and headed for the back porch.

I opened the screen door and crawled outside. I sat next to the dog of the house. His name was Manny More. He was one of those shepherd-mix dogs that wore a red bandana and rode in the backs of pickup trucks. In his younger days he probably chased Frisbees on the beach. Now he was content to do what most country dogs end up doing—panting and scratching.

I didn't know this dog well. A couple of pats here and there and maybe a potato chip passed to him under the table. I felt like there was no time like the present to bridge the gap. I began talking to him. I said, "Manny, you are so wise. So noble. We haven't spent a lot of time together. I just wanted to take this opportunity to change that, here, on this beautiful night. I envy your tranquility, your peace of mind."

Manny turned toward me and said, "Stephen, I have no peace of mind. You have no idea what you're talking about. We both look out into the night but from different perspectives. I have keener senses than you do. With my sense of smell and my hearing, I know, for example, that there is a coyote right behind that clump of trees, just waiting for me to go too far from the house. These mountains are filled with predatory birds. Hawks, owls. There's danger everywhere in the dark that I can sense, but you have no idea is even there. That's why you romanticize the night. I don't. I know the night for what it is. But you humans—all of your poetry, your art, your music arise from your weaknesses: your desire to romanticize the night."

"Wow. Manny, you're right."

Here I recalled Rule Number Three of using drugs: *If the dog talks to you, listen. Always listen to the dog.*

Another wave of laughter from inside the house interrupted my moment with Manny More. I stood up for the first time in what seemed like hours and walked back to see what I was missing. And I had missed a lot. Someone had set the house on fire.

There was a line of all my friends laughing uproariously as they shook their beers and tried to "squirt" the fire out. Our host and hostess threw pans of water on the wall leaving a smoldering, wet, black mess.

Here, Rule Number Four of using drugs came into play. It is perhaps the most important rule of all: *No one is to blame. For anything. Ever. It is a world without consequences.*

This rule, I believe, is the key to all addiction. Physical dependence can be overcome through abstinence. But drugs create a more enticing arena where we can become addicted to the drama of our own bad choices.

I wandered away from the group and into the deserted living room. I sat on the floor and watched my friends, the Christmas tree, the smoke. I looked at the ornaments, some handmade. I thought about Christmas and what a special time of year it is. I thought about how far we had come since that first Christmas so long ago in Bethlehem. But then I thought, maybe not. Maybe we haven't traveled that far at all. Jesus was born in a stable—not unlike Topanga—sort of. Animals figured prominently in that story, too. And in most Renaissance paintings, Joseph is alone, wearing a blue turban, with a confused look on his face.

The first rays of the sun came up over the Santa Monica Mountains. Night was over. The Fifth Rule of doing drugs: *The sun will eventually rise. The party will eventually end.*

Return to the world of consequences and regret is inevitable. And inevitability, after all, was the bottom line. For the person who doesn't believe in God, for the person who has no faith, the handiest substitute for the eternal is the inevitable. And for that, the sun will do as well as any deity.

I staggered out to my car. My thighs ached. My hostess explained that was caused by the strychnine used in the making of LSD. It would make my legs sore for the next two or three days, a small price to pay for an evening that set a new benchmark for terror and personal shame.

I took a deep breath. It was Christmas morning. The road would be empty. The highway would belong to me. In the quiet of the car I recalled the final rule of using drugs: *Conserve your strength. You'll need all of your energy to try to forget what just happened.*

I backed out of the dirt driveway and, as I headed for the main road, through my rearview mirror, I saw a patch of red moving through the tall brush. It was a bandana. I stopped and turned to look. Through the rising dust, I saw Manny More. He was wandering off into the foothills. Off to explore by light of day the dangers that we could only romanticize at night.

12.

MISS HARD TO GET

W**HEN YOU ARE** young, the biggest event in your life is school, and at school there is hardly anything more newsworthy than "new kids." I was in second grade when we merged classes. The kids from the other first-grade class were now a part of my world.

Mrs. Cooper was our teacher. She had a system to keep everything in order. We kids were organized alphabetically and by height. I was always tall for my age. The practical application of the Cooper System meant that I was surrounded by tall girls whose name began with letters at the end of the alphabet: Reynolds, Rice, Richards, Sims, Simmons.

I probably should have been seatmates with Sylvia Sims or Phyllis Simmons, but they were too short. Part two of the Cooper System—the height variable—paired me with Claire Richards.

Being almost as tall as I, Claire always sat right in front of me. She was always standing ahead of me in line. I would like to say that I was fond of her smile—which was sunny—or thrilled by her laugh and her conversation—except she didn't talk to me. She was from the other class, and I was a boy. But because of our relative positions in life, I became enchanted with the back of her head.

She had honey-brown hair. Shoulder-length. When we walked down the hallway, it swayed in front of me. I started feeling like our cat, Tom, eyeing a piece of string, wanting to paw at it. This was the extent of our relationship for the first few weeks at school. One day everything changed.

That day was Uniform Day. It was ordained that if you were in the Cub Scouts or Girl Scouts, or Brownies, one day a week you could wear your outfits. Claire, I discovered, was a Bluebird. She showed up at school in her red and blue Bluebird outfit and cap.

On Uniform Day, Claire wore her hair in a ponytail that she pulled out a hole cut in the back of her Bluebird cap. When she walked down the hallway, her ponytail swung back and forth. I noticed a funny something happen in my stomach. I got a nervous feeling when I watched that ponytail swing through that Bluebird cap. A little voice inside me was saying, "Man, I don't know what that is—but I like it."

The next big change in our relationship happened in music class. Fridays were talent days. People could get up and play a piece, usually on the piano. Claire got up and started playing a version of "Pickin' Up Paw Paws" that was so rousing the class started clapping and stomping in time. The music teacher applauded at its conclusion and demanded that she play it again. To this day it was one of the greatest performances I have seen, just for the moving effect the music had on its audience.

I was a goner. I was smitten, not just by Claire, but by music. I dreamed about music. I pretended I was a pianist in class and played "Pickin' Up Paw Paws" on my desk. Mrs. Cooper scolded me and told me not to thump. I couldn't help it. Not only was I not going to stop, my repertoire was expanding. I started including wild pianistic works that only existed in my brain, played on my desk for the back of Claire's head.

Mrs. Cooper reached the breaking point. She chastised me in front of the class for "being disruptive." She made me stand at the front of the room with my nose in a chalk circle she drew on the blackboard. But I didn't care. I knew what I was going to do the rest of my life. I would play the piano and marry Claire. It felt good getting those big decisions out of the way.

After Sunday school our family would occasionally go over to my Uncle Hymie's house. He had the greatest treasure of all, a grand piano. The house would fill with all my relatives eating brisket and sweet potatoes and talking. I would come in and sit down at that huge, beautiful piano and start playing. I didn't know how to play. I would just hit notes and try to tell a story with the sounds. I would hit a mass of bass notes and stomp on the pedal and in my head there were roars of something dangerous coming. Then, I would touch the treble keys, and I would see a girl running up the stairs for protection and shouting from a tower for help.

My improvisations drove all the grown-ups out of the room grumbling, except for my Aunt Hermine. She would move closer. She sat on the couch and listened. When I finished she applauded and asked me what I was playing. I told her the story. She nodded and said, "That's really quite good."

My Aunt Hermine was always a hero of mine. She was a smart, no-nonsense woman. I learned she wrote and worked to pass the Equal Rights Amendment to the Texas Constitution. Later she co-authored the National Equal Rights Amendment that failed to get passage. I had no idea when I was eight that she had been threatened and shot at because of her causes. She always stood up for the underdog. As far as I was concerned, her main achievement was being my musical patron.

She talked to Mom and Dad about having a budding pianist in their midst. After what seemed like months of requests, Mom and Dad agreed to let me take piano lessons. They bought an Acrosonic piano, which was as small and inexpensive a piano as could be had back then. Mom set up lessons with Miss Hamby, a gentle older woman who lived with her sister. My mother would drive me to Miss Hamby's house once a week. There wasn't enough time for her to drive home and drive all the way back again, so Mom would sit in her car and read until I was done. She never complained.

When you start taking piano lessons, you realize the distance between dreams and reality. Not just for the young pianist, but for the parents. For the child, he or she discovers they may be years away from a hands-together version of "Silent Night," decades away from "Pickin' Up Paw Paws." As for Mozart or Beethoven, well, that was witchcraft.

For the parents, you would think the biggest nightmare would be buying a piano and paying for lessons, and then having the child protest that they wanted to go outside and play and not practice, making the enterprise a waste of money. Right? But in reality the bigger problem is when the child *does* practice and he's terrible and he's loud and you've been working all day at the office and you want to just sit and relax and watch television and the child slogs away at "Big Chief Wahoo" for the twentieth time in a row. I'm sure it can make someone homicidal. That was me.

I practiced for the next two years. Not only did Dad have to endure the noise at home, it was now his parental duty to go to the recitals. He got to hear twenty other children who didn't know how to play, banging and stumbling through terrible pieces.

I would like to say that I was faithful to my talent or lack of it. But I wasn't. In fourth grade I started getting the idea that maybe the piano was not my instrument. Maybe I should allow myself to branch out. At one school talent show I saw sixth-grader Bobby Caldwell pull out a clarinet. Again I was swept away by the magic of the notes falling on top of one another in such a clever way. Perhaps the clarinet was the instrument for me.

Through the school, I signed up to rent a clarinet for six weeks. When Mom saw the bill she asked me why I was getting a clarinet and what about my piano lessons? I assured her that I would continue with Miss Hamby, but I just might be a double threat. And I was.

I showed up to band practice in the morning with my new clarinet. It was a foregone conclusion that I couldn't play the thing. I had never held one. When I opened the case I was shocked when I saw that it came in pieces. I had no idea how to put one together. Bobby Caldwell graciously showed me how to assemble it. And then I started playing. Like my piano playing at Uncle Hymie's, I just blew and moved my fingers. Instead of music a horrific series of shrieks and squeaks tore through the room. I sounded like a parrot being run over by a lawnmower.

In the band room I had no Aunt Hermine to protect me. I had Mr. Graham, the bandleader. He quieted everyone and looked at me with absolute mystification.

"Stephen, what are you doing?"

"I'm playing."

"Do you know how to play a clarinet?"

"No, sir. Not yet."

"Well, I think you should come back after you've had some lessons. Then you can play with us."

"Yes, sir."

I was back at band practice the next morning. Everyone looked at me. I sat down, put my clarinet together, and started playing. Mr. Graham heard the shrieks and squeaks and stared at me.

"Stephen, you're back."

"Yes, sir."

"I thought you were going to learn how to play first."

"Yes, sir. I thought Bobby could teach me something."

Mr. Graham nodded and said, "Bobby, why don't you take Stephen over to the other side of the room and show him how to hold a clarinet."

Bobby smiled and said, "Sure."

Bobby Caldwell was the best player in the band and an expert at the clarinet. He not only showed me how to hold a clarinet but that morning he taught me how to play "This Old Man." I was playing music! I rushed home from school that day and gave Mom a private concert. She laughed and clapped. My rapid progress impressed her. One day, one recognizable song.

I showed up the next morning. Mr. Graham looked exasperated. He said stoically, "Stephen, the band has to practice today, so it would help us out if you just pretend to play."

I nodded. I sat next to Bobby Caldwell. I put my clarinet together and smiled. The band started a song. I pretended to blow in the clarinet and move my fingers like Bobby's. After a moment or two, it was too much. The music was overwhelming and I had to play. I just tried to play softly and mimic Bobby's finger placements. At the end of the song I was so excited. I had played it! Without being able to read a note of music I played it and it sounded good. I turned to Bobby and said, "I did it. I did it, Bobby. I played the song." Bobby smiled and shook his head. "No, you didn't."

Mr. Graham said I had to leave the band room. I was disrupting the practice. There was a school concert coming up at the end of the week. It was unfair to the rest of the band. I felt like I was standing in Mrs. Cooper's room again with my nose in a chalk circle. Mr. Graham told me to leave and learn to play the clarinet. I could audition for the band next year. I nodded.

The next morning I showed up at band practice and started putting together my clarinet. When Mr. Graham walked in and saw me, he changed colors from normal to red to white and to red again. I realize in hindsight, that morning I probably got the benefit of Mr. Graham being a good Christian man. He asked me once again to step into the hallway. "Stephen, this has got to stop. What are you doing here?"

"I just enjoy the practice."

"Stephen, you are not in the band. You won't be in the band until you know how to play a musical instrument. Go home. Take lessons. Come back in a year. If you can play then, you can come to practice."

"What are you going to work on today?"

"We're working on songs for the concert. We'll be arranging where everyone is sitting and the order of the show."

"Where do you want me to sit?"

Mr. Graham took a beat of silence, then a moment of prayer, then a pause for reflection, and just said quietly, "In the audience. I want you to sit in the audience." I didn't go back to band practice for the rest of the week.

The day of the concert when our class marched into the auditorium, I brought my clarinet. Mark Wright asked me what was in the case. I told him it was a clarinet. Mr. Graham wanted me in the audience. We sat down, and I started assembling my clarinet. I ran my fingers over the stops readying myself for whatever Mr. Graham would ask me to do.

The other kids around me were looking over, staring, wondering what I was doing. The concert began. Bobby Caldwell played a featured solo with the band backing him. Everyone applauded. I figured maybe I would be doing "This Old Man." I started to go through my piece, mentally. The band launched into the second number and the third—still no indication from Mr. Graham that I was needed. Mark Wright looked over at me and shook his head. Roy Scott turned around and asked what I was doing with the clarinet. I told him that I would be playing soon. "No, you won't," he said.

He was right. The concert concluded. I saw Claire Richards looking at me as I disassembled my clarinet. "Mr. Graham never called on me. I guess he forgot," I said. Claire nodded. That was the end of my clarinet adventure. I continued the piano with a renewed passion.

I studied with Miss Hamby from ages eight to fourteen. I was now playing beginning classical works by Clementi and Mozart and some simple preludes by Chopin. In the same period of time, Claire became one of the better young pianists in Dallas. She played major concert works in competition.

Despite my longing for greatness, I couldn't jump the high bar at the piano. I would never approach the breadth of talent of someone like Claire. She could transport an audience and transform music into some higher form of spiritual matter. I had the ability to sound like I could play but not much more.

That's what I thought. Then magic struck at my final recital for Miss Hamby. Recitals were performed onstage at an old mansion in our area. There were always about twenty nervous performers and forty or so equally nervous parents at these events. The little ones played "Big Chief Wahoo" and "Piccolo Pete" like I did so long ago. Over the years as I became more advanced, I was moved further and further into the program. Jack Nunn was the closer. He was actually good. I had moved into the honored semifinal slot.

I played Valse in E-flat by Auguste Durand. It was a fast piece, flashy, with lots of familiar parts you've heard a thousand times before even though you never knew it came from this piece. In the first section there are three ascending arpeggios with dramatic chords that set up the light, delightful waltz section that follows. I played these arpeggios with such passion and such flair and so perfectly (for once), I was feeling so good—I decided to add a fourth arpeggio, one that ascended even higher, even more dramatically. As I played, I ran out of piano keys and fell off the end of the bench onto the floor.

The audience gasped. I sprung to my feet. I called out to the crowd, "No need to be alarmed. It's all part of the piece." The audience laughed. I grabbed the music and showed them the page of notes and pointed. "See. Right here it says, 'Pianist falls.'" They laughed harder. I bowed and they all applauded. I sat back down at the piano and continued playing. And at that moment magic descended. The audience was transformed. I had done it. I filled them with terror and within a moment changed it to delight. I had talent. I was just in the wrong field. Right after that I auditioned for my first school play. A comedy.

———

IT SHOULD BE mentioned that I believe in love at first sight. It is not a good thing or a nice thing, but it is a real thing. It was the beginning of my sophomore year in college, the day the new students arrived. The green room at the theater department at Southern Methodist University filled with all sorts of new faces. There were lots of pale, angst-ridden young women with stringy hair wearing black leotard tops. There were young gay men wearing powder-blue sweaters and corduroy pants. They were all away from home for the first time.

The energy in the room was too much for me. I climbed the spiral staircases to the dark, empty theaters upstairs. To the left was the large proscenium theater, the Bob Hope, and to the right was the experimental theater, the Margo Jones. I went to the right. The

Margo Jones was considered experimental not because of the plays performed there, but because the seats were on rollers and could be arranged in different configurations—which they never configured. So it remained an "experiment-waiting-to-happen" theater.

I climbed to the back of one of the banks of seats and sat and looked at the stage, which was lit by what they call a ghost light, a single bulb on a movable stand in the middle of the stage. I sat in the darkness wondering what my future would be. Would I get cast in a play this year? Would the gods smile on me? Would I gain favor?

A stage door opening and closing interrupted my reverie. I heard footsteps backstage. A girl, looking uncertain, peered around one of the curtains at the empty space. She stood there taking in the room. She never saw me in the dark.

She crept around the curtain and stood alone onstage. I imagined she was like me, wondering what her future would be, and if this empty space would be a starting point for something extraordinary. But then, unlike me, she took a pose as if she were a tightrope walker—arms extended—tottering as if she were losing her balance. She acted like she regained her composure on the high wire and started to make her way across the stage, step by step. I watched her focus on moving from one point of imaginary safety to another. And as I watched, I fell in love.

I can't explain how or why, but I did. I remained silent—the perfect audience—involved and transformed. I found out her name was Beth. She was from Jackson, Mississippi. That was odd. I never expected to meet anyone from Mississippi, let alone fall in love with someone from there.

I became aware of several practical difficulties with love at first sight. First of all, almost by definition, you are already in the deep end of the pool and the other person doesn't even know your name. That's always tough on a relationship. Another problem is that it's hard to start an introductory conversation without sounding creepy. "Hello, Beth, I got your name from a teacher. You didn't know it, but I was sitting in the dark, watching you in the empty theater the other day." Creepy.

I ended up trying to find a way to drop in and meet her "at work." Everyone in the theater department worked after classes doing some form of manual labor related to the theater: building sets, making costumes, hanging lights. Beth worked on sets that semester. The previous year I had worked on sets. I knew the head of the shop, R.B. Hill. R.B. was a loud, funny, gregarious man who was never shy about giving his opinions. I remember when I was on his crew the previous year he told me that he had worked with a lot of five-thumbed idiots before, but I was the first six-thumbed idiot he had ever met.

R.B. was surprised to see me back in the shop. I introduced myself to Beth as one of R.B.'s right-hand men. R.B. grumbled that I didn't even qualify as a foot. I managed to tag along with Beth to the cafeteria for dinner that night. We ate peanut butter sandwiches. She told me she was an orphan, information I didn't know how to process. I later found out she wasn't. Her father was a state senator, and she enjoyed spinning yarns as a somewhat dangerous recreational activity, like waterskiing.

I think she could sense I liked her. It flattered her. But she wanted nothing to do with me. She told me I was not her type. I was crushed, but I kept smiling as if the whole conversation were still some sort of joke. I asked why. What was her type? She said the man she would fall in love with had to have four characteristics. "He has to be a genius, he has to be either radically liberal or radically conservative, he has to have a beard or a mustache, and he has to have acne scars."

In other words, Edward James Olmos. But we didn't know him, so I still had a shot.

I would ask her about her life. Growing up. I would get indecipherable pieces of a puzzle. She said she lived in a closet. She cut out pictures of people in love from magazines so she would know what it looked like when she saw it. She swore the only man she ever loved was Chico Bambico. She kept his picture in a locket she wore on her heart.

I was jealous of this Bambico person, whoever he was. I kept asking her questions about him. Beth whispered that he was the only real man she knew. I finally got her to open the locket one day. Chico Bambico was a hound dog.

She said she loved snow. She hated telephones. Her eyes would flash joy and then I would see her fall into a hole of despair. I never could get a handle on who she was. And I don't think I was being dense. I just think she was hard to get.

I kept seeing her. I kept showing up. Just like with the clarinet, I didn't know the notes, but I knew how it would sound if I did. I just kept moving my hands over the stops like someone who could play, hoping at the end of the process I would have a tune of some kind, even if it was only "This Old Man."

I visited Beth at her dorm. I would have dinner with her. I would walk her to class. I never touched her. I never held her hand. It all meant too much to me. If I did something that made her say once and for all, "Go away. I don't want you," I didn't know what I would do.

Love can be a hopeless thing. And love without expression can be a killing thing. One day I was walking through the green room of the theater department after class. I knew Beth was in the cafeteria having lunch. Instead of following my usual instinct to run to meet her, I took a turn down a different hallway and ended up in another part of the building.

I wandered down a strange dark corridor with row upon row of wooden cubicles. Then I heard piano music. I was in the music wing and these were practice rooms. I walked down another narrow hallway and saw an open door. Inside the tiny, dark room was a piano and a chair. I went inside, turned on the light, and closed the door. I sat down and started to play. I played some of the old recital songs I learned at Miss Hamby's. Then I regressed and played the kinds of make-believe tunes that used to drive audiences out of the room at Uncle Hymie's. And out of that mess I heard a chord and a pattern that I liked. I repeated it. I added to it. A couple of hours later I had a song. I called it "Snow Song." It was an inconsiderable thing, but "'twas mine own."

That evening I went over to Beth's dorm. I called up to her room and asked if she would come down to the lobby. The lobby of Boaz Hall was a cozy open room with a few odd couches and chairs. Boys and girls could talk freely in a highly supervised, armed-guard environment.

Beth came down. She was upset that I didn't have lunch with her. She thought maybe I was mad at her. I told her I wasn't. I was busy and had something to show her. I led her over to the old grand piano in the middle of the lobby. I asked her to sit on the bench. I sat beside her. My hands moved trembling to the keys. I played "Snow Song." I told her I wrote it for her because she loved snow. It was her song. Her eyes flashed joy. She told me no one had ever written a song for her. I told her, "Now they have." She looked at me for a long moment and smiled and said, "You *are* a genius."

We moved our conversation over to one of the couches in the lobby. We weren't talking about anything significant. We weren't even looking at each other. But at one moment, my finger touched her hand. She didn't move away. I was on fire. I moved my finger on top of hers. She moved her hand closer. I gently moved my fingers on top of hers. Her eyes filled with tears. Neither of us said a thing. We sat in silence, holding hands for an hour.

It was a love story that occurred in geologic time, at glacial pace. Imperceptible to the naked eye, it shook us both with metamorphic power. We were now an item. As I said, love at first sight is not necessarily a good thing or a nice thing, but it is a true thing. I had been honored to enter the heart of Miss Hard to Get. A place I shared with no one—except Chico Bambico.

We never had much money. For dates we went on walks. Or we improvised. One night we walked through the quad past McFarlin Auditorium, the big two-thousand-seat venue for shows on campus. We saw a couple hundred people milling around outside the doors. We wondered what all the excitement was about. It was a concert. We arrived at intermission. We thought, "Why not? Nothing ventured, nothing gained." Beth and I grabbed a couple of programs on the ground and walked in not knowing what the show was. We ran up to the second balcony where we figured we would be safe from sitting in someone else's seats and getting thrown out by the ushers.

Onstage there was a single grand piano. My heart started beating hard. The curtains opened, revealing an orchestra. The lights dimmed. A tall, thin man walked onto the stage. I looked at the program. It was Van Cliburn. He was going to play a piece by Rachmaninoff. The Third Piano Concerto. I had never heard it. I had never heard him play it. He adjusted the bench. Looked at the keys. Flexed his gigantic hands and nodded to the conductor. The music started. Within seconds I was transported, so moved I couldn't breathe. Neither could Beth. I held her hand tightly to steady myself, unsure as to whether the real Miss Hard to Get was sitting beside me or was as untouchable as the beauty in the air around us.

13.

CHAOS THEORY

I ALWAYS WANTED to be in love. As long as I could remember I wanted to be married and have a family. I don't know why. I don't think it was because we had an ideal homelife growing up. I think it more likely that I was born a traditionalist. Either that, or I saw too many Jimmy Stewart movies when I was little.

I remember my first marriage proposal. I was five. I climbed up the mimosa tree in our front yard and picked some mimosa blossoms and ran over to Alice Nell Allen's house. She was a pretty girl who lived down the street. She was also five. She had long brown hair. On occasion she wore a yellow flannel shirt with wildflowers on it.

I actually had misunderstood her name the entire time I knew her. Instead of Alice Nell I thought her mother was calling her Alice Snail. I loved snails. I ran over to her house with the mimosa flowers. I asked her to marry me. She said yes. I kissed her on the cheek. I still remember how warm and soft that cheek was.

I knew from the movies that kissing a girl would be an important skill for me to learn. At night I would practice on my pillow. It didn't feel anything like Alice Snail's cheek. I needed to move up to something more girl-like. I switched to the stuffed rabbit I had in my bed.

It was missing an eye and an ear. But it did have a mouth of sorts so it was a step up from the pillow.

This was about all the preparation I had for the world of women. I was lucky that the person I fell in love with in college was Beth. She seemed to have as little preparation for a relationship as I did.

Years of kissing bunnies and pillows could not have prepared me for Beth. Perhaps a conversation with Stephen Hawking on the nature and behavior of unstable atomic particles could have helped. Beth was nothing like Grace Kelly or Donna Reed.

Beth's physical appearance to the world at large conveyed a mismatch of several different mythologies. She wore blue jeans with a miniskirt over them. She wore long underwear to class as a sort of fashion statement. She was modest but would model nude for art classes. She was shy and small, but on occasion, without warning, would beat me with her purse and throw me into a hedge.

She was a force of chaos, which could be destructive or inspirational, depending. As I said, I was a traditionalist. My life had always been structured. I was in bed by eight when I was a child. I always did my homework. I always had good grades. I always went to Sunday school and later Saturday school and later Saturday and Sunday schools, and I believed it all. Beth was a different animal altogether.

I remember once when she and I were sitting in the lobby of her dorm, after I had played "Snow Song," a song I had written for her and that was a constant request. She asked what I wanted in life. I said, "A home."

She looked at me as if I just said something in Arabic. She shook her head and said, "What's that?"

"It's having a wife and children and four walls and maybe even a fireplace. It can be anywhere. But it's warm and safe."

She looked away. Her eyes became dark. She stared at some invisible specter in the corner of the room. Then she said, "That doesn't exist. There is no place like that. No place that's safe."

"You don't think a place can be safe if two people love each other?" I said.

"No. Because how do you know if you are in love? How do you

know you just won't wake up one morning and want to pack up and leave? That's why I'll never marry you. I want us to be free to leave each other whenever we want."

There it was. The unimaginable distance between two people. I was too young to know it then, but I have since learned that some chasms can never be bridged, even with good intentions.

Ralph Waldo Emerson once said something to the effect that, "What you are thunders so loud I cannot hear what you say." When you date various people you tend to be defined by the things you say. But when you cross the line and start a relationship, you are defined by the things you do. And what you do is often determined by what you value. What you hold to be the center of your life.

I may have been clinging on to a vision of life I gleaned from Broadway musicals and the Dick and Jane series we read in first grade. As safe as that sounds, it had inherent dangers. The person who fashions his life after something he has seen runs the risk of worshipping form at the expense of content. But Beth held on to an equally dangerous model. She embraced the storm, or worse, the eye of the storm: the appearance of calm with the promise of disaster.

Chaos, as an inspiration, led Beth to suggest she "wanted to get away. Get away from it all." As long as it wasn't planned. That wish became a series of weekend trips I could have turned into a coffee table book entitled *Insignificant Texas: A Tour of the Townships Within a Three-Hundred-Mile Radius of Dallas.*

We would go to the Greyhound station on a Saturday and pick a town at random. We would buy bus tickets on the spot and go there for a day. There is an expression in Texas about "going nowhere fast." Not us. We went nowhere at fifty-five miles per hour. We would go to a town we'd never heard of, walk around, eat at a diner, talk to people, spend a night in a motel, and then return the following day.

Occasionally there were dramatic events on our trips. Once I bought a partial set of an encyclopedia for ten dollars. Once Beth and I got married in a field during a thunderstorm, by ourselves, of course, nothing legal or binding. The forces of chaos would never approve of that.

And sometimes the universe would throw us a curveball. On the way home from Mount Vernon, Texas, the Greyhound bus broke down about two and a half hours from Dallas. The driver told us that another bus would have to come to take us home. We could plan on being out for at least another six hours. That was way too much of a commitment to standing still. Beth suggested we leave the bus and hitchhike home.

I had never hitchhiked before, but I said nothing. We walked away from the downed bus and held out our thumbs. There was not much traffic. I realized if no one picked us up, we were heading on a course of action that could end up being unimaginably disastrous. The odds were against us. I felt like we just jumped off of an ocean liner hoping to catch a ride to Italy on a dolphin.

Just as I began to suggest we head back to the safety of the Greyhound, a beat-up red van pulled off onto the shoulder of the highway right in front of us. The side door slid open. Beth and I jumped inside the van and slammed the door shut. The van was full of black people. A man and woman were in the front seat. We were in the back with an old woman and two small children.

I said, "Hey." There was no response. I continued, "I hope you're heading for Dallas. That's where we were heading. Thanks for stopping." The man driving didn't say a word. He just looked at me in the rearview mirror. He started the engine.

I repeated, "You are going to Dallas, aren't you?" He just looked at me again in the rearview, put the car into gear, and off we went. I watched the bus get smaller and smaller out the back window and I thought how clever we were. I started talking to the people in the back of the van. The old woman put her hand on one of the children to quiet any urge to speak. Silence. No one looked at Beth or me. It was tense. Now I wondered how this ride would end.

Around sundown, the van pulled off the road in the outskirts of Dallas. The man driving said, "We're not going any farther. You have to get out here." I nodded and opened the van door.

"Hey, thanks for the lift," I said. "I was afraid no one would pick up hitchhikers anymore."

"What? You were hitchhiking? We never even saw you. We had just pulled over to change drivers. You jumped into the car and said, 'Drive us to Dallas.' We thought you were kidnappers."

Identity confusion can be a dangerous side effect of the chaos-centered life.

FOR PEOPLE WHO never made plans, it was odd that Beth and I forged a relationship that always involved travel. We decided to go to Boulder, Colorado, because Beth liked the name. That fell through. Then we changed gears and thought a trip to London and Paris sounded like a good idea. We bought plane tickets and Eurail passes. As for details like hotels, theater tickets, ground transportation—we left those matters up to the universe.

We had no idea what to take. So we took everything. We needed Sherpas to get to the plane. Beth's green suitcase must have weighed four hundred pounds. She couldn't carry it. The sensible thing would have been to tell her straight out: "You pack what you can carry." But I learned everything I knew about life from *The Andy Griffith Show* so I asked myself, "What would Andy do for Miss Helen?"

I ended up carrying Beth's suitcase and my equally huge bag for the entire trip. I developed a new posture for slogging around the luggage. With bent knees and straight arms I could have been mistaken for an orangutan.

Beth and I arrived in London. We had no idea where to go, so we took a subway to the Paddington stop where a friend of ours told us he had found a hotel. We got out and walked up and down the streets, Beth holding her pillow from home and me grunting behind her with the two suitcases. We came to rest at a hotel aptly named the Nomad.

The hotel was far from elegant. It was something in between a youth hostel and a building tagged for demolition. The manager wanted to be paid in advance. As I was shelling out the pounds, he told me that there was one bathroom at the end of each floor. I stopped. I assumed being in England we were still in the "civilized world." We would need a private toilet, I told him.

He sneered and said, "That's not romantic."

"Regardless of the romance, we want our own potty."

He told me that costs extra. I expected as much from the Nomad.

We paid the money and ended up with a single room that connected to something in the corner that resembled a ride at the fair. You walked up three steps to a tiny cubicle, shut the door. To flush, you pulled a piece of bicycle chain connected to a tank that somehow diverted the River Thames into the potty for eight seconds. The floor shook. The roar deafened. I could have used a seat belt.

Traditional science based a lot of principles on the assumption that objects and forces seek equilibrium, keeping everything in balance. New scientific thinking has chucked that and embraces nonlinear systems called the "science of Becoming." The focus of these experiments is not balance at all, but spontaneous ordering and the emergence of novelty. That was us. We were the New Scientists.

If there was an opportunity in London to go to the theater, we took it. We saw ten plays that week that happened to star the great Laurence Olivier, Joan Plowright, Frank Finlay, Paul Scofield, John Gielgud, Tom Courtenay, as well as a young Michael Crawford and Michael Gambon. All by chance. All by walking up and getting cancellations or whatever happened to be available.

Every place in London became an opportunity. If the doors opened, we walked in.

We saw pictures of T. E. Lawrence and George Bernard Shaw at the National Portrait Gallery.

We ate something called "American pancakes" at a British breakfast house. "It" was to "food" like "nightmare" is to "dream." It was a stack of flapjacks covered by a steak (a small rib eye) covered by potatoes and brown gravy. I asked our waitress if I could have just the pancakes with butter and syrup. She was horrified.

We went to the Tate Gallery and saw the haunting painting of *Hope*. It portrays a blindfolded woman sitting alone atop a desolate world plucking the string of a harp. Beth stared at the picture for a long time. She murmured, "It's beautiful." I found the painting terrifying. From completely different vantage points we were ambushed by its power.

One afternoon we had thirty free minutes, so we ran into the British Museum. By chance, before us was the Rosetta Stone: a fitting artifact for two people trying to understand a common meaning in the indecipherable.

Just as the Chaos Theory giveth, it also taketh away.

A few days later we used our Eurail passes to go to Paris. We arrived not knowing we already had two strikes against us: one, we were in France where they didn't speak English, and two, we were in France.

When we got into the train station in Paris, we were directed to go to a window called "Passport Authority." It was just like in the movies where they had men with guns who checked your papers. A policeman looked at us with the fish eye and asked in English with a French accent, "Where are you staying while you're in Paris?"

"I don't know," I said. "I figured we'd walk around until we found a place with a bathroom." That was not the right answer. As ambassadors of the chaos-centered life, we were instructed to take our two gigantic suitcases and stand in an enormous line and be assigned a room.

We waited in line for over two hours. When we got to the front, several disgusted French civil servants assigned us a place to stay. They gave us an official slip of paper with an address and directions. We gave the slip of paper to a cab driver who didn't understand English. I didn't speak French. He said, *"Ich spreche nur Deutsch."* He was German! I noticed he had a new black leather jacket on so it enabled me to use one of the two sentences I knew in German, *"Ich müss mir eine neue Jacke kaufen!!"* ("I must buy a new jacket.") He looked at me in the rearview with a certain amount of confusion and continued on to our destination.

We got out. I grabbed the two suitcases and started slogging my way down the block to the hotel. I noticed I was receiving many fetching looks from all the single women walking around our neighborhood. At first, I thought maybe it was the suitcases. My strength indicated virility. Perhaps it was my Russian good looks. Then it dawned on me that we were in the middle of the red-light district. The women were prostitutes and our "hotel" was a brothel. My first conversation with the madame was to explain that Beth was not one of her new girls. We weren't renting the room by the hour. I showed her the official government slip of paper ordering us to stay there. She disliked us at first glance. That was as good as our relationship ever got.

We didn't spend much time in the room. We were out on the town. We went to the Louvre and saw the *Mona Lisa*. We went to the Paris Opera. I sprang for the expensive seats to see *The Marriage of Figaro*. I could have saved the francs. It was an experimental production that staged all of act two in the dark. We went to Shakespeare and Company bookstore. We rode on the Batobus up and down the Seine.

One night we went to the Moulin Rouge, the famous nightclub where they featured a variety of dance routines with topless women interspersed with jugglers and dog acts like the ones on *The Ed Sullivan Show*. To get in you had to buy one of three ticket packages. Beth and I got the cheapest one. Our ticket included the show and a bottle of inexpensive champagne.

We sat at a table with two other Americans, George and Marion, a middle-aged married couple from Maine. Marion was elegant. She had short black hair and wore a flowing flower-print dress and dangling earrings. George had a sort of professorial look complete with a handsome tweed jacket and tortoise shell glasses. He explained they had been here before and just loved the show. They had ordered the most expensive package that included a full seven-course dinner, referred to as the "French Feast."

Beth and I sipped on our champagne as they ate their soup. Marion felt guilty for eating in front of us to the point of offering us a taste. We told them not to worry. Enjoy. That's when George muttered, "Oh no." And a torrent of blood blasted out of his nose into his soup. He politely noted that he was afraid this might happen. He excused himself from the table. He ran for the men's room with a handkerchief pressed up against his nose. Marion continued calmly, "George has a problem with his nose." Beth and I looked at each other.

The waiter removed George's soup and replaced it with his salad. Marion asked what we were doing in Paris. Beth told her a bit about our travels. Marion was inspired by how romantic it all sounded, taking off on a whim, with no job, no money, no preparations. Marion mentioned that the world would be better if people were a little more impulsive and not so calculating. The waiters removed George's untouched salad and brought his fish plate. George returned from the men's room with wads of toilet paper jammed up his nostrils.

He smiled and apologized, saying that he was hoping for a quiet evening with his nose. He chuckled and added that he guessed that wasn't in the cards. He picked up his knife and fork. He started cutting his fish when he gave out another little groan and a sort of hard sneeze, blasting the toilet paper wads into my lap and spraying the filet of sole and the table in a shower of blood.

George gritted his teeth and grinned. "Oops, here we go again." I started mopping up my side of the table with a nonchalant, "No problem, no problem at all." George ran back to the men's room.

Marion didn't bat an eyelash and continued, "So what do you two study in college?"

"Theater." The dance orchestra started up with an Edith Piaf tango. Marion asked Beth if it would be all right if she borrowed me for a dance. Beth found this enormously entertaining because she knew I couldn't dance. She said it was perfectly fine as long as she could watch.

I got up and faked it as George came back from the men's room. He saw his wife and me dancing a sort of fox-trot cha-cha to the tango music. He offered his hand to Beth. I found this delightful because I knew that Beth couldn't dance, either, plus there was the added suspense of dancing with George. We all danced together at the Moulin Rouge. Beth shot a look to me and then a look at the wads of tissue up George's nose.

The song ended. We got back to the table just in time for the meat course and George's next hemorrhage. He ran from the table, never to have touched a bite of his seven-course French Feast and never to be seen again.

We returned that evening to find our luggage in the hallway. The madame in charge of the hotel explained that we were being thrown out of our room because I punched the toilet with my fist and smashed it. I don't know how many times you have felt the need to punch a toilet. I never have. My French was not sufficient to answer such a charge except with the five reporter questions: how, when, what, where, and why? The madame assured me that my punching of the toilet was witnessed by the maid, which led me to my own conclusions.

We were out on the street. One of the advantages of the Chaos Theory is that it doesn't look at events like these as negatives. They just provide more chaos for the engine to operate. We jumped on a train and headed for Versailles, where we spent a couple of lovely days before we decided to head back to England.

The plan was that we would take a train from Paris to the port town of Calais, then a ferry across the English Channel, and then take a train to London. Believe it or not, there was no longer room in our massive bags for my two Pierre Cardin suits to fit without getting crushed. I thought they would travel better if I wore them—both.

Wearing two suits and slogging along with both suitcases, we boarded our train to Calais. As holders of a Eurail pass you get first-class travel anywhere in Europe. Unless you lose the Eurail pass. Then whoever finds your pass gets free first-class travel anywhere in Europe.

We had settled into our first-class seats when Beth whispered to me that she had lost her pass. She had no idea where it was. I saw the conductor coming down the aisle. I told her to go back to the bathroom. I would show the conductor my pass and tell him that she had the same. That didn't work. The conductor said he would wait for Beth to come back to her seat. I excused myself saying I would go get her.

I got her out of the bathroom and we moved to the second-class cabin. That worked for about five minutes. I saw the conductor headed our way. We got up and strolled back to the third-class cabin. Third class was jammed with humanity. There were no seats. It was sweltering. In my two Pierre Cardin suits, I was starting to sweat.

We walked back into the club car and ordered lunch. We ate our french fries and ham sandwiches as slowly as we could. The waiter eventually told us we would have to leave to let others come and eat. We started to head back into the train when I saw the conductor making his way to the club car. Beth and I turned and kept walking toward the back of the train. We walked through the kitchen and out the back door. Now we were sitting outside the train on the iron couplings that held the passenger section to the baggage cars.

Just when I was starting to feel sorry for myself, possessing a first-class ticket but having to ride outside the dining car of a speeding train in two Pierre Cardin suits, a busboy opened the back door, muttered a curse in French, and threw a bucket of food scraps on me. I was in shock. And just when I started to feel sorry for myself riding outside a dining car of a fast-moving train wearing two Pierre Cardin suits covered with food scraps, it started to rain.

The wet wool mixed with partially eaten potatoes au gratin made me snap. I yelled at Beth. We had to get out of the rain. The only way was back into the baggage compartment.

Riding in the baggage compartment of a rapidly moving train is a lot like riding on the freeway in the back of a pickup truck with a lawn mower and a pit bull. Besides being tossed from one end of a metal car to another, you also have heavy bags being thrown at you, on you, with you, under you, around you, and all the time you know that you have a first-class ticket in your pocket.

We arrived at the port of Calais. I stumbled out of the baggage car looking like a tossed Cobb salad. We made it to the ferry to take us across the English Channel. That was where we met Michael. I'll never forget him. He had dark hair and dark eyes. He bathed infrequently. He said he was a young German art student who was on his way to New York to see the art galleries to learn from the masters. That's what he told me right before he got seasick and threw up on me.

I have encountered genuine disgust in my life. I know the look in the eyes: the look from my anti-Semitic classmates in seventh grade when they found out I was Jewish, the look of kindergarten teachers when I unknowingly tossed off sexually explicit comments in Spanish to a group of children. The look of an East German border guard pushing me up against a wall with his machine gun as I tried to cross into Berlin in 1970. But nothing tops the looks I got that day getting off the boat wearing two wet wool suits, covered with food and vomit, shuffling down the gangplank, groaning under the weight of the two gigantic suitcases.

There are two ways of viewing existence. One is that we live in a world of cause and effect. The other is that we live in a world of probability. I had discovered a third. Living with Beth you could also live in a world of possibility where there were no rules at all—except gravity. And we were working on that one.

14.

THE SOUND OF SURPRISE

THERE ARE TWO ways of going through life: you can be a master or a student. Being a master is more difficult. The expectations are higher and the wardrobe is more expensive. I have always chosen to be a student. It's fun to learn. When I got out of school and started acting professionally, the first thing I learned was that I had no idea what I was doing. I had to start learning all over again. Working on a film or television was different than doing class scenes.

What was the difference? It's one of those questions whose answer seems apparent. Theater is live. Movies and television aren't. In movies, theoretically, you have unlimited attempts at getting a scene right. In theater you have one shot every night and twice on Wednesdays and Saturdays.

Because of the demands on the actor, theater has something called a "rehearsal period." It can often go on longer than the run of the play, especially in high school. My friend Julie Hagerty is involved with a production of Ibsen's play *The Master Builder* that has literally been rehearsing for over twelve years. At that point if a show doesn't open, it should at least get bar mitzvahed. They recently performed for a limited run in an art gallery in lower Manhattan. It was wonderful. It demonstrated what my grandmother always said: "Sometimes it's better if it stays in the pot a long time."

Compare that to film. Recently, I worked on an episode of the television program *Californication*. The director told us where we were to stand. He told Pam Adlon, who plays my wife, Marcy, where to enter. Then, without any rehearsal, he laughed and said, "Shall we just try one and see what happens?"

I used to think that filmed productions didn't rehearse as much as theater because they didn't have the time, the money, or the interest. I had a theater actor's prejudice. Now I am ready to admit I was wrong. Film directors are very interested—just not necessarily in what I was doing.

In theater, the actor tells the story. The actor must learn lines, movements, and timing to create the piece's reality. In a film, the technical people tell the story. The director creates the reality using actors as only one element.

The "wow factor" of theater is seamlessness. The "wow factor" of a film is surprise. And to that end, film directors focus rehearsal on the technical aspects so they can record the sound of surprise. If an actor rehearses too much for a film and gets too comfortable, it may be counterproductive to a good film performance.

I can think of an exception that proves the rule. In *Single White Female* we had a rehearsal period of more than a month. That almost never happens. We even rehearsed in sequence, which is as rare as finding a real diamond ring in a box of Cracker Jacks. We reached a scene near the end of the movie where I attempt to rape Bridget Fonda. Bridget repels my advances by kicking me in the crotch. This is the kind of scene you would spend days rehearsing if it were a play. On stage you would have to meticulously work out how and where I grab Bridget. What do I do to act like an authentic rapist? How do I do it without looking silly or getting sued by her people? How does she get out of my grasp? And most importantly, how do we negotiate her kneeing me in the nuts?

Our director, Barbet Schroeder, curiously stopped rehearsal at this point. He said we would practice the rape and the kneeing in the groin later with a fight expert. Barbet told me not to worry about my privates. It would all be safe and "beautifully choreographed." At this point I wasn't expecting *Swan Lake*. I hoped to remain a baritone.

However, once we started principal photography, we never rehearsed again. There was no fight choreography. No *Swan Lake*. We shot for the next two and a half months. On the day Bridget and I were to shoot the rape scene, I went into my trailer and found a brown paper bag on my dresser. Inside was a hard protective athletic cup with a picture of a hockey player on it.

The fight expert stuck his head in the door and said, "Good. You found it. Just slide that puppy into your shorts. Cover up your jollies. We'll tell Bridget not to whale on you. Don't worry, man. Everything should be cool."

That was it. That was the extent of the fight choreography. Bridget and I would wing it. The safety net would be a hockey cup purchased at Big 5 Sporting Goods and my wife, Ann. Ann decided to come to the set that day to "supervise" the rape. She exchanged a bit of girl talk with Bridget before we started shooting. She explained she wanted me returned home with the factory equipment intact. Bridget smiled. Message received.

We started to shoot the rape section of the scene. Bridget came up to me and whispered, "Stephen, it would really help me if you could put your hand under my blouse and pinch my nipple. Hard. That gets me really angry."

This is where it helps to be a good student. They don't teach things like this at the university. Being a classically trained Method actor, I assured Bridget I could deliver the necessary pinch. Of course, I wasn't sure how angry I wanted to get her. The "knee to the nuts" part of the scene was only a page away.

We shot for three hours. There were over thirty takes of nipple twisting and nut kneeing. Bridget, with almost ninjalike skill, came full force into my lower forty-eight and always stopped one half of an inch from disaster. I have worked with hundreds of actresses in my career. The best two technical actresses without question were

Meryl Streep and Bridget Fonda. I would trust them with my life or, in this case, my unborn children.

I have to admit, at the time, I thought the lack of rape rehearsal was poor planning bordering on recklessness. I recognized some years later that Barbet wanted to preserve the surprise. A movie is pieced together months after filming. After editing, sound editing, special effects, and scoring, it can die unless the performances carry spontaneity that grabs the audience.

Ridley Scott is a great general of all the film elements. I worked with him on *Thelma & Louise*. Before each scene he called a meeting with the actors to discuss what we wanted to do. I played Max, the head of the FBI team in charge of tracking down the women. In my first scene I come into Thelma's house with all of my men. Ridley suggested, "I think you should take over the room."

"Absolutely," I said.

Of course I had no idea what "take over the room" meant so I just did what a lot of actors do. I copied things I had seen on reruns of other cop shows. During camera rehearsal I came in quickly. I ordered each one of my men to do a certain task using their last names. Using last names is very coplike. Things like "Morgan, put a wiretap on line one. Johnson, I want a T1 line set up to base." All sorts of butch commands like that.

Ridley nodded. He said, "Fine. Shall we shoot one?" We all said sure. I went outside the front door and got ready to make my entrance when the spirit of surprise started whispering in my ear, "Stephen, that was terrible. Derivative. Phony." (I should mention that myself is very hard on me sometimes.) I continued, "When you direct a play you don't walk in and say, 'All right, Carol, go design the costumes. John Lee, make the sets. Pat, learn your lines. Let's do this play!' You assume everyone knows his or her job."

On the set I could hear the AD calling places and telling the cameras to roll. I continued talking to myself, "What do *you* care about when *you* run things? Come on, man, I need an answer fast!" I answered myself, "Okay. Okay. Snacks. I care about snacks." The First AD yelled, "Action!" I entered.

I walked into the room, looked around, and ad-libbed, "People, attention." The room got quiet and everyone looked at me. I continued with an FBI sort of confidence, "I'm going on a deli run. Who wants turkey? Morgan, you want roast beef again? Cole slaw?" The other actors looked perplexed. I continued, "I'm going with the turkey, rye, Swiss, anyone else?" There was a momentary pause and then miraculously the other actors started giving me food orders! Ridley called, "Cut!" He ran up from behind the camera yelling ecstatically, "I love it, I love it!"

From then on Ridley wanted me eating different food in every scene. The gods of surprise formed a dramatic narrative. It christened Ridley and my character, Max, at the same moment. If we had rehearsed the scene for a week, it never would have happened. Ridley Scott is one of the great directors working today. Many other directors might not have liked the food bit, and I could have gotten fired or just told to come in with more of the *Law & Order* stuff. I have found the greater the director, the greater the likelihood they enjoy being surprised.

SOMETIMES REHEARSAL ON a film is a dangerous waste of time. Or worse. I was hired for a one-day part on the film *National Security*, starring Martin Lawrence and Steve Zahn. I played a machine shop guy delivering some crucial story points about the metallic composition of a beer keg. Our set was an actual blast furnace in a part of L.A. that was so scary, so nasty, that I petitioned to have the area banned from Google Earth in the public interest.

There was nothing in this shop that couldn't kill or maim you in less than a minute. The foreman of the shop was our safety monitor. He told us, "Stay away from that furnace. It heats up to six thousand degrees."

I raised my hand. "Six thousand degrees? Isn't that like the surface of Mercury?" He didn't answer. He just stared at me and continued on the safety tour.

He pointed to another red-hot oven and told us, "If a shard comes out of this oven and lands on your shoe, it'll melt your foot." He pointed to the back of the shop. "Don't open that door, the light in that room is so bright it'll burn your retinas." He gestured to another corner of the set. "Don't walk in that part of the shop. The fumes will eat your lungs out." Into this intoxicating mix we added one final unstable element: people.

I was advised that Martin Lawrence was traveling with his assistants who also worked as his personal bodyguards. The AD called a rehearsal for the first part of the scene. The director called action. Steve and Martin entered the shop followed by Martin's posse: four guys with long sports jerseys, baggy jeans, and gold chains. I felt like I was in an MTV video.

We started the dialogue. Instead of just watching the scene, Martin's posse walked toward me. I kept acting and got to the point in the scene where I walk over and put my arm around Martin. His bodyguards reached into the waistbands of their pants and pulled out guns and aimed them at me. I put my hands in the air and froze. Martin, to his credit, yelled out, "Guys! Chill! It's cool. It's cool. We're just rehearsing. This is part of the movie."

I was still frozen. "Yes. Guys, let's just chill. We're acting here. This is just acting." The guys put their weapons back in their pants.

"Shall we continue?" the director asked. Martin, again to his credit, said, "Why don't we just shoot one." I agreed. If someone's gonna bust a cap in yo' ass, might as well be for the real thing and not just a rehearsal.

There is one time on a movie you don't want to capture surprise—when you work with explosives. In the movie DMZ I played a sergeant on my last day of duty on the border between North and South Korea. In the scene a group of North Korean peasants were supposed to make a desperate run for freedom through the DMZ while being shot at and blasted by the soldiers of the North. The producers brought in real Koreans to play the escaping Koreans because they thought it would be "more authentic."

We rehearsed the scene for hours. Special-effects people planted dynamite in the ground and marked each explosive with a small bit of white powder as a visual reference. A Korean translator walked through the path with the extras, demonstrating the serpentine course they had to run to avoid getting blown up. They rehearsed the "run to freedom" in slow motion several times.

Everything was perfect until the director yelled, "Action!" Either the sound of his voice in the megaphone was too loud or the word "Action" meant something different in Korean. Panic ensued. The extras screamed and ran straight through the pass in a nonserpentine fashion getting blown to bits.

The good news was we got great footage. And fortunately, there were no casualties. Injuries, yes. Deaths, no.

It boggled my mind to imagine the hardships these people went through: leaving Korea, coming to America, only to get blown up in a movie where they pretend they're back in Korea coming to America. It hurt my brain to think about it.

IF WE OPERATE on the assumption that the goal of a film is to preserve surprise, there would appear to be method in the madness of David Milch. I have had the privilege of working with David in various capacities on four projects from *L.A. Law* to *John from Cincinnati*. But I think David's most amazing achievement so far is the series *Deadwood*.

It was television, but it is misleading to call it a television program. It would be like calling the rings of Saturn space dust. The scope of *Deadwood* was beyond television in any number of categories: size, cost, quality, and profanity. *Deadwood* broke the mold in every way.

It may be an apocryphal story, but the way it was told to me was that David wanted to shoot a series about the rise of civilization during the Roman Empire. He wanted the drama performed by actors, in Latin, with subtitles. It would feature the unimaginable violence of the age coming into conflict with the inexorable forces of the future. He pitched it to HBO. They listened and said, "Well, David, what we're looking for is a Western." And David said, "It's the same thing." And *Deadwood* was born.

Instead of the actors speaking in Latin, he had characters speaking in streams of profanity, or in backward Shakespeare like my character, Hugo Jarry. Regular viewers of the show told me that they had to record each episode and listen to it over and over again to decipher what was happening.

The haiku that describes *Deadwood* was the infamous "cocksucker" scene. If you have seen it, you can't forget it. If you haven't you should rent the DVD just to see it. In the scene a Chinese worker is trying to warn his boss about a dangerous man arriving at the train station, but the only English word he knows is "cocksucker"—which is horrible and hilarious in its own right. The scene goes on for several minutes as the Chinese worker frantically repeats the word "cocksucker" with various inflections to his mystified boss. The levels of emotion and torment and danger and frustration in the scene are a perfect statement of the foreign film David wanted to create.

Physically, the show was gigantic. The shooting schedule for a one-hour television program in the 1990s could balloon into fourteen days. That was huge. Later in the decade, with the influx of inexpensive Canadian productions, shooting time shortened to seven days. That was brutal. I have worked on feature films shot in twenty-one to twenty-eight days. The final episode of *Deadwood* in season two took thirty days to film.

Deadwood often worked with two full-time crews, two cinematographers, and two directors, with David Milch overseeing everything. And they were always the top-line people. One of our camera crews included some of the team Alan Parker used on *Mississippi Burning*.

On a typical day at *Deadwood*, we would arrive at five a.m. and get breakfast. Rehearsal would begin in the dark, supervised by the director of the episode and David Milch. David liked to shoot in natural light as much as possible. He wanted to be ready to go at sunrise. We would rehearse and get the scene up to speed. Then David would toss in something like, "Oh, and we should have a cattle stampede going down Main Street somewhere in there." Once in season three, I was rehearsing a scene and we were just wrapping up when David left rehearsal saying, "Great, great—so, Stephen, when we shoot it, do it like a bird."

"Beg your pardon?" I said.

David said, "Do what you're doing, but just do it like a bird. You know, with wings and feathers and a beak. Just see what happens. Try to fly or something like that."

"Okay."

In one scene Tim Olyphant, as Sheriff Bullock, takes me to jail for protective custody. After watching rehearsal, David felt the street was too empty. He added a huge yoked bull to walk in front of us. During the take, the bull lifted his tail and took an enormous dump on me. Tim and I kept going, even though I squished when I walked.

When they yelled, "Cut," Tim busted a gut laughing. I complained to David that I got crapped on during the shot. David was thrilled. He said, "Are you kidding? You can't plan things like that! It was great! That was the best part of the scene. And he almost did it on cue! That's a print." As I started slogging my way back to my trailer, David yelled, "And remember, Stephen, we don't wash costumes on *Deadwood*." Which was true. David wanted the stains to match from week to week. That bull gave me a gift that kept giving for the rest of the season. At the end of two or three months, the clothes walked on their own.

More than once after rehearsal, David rushed off to rewrite the scene. Actors would sit in their trailers for hours only to be told there was a change of plan. "David hasn't finished rewriting, so we will shoot tomorrow's scene today and today's scene next week. I don't know. We'll call you."

The other popular scenario was when the AD called at eleven o'clock at night with the news that you were added to a scene that shoots tomorrow at dawn. Pages were being sent in an email. You run to your computer and find that you have a new six-page monologue of backward Shakespeare to learn. Then you cry. After the nervous breakdown you have a decision to make: Stay up all night and learn the scene? If you do, odds are David will just rewrite it after rehearsal. Should you just blow it off and get a good night's sleep in case they let a stampede of cattle loose, and you need the energy to run for your life? Once I offered to pay the AD a hundred dollars to move my scene to later in the day. He said, "Sorry, man. David wants to shoot you first."

It could have been David's way of injecting surprise into the process. Or it could have been that he was just nutty in a brilliant way or brilliant in a nutty way. Either way, it was the poetry of chaos.

Weather also injected surprise into the process. We never stopped what we were doing because of burning heat or torrential rains. I had one scene where I had to walk down Main Street and enter the Bella Union Saloon to meet Powers Boothe, who played Tolliver, for a bit of scheming and betrayal. The camera started with me outside and followed me through the swinging saloon doors.

The rain outside was incredible. It was more reminiscent of Calcutta than Los Angeles. Several inches had fallen that day, and there was no sign of a letup. The mud was a foot deep in the streets. On one take, a horse in the background had enough of being out in the weather and made a dash for the bar as well. He came walking through the swinging bar doors right behind me. Talk about the sound of surprise. The horse came up and stood at the bar with us. No one called, "Cut." Powers played the scene to me and the horse. I choked back tears of laughter as Powers, with deadly earnestness, told each of us what our part in the plot was, including the horse. They called, "Cut." Afterward Powers asked me if the horse was a last-second addition of David's.

One day David asked me how I felt about nudity. I told him I do it every day, briefly. He said he wanted to write a scene where I have sex in a bathtub with a prostitute at the Bella Union. "Why not," I said. I had only tried sex in a bathtub once in real life. It was not to be recommended, just for the sheer mop-up factor afterward. But this was fiction.

In one of many heartwarming father-and-daughter stories in Hollywood, Powers's daughter, Parisse, was playing a prostitute who worked for him. David chose Parisse to be the lucky girl to join me in the tub.

The irony was that Powers and I went to school together at SMU thirtysome-odd years before. Back in the old days I had spent some wonderful evenings with Powers and his wife, Pam, and their new baby, Parisse. One evening, after Powers had passed out, I was talking to Pam about horses and stained-glass windows. Pam went to get a couple more beers and asked me if I would diaper Parisse for her, who was a few months old at the time.

So in an unlikely turn of events, I was going to have simulated sex in a bubble bath with a woman I had diapered in my past. For those who believe in a universe of probability, the odds of this one have to be lesser than finding sushi in South Dakota.

Any day on *Deadwood* could be your last. We were shooting the first episode of season three. It was over a hundred degrees. We were behind schedule. We were shooting a street scene with two hundred townsfolk, children, dogs, and a runaway stagecoach. After a few rehearsals we were about to roll cameras when one of the extras apparently dropped dead.

They called for an ambulance. The filming stopped until help arrived and the man was put onto a stretcher and taken away. One of our assistant directors made an inspirational speech:

"Everybody, I know we're all in shock over what happened to"— the AD turned to his assistant who whispered, "Dan," in his ear— "Dan. Our old buddy Dan. I know he didn't regain consciousness and that's got us all worried. But we all know that Dan was a real fighter. And I have no doubt he is going to fight this heart attack thing with everything he's got. He's just that kind of guy. The good news is that the ambulance is already on the way with him to the trauma center. It's very close. They'll call us when Dan gets there. So . . . I would like to take ten seconds of silence for us all to pray for Dan." (He lowered his head for eight and a half seconds.) "And finally, I know the one thing Dan really loved was this show. *Deadwood* was his second home. And there's one thing Dan would want us to do if he were here right now. He would want us to finish this scene! SO EVERYBODY BACK TO PLACES. READY. ROLL CAMERAS."

It was cold.

If David didn't like the way a scene was coming together, he would just rewrite and reshoot it. This methodology did not thrill the money people at HBO. It led to exploding budgets and eventually the premature cancellation of the series.

But there was a moment during season three when I was shooting a scene with Gerald McRaney. We were on the rooftop of a building on Main Street at two a.m. There were no guardrails to prevent us from falling three stories into the night. We began the scene. In the background, on the street below, twenty horsemen rode in procession with burning torches. It was so beautiful it was almost holy. In the middle of one of Mac's speeches, we were hit by the sound of surprise. There was a screech and a family of white barn owls dove between us. Mac stopped midsentence. The birds flew around us and swooped down over the heads of the riders below. Mac looked back at me, raised his eyebrows, and said, "Well, that was something."

And it was.

Deadwood exemplified the temporary nature of the extraordinary. In that insignificant moment, in a make-believe town, I felt transported. I left my body behind for another time and another place. All I was really experiencing was the power of poetry, coming close to a thing of beauty without falling into the blackness.

15.

CONFERENCE HOUR

EVERY TUESDAY AND Thursday in the drama department at Southern Methodist University they had what was called Conference Hour. All of the drama students could come to the Margo Jones Theatre and hear someone speak. It could be a former student who made it good, such as Sharon Ullrick, who was in *The Last Picture Show* and then headed off to New York. It could be famous makeup artist Richard Corson talking about his new book. At this particular Conference Hour, the head of the acting curriculum, Professor Jack Clay, spoke on what all actors needed to know to be a success.

Mr. Clay was a distinguished man in his late forties. He was very formal. Very formidable. A solemn duke from a Grimm's fairy tale. He spoke seriously about the proper education of the modern theater student and how "woefully inadequate" it was. To be an actor, he said, one must be expert in five things: comedy, Shakespeare, singing, dancing, and fencing.

All of us took Mr. Clay's word as gospel. I signed up for singing and dancing lessons, tap and jazz. My friend Jim McLure and I took fencing with Hungarian champion Emeric DeGall. We were not allowed to take Shakespeare or comedy classes. We were only sophomores.

Those classes were part of what was called the Professional Acting Program, reserved for juniors, seniors, and graduate students accepted into the theater department's advanced acting curriculum.

At that Conference Hour we were also introduced to a new acting professor. Her name was Joan Potter. We were all excited to meet her. She was special. Unlike most acting teachers, she was no academic. She had been a real actress at the famous Actors Studio in New York. She studied under Lee Strasberg. She had been in his world-famous production of Chekhov's *The Three Sisters*. She was in a movie with Richard Burton. She was as close as any of us had come to learning from a real professional actor.

At the conclusion of that first Conference Hour, my faculty advisor came running up to me. Burnet Hobgood, known affectionately to everyone as Hob, was not an acting teacher. He was the head of the entire theater department. If you subscribe to the theory that we freeze our appearance to the period in our life we were the hottest, you would have to think Hob must have been one hot beatnik. He had a little goatee. He always wore a beret adjusted at a sporty angle on his bald head. He smoked cigarettes from Europe. You would bet he had a set of bongo drums in his closet at home.

Very few students had Hob as their advisor. The reason for this was that, unlike Miss Potter, Hob was a true academic and consequently no one could understand what he was talking about.

He came up to me and whispered, "Tobo. Freshman auditions are at the end of the week. All of the new students are doing their pieces for Joan. Maybe it would be a good idea for you to do a piece to liven things up." He winked at me and elbowed me in the side.

In hindsight, I realize the wisdom of Hob's advice. He wanted me to audition with the freshmen to properly introduce myself as an actor to Joan Potter and all of the new directing students. However, I was a moron. I interpreted his wink and nudge and request to "liven things up" as my cue to do a "novelty piece."

I winked back at Hob and told him to count me in! I decided to do my old Shakespeare audition, a monologue of Orlando's from *As You Like It*, but with a twist. I would do it as a striptease. That Friday evening I came out onstage. I announced my piece. The audience settled in. I started taking off. Gasps. Shrieks. Shrieks of laughter. Stomping and hooting. I ended the monologue wearing nothing but boxer shorts. I turned around and revealed I had written "Hi Hob" on my butt. For the finale, I bent over, saluted the audience, and danced offstage.

I recognize that this was probably an error in judgment. It was in terrible taste. But it was novel. Beth was in the audience. She was not yet my girlfriend. Years later, she told me she was in shock watching my audition. She said she couldn't believe anyone would do something so crass. I thought it was harmless. It wasn't the first time I sold my soul for a laugh. I knew my audience and I figured this would work.

My initial assessment appeared to be right. The directing students and faculty were on the floor. Hob was laughing so hard I thought he would have to be carried out on a stretcher. I think the one person not amused was Joan Potter.

That semester Joan taught a beginning scene study class for the sophomores. I was doing an adapted scene from the novel *The Catcher in the Rye*. It went well. Joan was crying at the end. She asked for an essay on how we worked on our roles. I turned in a four-page paper that I'm sure was inarticulate. I had no methodology on acting at that point in time.

The next day Joan returned the papers. She gave me an F. An F! My heart stopped. It was the first F I had ever gotten in my life. It was the *only* F I had ever gotten. She said she wanted to see me after class. I met with her. She shook with fury. What did I think I was doing? she asked. Was I making fun of the process? I was terrified. I said, "No. No, ma'am. I don't know enough about the process to make fun of it." I told her I would redo the paper. Which I did. I turned in a new essay the next day. She took it and never gave it back.

The next morning after Theater History, Hob ran up to me in the hallway. He pulled me into the men's room and asked me, "What did you do to Joan?"

"Nothing. I don't know," I stammered.

"Well, she's furious. She said you have a bad attitude."

I felt as though I had fallen into a world where people spoke a different language. I had always been a good student. I had always been likable and agreeable to most teachers. Because I was tall they asked me to put books on high shelves. Because I was easygoing they paired me up with the new kids. Now I had become one of those kids that smoked cigarettes out by the woodshop.

"What should I do?" I asked.

"I don't know," said Hob. "Something different. Whatever you are doing, do the opposite. Just stay off of her bad side."

I took Hob's advice to heart. I did the opposite. I didn't make any jokes. I didn't try to stand out in any way. I followed the Taoist principle that "the ax falls on the tallest tree." I tried to be the smallest tree in the forest. The semester went on. Joan was not overtly hostile to me. Nor was she friendly. I felt like I had distanced myself from my earlier missteps.

Then something extraordinary happened. Near the end of the term the department announced that for the first time in SMU theater history they were going to present the work of our acting classes to the public. Each acting teacher could select two scenes from his or her class. The theater department would sell tickets for the showcase as the final production of the year.

Joan asked me if I would do my *Butterflies Are Free* scene. I played a blind songwriter meeting a girl for a first date. It was sweet and romantic. I played guitar and sang, which made the scene a little different from anything else on the program. I was so flattered. I told Joan how thrilled I was, and that I would love to do the scene.

Joan stepped close to me and lowered her voice. She told me she wanted to rehearse with me privately for a couple of hours. There were some little things she wanted to fix. "Absolutely," I said. "Whatever you want." She smiled at me and said, "Your work in this role is really extraordinary."

Victory. I felt like I had won Joan over. The bitterness from the beginning of the year was gone. Joan asked, "How about Thursday at three in the Margo Jones?" That was a problem. I told her I couldn't be there at three because I was part of the stage crew dismantling the *King Lear* set. I could be there at five. Joan looked concerned and told me that wouldn't work. She said she would write a personal note to the head of the crew and get permission for me to rehearse. I shrugged and said, "Sure."

The next day Joan told me it was done. She wrote the note. I was cleared to rehearse. They had more than enough help to tear down the set. I met her Thursday at three and we worked for a couple of hours alone. She was attentive and happy with the changes we made to the scene. I felt ready to perform.

The next morning Hob was waiting for me after first-period Theater History. He pulled me into the men's room and screamed, "Where were you?"

"What are you talking about?"

"Yesterday. Crew call. You missed crew call."

I relaxed. "Oh, that. Joan wanted me to rehearse for the show we're doing in the Margo Jones. It's all right. She wrote a note. She got me out of crew call."

Hob turned red. "There was no note! And it doesn't matter if there was! The bylaws of the theater department stipulate that a student can never miss a crew call. Under any circumstance. It's an automatic Unsatisfactory Critique. It goes on your permanent record! Two Unsatisfactories and you are expelled from the department."

The blood drained from my head. I couldn't understand what had happened. I showed up Friday for the opening night of our scene show. Joan never made eye contact with me. She didn't speak to me. I focused on the scene. I thought if the scene went well for the faculty, and the public, and Joan, this whole episode would go away. The evening was a success. We got a standing ovation. Joan never talked to me after the show.

The following Monday they posted a list on the bulletin board of students accepted into the Professional Acting Program. If they put your name on the list, you could return to the theater department for your junior year. It didn't really concern me. Everyone was automatically asked back. I wandered up to the board for a look. My roommate

Jim McLure was looking over the list. He turned to me and raised his eyebrows. "Sorry, man." I looked. My name wasn't on the list.

I ran to Hob's office. I was on fire. I walked past his secretary, Edna, who was asking me to wait while she checked to see if Hob was available. I blew past her into the inner sanctum. Hob was behind his desk. I could tell he already knew. He asked me to sit down. He said that it was wrong. He wrote on my file, "Hob does not approve." But all of the teachers had to vote "yes" for a student to be accepted in the Professional Acting Program. It was five to one. Joan voted me down. She had ammunition with the Unsatisfactory Critique.

"This is nuts. I didn't do anything. Have you looked at that list? There are people being accepted in the program that haven't shown up for half of the classes because they were too busy smoking pot and listening to *Abbey Road*. You saw the scene I did the other day. We closed the show. We got a standing ovation."

"I know, I know," said Hob. He shook his head. "I'm sorry. But my hands are tied. You need to calm down. We have to look at what you can do. Transferring to another school won't be a realistic option. With the Unsatisfactory on your record, no good school would take you." Hob leaned back in his chair. He appeared to be deep in thought as he played with his package of cigarettes on his desk. "The only real option would be to leave the department. Pick a different major. You can still take general theater courses. Theater History. Dramatic Literature. You can still audition for the plays. It's just the acting program and all the acting classes that are off-limits."

I didn't say a word. I left Hob's office. I headed back to my little room off campus. A sudden storm blew in and I walked through the freezing Texas wind. I didn't feel a thing. I burned with a mixture of fury and failure. It's a bad mix.

In that fifteen-minute walk I saw the end of all my dreams. Not to graduate, not to be an actor, shamed in front of all my friends, shamed in front of my new girlfriend, Beth. What would she think? I knew my parents would be sympathetic, but they weren't advocates. They never wanted me to be an actor. They wanted me to be a lawyer.

I got to my room and closed the door. I sat on my bed. Outside, the sun began to set. In the gathering darkness, I had the first real Conference Hour of my life. A Conference Hour with myself. I looked at all of my strengths and weaknesses. Truthfully. It was a Conference Hour with no answers, but no excuses either.

And in the silence, I remembered a phrase from religious school that I always thought was catchy. It was from the great Jewish teacher Hillel, who lived roughly at the same time Jesus did. He said:

If I am not for myself, who is?
If I am for myself alone, what am I?
And if not now, when?

I never knew what that last line meant. "If not now, when?" I realized Joan Potter had just taught me the meaning of those words. She didn't know it, but she gave me the gift of "when." When was now.

I devised a plan. A plan that was so outrageous it had no chance of working. I went to the registrar's office in the morning and enrolled for the next year. I signed up for all of the Professional Acting courses I wanted in spite of being thrown out of the department.

⸺

WHEN I WALKED into Joan Potter's intermediate scene study class the first day of my junior year, she almost had a stroke. She refused to look at me. She gave out scene assignments, omitting me. When she asked if there were any questions, I raised my hand. She ignored me and dismissed the class.

I got strange looks from the entire faculty for the rest of the day. Some were concerned. Some were confused. They double-checked their rosters. The next morning as I was leaving Theater History, the one class that was happy to have me, Hob came bustling up to me.

"I need to see you in my office. Now," he said. Hob walked off, looking shaken. I followed him. We entered his office in silence. I sat down. He closed the door and sat across from me. He cleared his throat and tried to find the right words. "Stephen. The Professional Acting Program is not an option for you. It's not what I want, but we can't allow you in those classes. You have to understand that if we let you in after being removed from the program, we have no control over who gets admitted in the future. That's the way it is. I'm sorry."

I stared at Hob. I felt his pronouncement settle in the room like mustard gas on a World War I battlefield. I searched for the right words.

"Hob, I'm sorry. But your problems are of no concern to me. Who gets in or doesn't get in to your program is none of my business. The way I see it, I pay you. You accepted my tuition money, so I pay your salary, and Joan Potter's salary, and Jack Clay's salary. So I will be in class. You have rules, but this is my life. I always wanted to be an actor. You people aren't going to stop me." I got up and stopped at the doorway. "Again, Hob. I'm sorry."

I showed up the next day for class. Again, the teachers looked confused. Joan continued to ignore me. Over the next two months, I was never given an assignment. I was never called on in class. My tests went ungraded, my essays were returned unmarked. I still showed up. Some teachers looked at me with irritation. Some, like Joan Potter, only smiled and continued to shut me out. I was not cast in any plays my junior year.

Near the end of the semester Hob was waiting for me once more after first period. He nudged me into the men's room. We stood at the urinals. Hob unzipped and started to pee. I was unsure of the proper etiquette so I unzipped, too, and joined him. It seemed like the only polite thing to do. He said, "I think she's going to do something else."

"What?"

"I don't know. In the faculty meeting she asked what the requirement was to get someone removed from the school permanently. I told her two Unsatisfactories."

"Hob, I don't know what else I can do that's unsatisfactory. I'm not in any plays so I can't miss any rehearsals. I've turned in all my assignments. It's not my fault they haven't been graded."

"I know. I'm just warning you. She's going to try to get you kicked out."

"Thanks, Hob. I appreciate it." We zipped and went our separate ways.

I thought through my world of limited options. I learned the first real lesson of my time in school: never underestimate the power of being underestimated. I went to see Tony Graham-White, my Theater History teacher. He was a short, terribly bright, terribly idiosyncratic Englishman. He asked what he could do for me. I said, "A lot, Tony, a lot. As a member of the faculty you can give the Theater Comprehensive Exam, right?" The Comprehensive was the graduate test everyone had to take senior year to get a degree. People studied for it forever and hated it. Tony looked a little surprised and said yes. He was giving it to the seniors in about a month.

"Tony, there are no bylaws in the theater department against me taking the test early, are there?"

He shook his head nervously. "Are you kidding? People hate the bloody thing. Why would anyone want to take it early? You can take it whenever you want."

"Good. I'm sure you know about the problems I'm having with one teacher in the department." Tony raised his eyebrows. "I want to make sure I take that test next month. But, Tony, this is important, no one can know I'm taking it. My name can't be on any list. No one else in the faculty can know. You can't tell anyone, not your friends, not even your family." Tony's eyes widened. This was as close as he had ever been to being in a James Bond movie. "One more thing, Tony. When I finish the test, I want you to grade it. Only you. And whatever happens—win, lose, or draw—save it for me in case I need it."

Tony shoved his hands in his pockets and rocked on his heels. He nodded and said, "I could do that. Not a problem."

I studied for the next month and took the Comprehensive Exam for three hours one Saturday morning. About a week later, in the hallway, Tony cruised up alongside me. He gave me a thumbs-up and whispered, "Graded the test. Flying colors," before he changed course and scurried off.

It was a minor victory in this completely undefined war. My moment of triumph was short-lived. I arrived in Joan's Oral Interpretation class and I got another essay back ungraded. Nothing had changed. That's when the weight of the last year crushed me. I had never felt so much despair. The next day I had an assignment due in Jack Clay's comedy class. We were working on songs. I was going to do "Reviewing the Situation" from *Oliver*. That night I started to look at the lyrics, and made an uncharacteristic decision. I blew it off. I could no longer muster the energy to prepare another useless assignment.

I went into Professor Clay's class and settled in for a big helping of being overlooked. This time I was counting on it. Mr. Clay said, "Who's first up with their song?" Several students who loved show tunes raised their hands with such enthusiasm they almost fell out of their chairs. Mr. Clay looked past them and fixed his gaze on me. "Mr. Tobolowsky. Why don't you show us what you've worked on?"

Silence. I didn't move. I was in shock. The only preparation I had done was singing the song in the shower two weeks ago. I walked to the front of the class and began to wing it. I stumbled through the first verse and part of the chorus when Mr. Clay called out, "Stop, stop, stop! This is unacceptable. This is shoddy and unprofessional. I won't have it. Did you work on this at all?"

I shifted on my feet, ashamed. "No, sir. No. I didn't." Mr. Clay never let down his gaze. He looked right through me. Under his breath he muttered, "Well, at least you're honest about it." He pulled out his little book and a pencil and pretended to write something.

He looked up at me again. "Next class you will bring in this song—finished—and you will bring in another song as well. Do you understand?"

"Yes, sir."

"You will never come in this class unprepared again. Do you understand me?"

"Yes, sir."

The next Monday was Mr. Clay's Shakespeare class. I was prepared. It was a good thing, too. He called on me first once again. I went up and performed a short monologue of Leontes's from *The Winter's Tale*.

Mr. Clay observed me, coolly. He damned me with faint praise saying it was decent for a first time through, but that I was just scratching the surface of the character. For the next class he wanted me to take it to the next level. I headed back to my seat. Mr. Clay stopped me. "I'm not finished. For the next class I want you to prepare two more monologues: the Leontes act five speech from *The Winter's Tale* and the speech of the Ghost in *Hamlet*. You are to be off book for both. Do you understand?"

"Yes, sir."

Again, his gaze.

The class was embarrassed for me. They thought I had just been publicly chided. They had no idea that they were witness to an act of almost unbearable kindness. I walked back to my seat, looking at Mr. Clay. He met my eye and once again pretended to write something down in his little book. For the rest of the year and throughout my senior year, Jack Clay doubled and tripled my workload. He gave me extra reading. He criticized me continually, but fairly.

Professor Clay gave me hope when there was absolutely none. His attention to me was unsolicited and unexpected, and it dismantled Joan Potter's attacks. Years later, when I worked on *Groundhog Day*, Harold Ramis told me show business is impossible. To succeed you need at least four heroes. Alan Parker, as I mentioned, is one of my heroes. Jack Clay is another.

Two curious details also marked these years at SMU. First is the attitude of my fellow students. They considered the events happening to me as unrelated to them as a tornado in the next county. They still pursued Joan's favor. Everyone remained friendly but no one stood up for me for fear of getting the same treatment.

And even though Joan never graded my papers, she gave me A's in her classes. It's perplexing. Every movie made about abusive teachers centers around giving a student bad grades. Not Joan. I have no answers, only theories. Perhaps she had good days and bad days. Perhaps she was bipolar. Or perhaps she knew an artificially low grade would be a tip-off to parents or administrators that something untoward was going on in the drama department. Perhaps she had deeper, darker plans for me. A's in her classes would provide a perfect cover.

Her final assault came a month before the end of my senior year. Hob called me into his office. He asked me to sit down. He said he had bad news. Joan Potter had given me a second Unsatisfactory Critique.

"What on earth for?" I asked.

Hob pulled out my file and read, "For having a poor attitude in her class." Hob tossed my file on his desk. "She waited until the end of the term. There's not much we can do about it. With the previous Unsatisfactory Critique it means, unfortunately, that you won't be able to graduate."

"Why?"

"Well, you have the hours and the grades, but now that you are officially expelled from the school you won't be able to take the Comprehensive Exam."

"But, Hob, I've taken the Comprehensive."

"That's impossible. We haven't given it yet."

"I took it last year, as a junior. It's in Tony Graham-White's office."

Hob was incredulous. "Really?"

"Yes."

Hob tapped his fingers on his desk. "If that's true, that would change everything."

Hob picked up his phone and dialed a number. "Tony? Hob here. I heard that Stephen Tobolowsky has already taken the Comprehensive Exam?" Pause. I could hear electronic jabber with an English accent on the other end of the line. "Well, do you have it?" Pause. I sat in the chair crossing everything I could cross for luck. Hob raised his eyebrows and hung up the phone. We sat in excruciating silence. A couple of minutes later Tony Graham-White sauntered into the office with a large manila envelope. He had saved it for me for over a year. He tossed it on Hob's desk, turned, and gave me a devil-may-care salute and left. Hob opened the envelope. I had made an A on the test.

I graduated first in my class from the SMU Theater Department, due in large part to all of the A's Joan Potter gave me.

In 1982 I did my first Broadway play. I heard a familiar voice backstage. Joan had come to congratulate all the SMU alums in the show. I saw her in the hallway outside my dressing room. We caught each other's eye in my makeup mirror. She stuck her head into my dressing room and said over the din backstage, "You're still no good."

In 2008, Joan passed away. I tried to make sense of what happened. The years tell a story. After I graduated Joan continued to teach at SMU. She taught in Westchester, New York, and many of her students considered her to be their favorite acting teacher.

I have no idea why I became the focus of so much of Joan's energy for three years. From the Shakespeare Jack Clay made me study, I can only cite *Julius Caesar*, act three, scene two: "The evil that men do lives after them / The good is oft interred with their bones."

In 2010, SMU invited me back to be the featured speaker at Conference Hour. I looked at all those faces and wondered if I was ever that young. Faces filled with such hope and terror. I started to talk about Hollywood and auditions when one girl raised her hand. She asked, "What is the most important thing an actor needs to know to be successful?"

"Not fencing," I told her. "And probably not even Shakespeare, even though it got me through *Deadwood*. But seriously, the most important thing for you to learn is something I was lucky enough to learn here. Along the way many people will tell you, 'No. You can't do it. You have to go home.' You have to survive that. You have to stand up to that, and say, 'This is my life and this is what I'm doing.'"

Fairly or unfairly, many people are tried in life. The mistake people make is that they think the trial is a sign of failure. It's not. It's only a doorway that leads to who you really are.

16.

LOST IN ACT ONE

ONE REASON WHY studying acting at a university will always be misguided is because you will inevitably work on plays written by Shakespeare, Molière, Chekhov, Tennessee Williams, Eugene O'Neill, and Neil Simon. These authors' primary aim was to write material that made sense. When you get into the professional world, producers and writers have actors work on projects that make no sense at all. They do this without remorse.

There are many reasons. Sometimes the producers can't help it. One of the first professional jobs I got in Los Angeles was performing in a Japanese commercial. I played the role of "Yankee Sailor Man." The commercial had no script. I was brought into a room in West Los Angeles. Three Japanese clients in expensive suits sat in school desks. They never made eye contact with me. An American casting director pointed to a line of white tape on the floor at the front of the room. He told me to stand on it. I did. The casting director tossed me a sailor's cap and told me to "put it on and move around."

I took the cap and pretended to look into a mirror. I placed it on my head. I smiled in the pretend mirror and made different faces, straightening and repositioning the cap. Then I walked around the front of the room. I picked up a make-believe mop and pretended to mop the deck. When that idea ran its course (about four seconds later), I started singing "I'm Popeye the Sailor Man" and making muscles. The clients seemed to like the Popeye song. They laughed and started whispering to one another in Japanese.

I got the part. I celebrated. Beth and I opened a bottle of champagne and toasted the coming of the Golden Days. I called Mom and Dad to tell them I was a success in Hollywood even though I still had no idea what the commercial was.

On the set I put on my white sailor suit. I got a doughnut and coffee and headed for the makeup trailer. Sitting in the trailer were three beautiful models: a blonde, a brunette, and a redhead in high heels and miniskirts. They were already made up and now getting their hair blown out. Our Japanese director briefed them on the story of the commercial. English was not his strong suit. He spoke in a hybrid language that fell somewhere in the middle of the Pacific Ocean. He came over and shook my hand warmly. He started filling me in on my role.

"You sailor man. You want the woman. Many, many woman. You chase the woman." Despite the choppy English I recognized the director was referring to what the famous cartoon skunk, Pepe Le Pew, called the "international language of love."

The director handed me a script. My line went something like this: "We American sailor like girls in big city. They nice and all right. But not like girl in backcountry. No. No. But we American sailor man like the pretty girls, yes, yes indeed."

I broke out into a flop sweat. There was nothing in my training at SMU or the University of Illinois graduate program that could prepare me for this. I walked around on the roof of a nearby parking garage and tried different approaches to the material. I thought, "What if I'm drunk? What if I'm laughing? What if I'm Robert De Niro?" Nothing worked. The director took me out to the set and explained the scene. "You chase the womans down the street. You try grab the womans. But they too quick. And then you get by camera, stop, and say line."

The models started running down a steep hill with me in hot pursuit. I had to pretend to run. It was hard for them to get up to speed in their high heels. The girls ran past the camera. I stopped and tried to say my line. "We American sailor like girls in big city. They nice and all right—"

The director interrupted, "Stop. Stop. Stop. You too tall. Need to be small to get on camera. Can you run smaller?" I looked over to the models. They looked at me with no compassion at all.

"Yes. I will run smaller." We did another take. I stooped over and bent my knees so I looked like Igor, the hunchback in the *Frankenstein* movies. I chased the girls again. I got to the camera and scooted into frame. "We American sailors like the girls in big city . . ." I started laughing, ruining the take. The director was perplexed. He called cut. I tried to be diplomatic. "Uh, these lines are a little odd in English. Can I rewrite them a bit?"

He said, "You say whatever you want 'cause we put Japanese over you face."

I realized I was going to be like a Japanese actor in a *Godzilla* film. That made me feel better. We did the scene again. The models ran. I squatted. I waddled into frame at an appropriate height and started a speech from *Hamlet*:

Oh that this too, too solid flesh would melt,
thaw, and resolve itself into a dew!
Or that the Everlasting had not fixed
His canon 'gainst self slaughter! Oh God, God. . . .
That it should come to this.

The director loved it. It was a print. Ironically, it remains the only time I ever performed Shakespeare in Los Angeles.

Sometimes an actor has no idea what he or she is doing because no one has any idea. This happens a lot when you work on special-effects projects. Usually special effects are added after principal photography, so no one really knows what's chasing them. I'm always amused when I see a scene in a science fiction movie in which the New York police fight a giant demon from the underworld with spider legs and a dog's head. The actors playing cops always have a "business as usual" expression on their faces. Maybe in New York that's business as usual, but my bet is that neither the actors nor the director had any idea what the final object of their pursuit would look like.

My first encounter with special-effects acting was in *The Philadelphia Experiment*. I played Barney, the computer tech guy. I come out of a truck and see something referred to in the script as "the Vortex." When I see it, I utter the line, "Oh my God!"

I had no idea what a vortex was or what it looked like. I figured it was just another one of those rips in the time-space continuum. Stewart Raffill, the director, also didn't know what the final effect would look like. Stewart told me he would talk me through it. I nodded and prepared to step out of the truck. They called, "Action!" I came out and Stewart started coaching me.

"All right, Stephen, you look up. It's like nothing you've ever seen before, it's big and you say—"

I dropped my jaw and said, "Oh my God."

There was a pause.

Stewart was disappointed. "Stephen, let's try it again. And *action*! You come out of the truck and you see it and it's big. It's enormous. You are *terrified* and you say—"

"Oh my God!"

"Bigger, Stephen, it's HUGE."

"OH—MY—GOD!!!"

"Okay, Stephen, maybe it's not so big. Maybe it's small but very, very sinister."

"Oh . . . my . . . God."

I gave the director four flavors of nothing. It is also a reason why movies aren't what they used to be. As the special effects become the main course and not the side dish, the performances become less affecting. The actors have no idea what they're doing.

Another common reason for actors having no idea what they are doing is secrecy. Producers are afraid that if a script of a particular project gets out it will either be stolen by another producer or auctioned on eBay. As a result the actors only get to see snippets before the audition. These little pages are called "sides." Sometimes the sides are enough to glean who you are and what you are talking about. Other times, it's hopeless.

I got an audition with one of my favorite directors of all time, Michael Mann, for the film that became *The Insider*. When I auditioned, the movie had no title and no available script. They sent me sides for a part named "Clerk." Already a bad sign—no first or last name. The page of dialogue was incomprehensible. I had no idea what I was clerk of, what I was talking about, why I was talking about it, or to whom I was speaking. I might as well have been saying "Oh my God" to the Vortex.

I debated long and hard as to what I should do. I asked my agent for a script. "No one is getting a script," he told me. I asked for more information. That was a nonstarter. No one knew anything.

I sat in the waiting room for two hours trying to manage some sort of performance out of my lines. It was like trying to walk in an earthquake. When the rumbling starts and your house shakes and the floor buckles, you want to run to safety. But you can't. You can't move. It is the cruelty of physics. You realize the only reason you are able to walk is that your feet are in contact with the ground. Remove that contact and you don't go anywhere. When you try to act without knowing who you are or what you want, you go nowhere.

I got called in to meet Michael. He asked me to have a seat. He turned on a camera to record the audition. He said, "Let's read the scene, shall we?" I paused and said, "Let's not." He looked at me with a bit of a smile and asked, "Why not?" I said, "Because I don't have a clue what's going on. It would be a huge waste of both of our time." He chuckled and said, "Should I explain what's happening?"

I said, "I have a better idea. Let me read a script." He said, "No one has a script." I said, "I understand. Let me explain it this way. How would you feel, Michael, if someone said they wanted you to direct a suspense movie and wanted to know how you would do it, but they refused to tell you who the main actors were, what era the movie took place, and what your budget was. You would probably say, 'No can do.' The only thing I have to offer as an actor is my point of view. Without a script, I have no point and no view."

Michael pulled out a script and a contract from a drawer in his desk. The contract stipulated that if I told anyone the contents, the character, the story of the movie, I would be murdered and then sued. I signed it.

I went home and read the script and came back the next day. Michael asked what I thought. I said, "It could be the best script I have ever read. Who wrote it?" Michael smiled and said, "Me and Eric Roth."

"So I guess it's good I said it was a great script."

Michael laughed. "Let's read."

I read three different parts. It was easy to do because I knew who all the people were and what they wanted. I handed the script back to Michael with a sigh of relief. I got cast in the movie.

That was a happy story. There are many, many unhappy ones, too, that all revolve around the actor not having a clue as to what to do. I have not done "on camera" commercials since I started doing movies. I got a phone call from my commercial agent. She said, "Stephen, I know you don't do commercials but this one is big, you have to do it. It is on-the-air and in-print for Universal Theme Park, Orlando. It could be multiple spots. This could be a seven-figure job." Seven-figure meant over a million dollars. I hung a U-turn over my convictions and headed for the casting office.

When I got there, I saw every bald-headed, middle-aged man I ever knew in Hollywood. There had to be fifty guys waiting. And they had to have been waiting forever. Most of them were asleep or nodding off. One guy in the corner was snoring. The casting director ran up to me and said, "Stephen, I'm so glad you decided to come."

I said, "My pleasure. Is there a script or sides?"

"No," she said. "We do have a storyboard on the wall. We'll want you to improvise."

"Absolutely." I gestured to all of the guys sleeping in folding chairs around me and whispered, "Now, I don't want to be a pain but I just found out about this audition, and I do have another meeting in a couple of hours, is there any way I could get in sooner rather than later?"

She was apologetic and said, "Yes, we'll get you right in. Just let me know when you're ready, and I'll get you in to meet Nigel, our director."

"Great. Thank you." I walked over to the storyboard on the wall. A storyboard is a sort of comic-book-style, frame-by-frame description of the commercial. This hieroglyph showed a family flying to Universal Orlando with a little boy looking out of the airplane window. His mother and his bald-headed father sat next to him, both asleep. Asleep! I looked back at the waiting room and I realized that all the guys there had not been waiting forever to go in. They were practicing!

I told the casting director I was definitely ready to see Nigel. She took me in. The room was empty except for a first-class airplane seat, a video camera, and Nigel. Nigel was about thirty, English with dirty Keith Richards hair, a skintight, torn T-shirt, and leopard-print tights. He got up grandly from his desk. "Hellllooo, Stephen. I absolutely loved you in *Groundhog Day*. One of my favorite films as a child. And your character was outrageous. Out-ra-geous! Shall we have a bit of fun?"

"You bet," I said.

"All right. Strap yourself into the hot seat."

I did. I sat in the airplane seat. I buckled my seat belt.

Nigel walked back and forth in front of me in director mode. "Here's the backstory. You are on a family trip to Orlando. You are a businessman and saved up for business-class seats for the family, maybe even first class. Your little boy is *so* excited he is about to pee his pants. You have just had your meal and the movie is starting, you have your headphones on and you decided to take, say, forty winks."

Pause.

"I'm asleep?"

"Right. Asleep. Shall we have a go at it?"

"Right. Now, Nigel, question. I'm totally asleep?"

"Yes. Dead out. Ready?"

I assumed an unconscious posture as Nigel called out, "Action!" I stayed unconscious for a few seconds before I felt inadequate and wondered if I should snore or drool. Or worse. Should I steal some of the stuff I saw the other guys practicing in the waiting room?

Nigel called, "Cut!" I opened my eyes. He was clearly disappointed that I didn't offer up some sort of comic gem. He said, "Shall we try another? Do something different this time."

I swallowed and said, "I'm still unconscious?"

"Right."

I nodded and wondered why I had not gone to law school like Mom wanted. He called out, "Action."

The only thing I could think to do was twitch or snore like Shemp in *The Three Stooges*. I did not get the part, nor was I ever invited back to that casting office. The experience reinforced what I always suspected: that in Hollywood, consciousness was a matter of perspective.

IF YOU TAKE sci-fi, secrecy, and calculated confusion to their furthest intersection on the horizon, you end up with the television series *Heroes*. I played a major role on the show throughout season two. I was Bob Bishop, the man who could turn things to gold, but for the life of me, I still have no idea what I was doing.

And I don't think anyone else had more of a clue than I did.

Madness was the method. Being on *Heroes* was like being in one of those comedies where the leading man wakes up hungover with a woman in his bed and a walrus in his bathtub and he shakes his head and says, "What happened?"

It was the biggest production I have ever been a part of. The show took over a good portion of an entire studio in Hollywood. We used seven different soundstages. On any given day we would be working on three scripts at once with three full-time crews and directors. Two directors would be shooting different episodes and another director would be shooting special effects for past, present, or future episodes. Sometimes we would get a massive rewrite for an episode we thought we had finished a month ago, and we would reshoot that while shooting the current episode that may also have just been rewritten to contradict everything we were reshooting in the previous episode. Got that?

I concluded that it was all right that I didn't know what I was doing. I decided the show required a "young brain" to absorb the rapid plot twists and liquid mythology. Its strength rested in the fact that it was incomprehensible.

I still have dreams, years later, like victims of post-traumatic stress disorder, that even though the show has been cancelled, they have just churned out another rewrite and they want to reshoot my death one more time. But just like a story line from *Heroes*, I have gotten ahead of myself. Let's go back in time.

In the beginning, there was the audition. I had three scenes to read for the producers. I couldn't get a script in advance because the show was such a phenomenon, the executives feared a future episode would end up in the hands of a "spoiler." Spoilers are people whose sole mission in life is to gain notoriety by revealing the punch line of someone else's joke.

I went in and read the three "Bob" scenes for the seven executive producers. I thought it went fine. The producers nodded and looked at one another and then one of the executives, Jeph Loeb, asked me if I could do it "funny." I had no idea what that meant. I didn't have a clue what I was doing or to whom I was speaking. I was trying to walk in an earthquake once again. The scene started. I just talked faster and ad-libbed that the person reading with me looked like he had food on his jacket. I brushed it off with my hand and examined it and said, "Just as I thought, gorgonzola." The producers smiled and nodded in confusion.

They asked me to be threatening. I threw a chair. That threatened them for sure. They asked me to be "mysterious," whatever that is. Try being "mysterious" sometime on your own and see what you end up with. At best you will look like a bad guy on *The Man from U.N.C.L.E.* If you do it at work, your boss will think you're stealing office supplies.

Two days later I got the news that I didn't get the part. I was depressed. But the next day I got the news that I may get the part after all. I was thrilled. And the next day I got the news that they were unsure as to whether the part would be "Robert Bishop" or "Roberta Bishop." They were looking at women for the role. Now I was depressed and had an identity crisis. It never changed, even after the next day when they told me I got the part.

When I arrived for my first day of work, I met several cast members in the makeup trailer. I had never seen so many attractive people in one place in my life. I was in a sort of sugar shock. If the *Heroes* cast were a vegetable garden, I was the potato. And this was before Kristen Bell was brought into the cast to play my daughter.

I met Sendhil Ramamurthy, who played Dr. Suresh. I was so happy to meet him. His last name was harder to spell than mine. Everyone in the cast was very warm. They asked me what I was doing on the show, and I answered I had no idea. One of the stars of the show, Greg Grunberg, laughed and said, "Get used to it."

Next, I stopped by Wardrobe for a costume fitting. The costumers also had no idea what my part was. They hadn't seen a script yet. They needed to know who my scenes were with so they could pick the right sports jacket for me to wear. I didn't follow the logic. The costume designer explained the color of my clothing was dependent on the hair color of the person in the scene with me. I was still lost.

I got a brief tutorial. Modern special effects are usually composite shots where they add something in the foreground or background of a frame in postproduction. For the wide shots in *Deadwood*, they erected a giant green screen five stories high and three hundred yards long at the end of Main Street. In postproduction they added South Dakota on that screen so you would see the Old West instead of the 14 Freeway.

The reason special-effects experts choose blue and green as the colors of their background screens is because these are the two colors not usually found in human skin tone. When they make a composite shot, anything with that color becomes invisible, leaving the added effect of a Vortex, or a spaceship, or a city you are flying over, wherever the green or blue screen was.

In *Heroes*, almost all of my scenes had special effects. That meant that the backdrop would be a blue screen—unless the person in the scene with me was blond, then they would use a green screen as a backdrop. The cinematographer determined that a green screen worked better for blondes after adding the special effects. Consequently, my clothes would have to avoid shades of blue or green accordingly, or I would be in danger of vanishing.

After my costume fitting I ran into one of our director-producers, Allan Arkush, and asked him who Bob was in the show. Allan smiled wickedly and said, "Think of Bob as a good guy, who may actually be a bad guy, who is pretending to be a good guy, who in essence is a bad guy who makes a turn on the show to be a good guy." Allan laughed, but I knew he wasn't kidding.

My first day shooting I had to use my superpower of turning something into gold for the first time. Greg Beeman, another executive producer and extraordinarily fun director, asked me, "Have you ever had superpowers in a movie?"

I thought back through my résumé. "I've been a ghost before," I told him.

He shook his head and said, "Different thing. On the show we have evolved that a 'hero' has to show a bit of exertion to use their power. The only way I can describe it is that it's more than a burp but less than a crap."

"Okay," I said. Again, this was something I never learned in acting class.

Greg said, "Give it a try. Show me."

I tried. Greg shook his head. "No. Too much effort. You just look constipated. Try a little less."

I focused on looking like I was about to hiccup but was able to hold it back. Greg said, "That's better. Keep it around there."

I shot four scenes that first day. I decided that Bob Bishop was a moral relativist. That way I could justify anything they asked me to do. But it was never that easy.

During the next episodes, I tried to find a cure for the deadly Shanti virus. Then the story revealed I was using the virus as a weapon. Then it was implied that I was trying to isolate the virus so it wouldn't fall into the wrong hands. Then it was discovered that I was developing new strains of the virus in a secret lab. I couldn't keep up.

Aristotle, one of the most influential people of the modern age, never gets the credit he's due. His ideas have permeated the Western world. This is because he was Alexander the Great's teacher. Everywhere Alexander conquered, the people adopted the ideas of Aristotle. Later, when the Romans conquered these lands, they took Aristotle's ideas and spread them from Britain to North Africa. We inherited those ideas without really being aware of it.

Aristotle's big invention was that every story has a beginning, a middle, and an end. Three acts: introduction—conflict—resolution. It seems like a no-brainer now, but if you look at literature written before Aristotle, it goes every which way.

The writing for *Heroes*, as well as other programs with a supernatural bent, doesn't follow Aristotle. Instead of true development, they redefine act one by introducing new characters, new rules to play by, new emotional geography, and new objectives. Even when they reach some sort of conclusion, like a secret code being discovered or a main character getting killed, we find out that the code didn't work or the character wasn't dead. Act one just extends further.

My agent sent me an article from *New York* magazine. It had my picture and a caption: "Meet the New Face of Evil on *Heroes.*" It was news to me. I wasn't sure what I had done that was evil yet. I was still lost in act one.

As the episodes rolled on, I felt like my real job on the show was to create the illusion that there was a plot. My scenes usually revolved around making an apology to various regular characters for my past deceptions. I tried to convince them to work with me on a vital new project. But as the scripts rolled through it became apparent that the projects never existed. By the time the audience started to wonder, we were on to the next.

I knew my days on the show were numbered during episode nine. I asked for my chair. They still didn't have a chair with my name on it. Instead they gave me a folding chair with a piece of duct tape on the back of it that had "Cast" written in magic marker. Tim Kring, the executive producer and creator, called me at home to tell me they were killing me off in the next script. It was embarrassing. When the word got out that I had become expendable, no one wanted to get near me. Death could be contagious.

Zachary Quinto, who played Sylar, murdered me in my office. Before he killed me he paralyzed me with his mind and delivered a sarcastic speech. That seemed a little unnecessary, I must say. The whole time I was pretending to be paralyzed I was thinking that it looked like he got his clothes at Bloomingdale's. As he continued to emote I imagined Sylar shopping for his jacket at the mall. I wondered if he was polite to the sales staff or sarcastic. I wondered if he paid in cash or credit, or just paralyzed them with his mind and shoplifted.

After the speech he sent some sort of ray that cut off the top of my head. Then he ate my brains. The scene took half a day to film. Most of the time I was covered in Karo syrup and red food coloring. At the end Zach came up to me with enormous concern. He helped me out of my office chair saying, "Stephen, I'm sorry. Are you all right?" I said, "Zach, I'm fine. You didn't really kill me. You just made me unemployed."

And that should have been the end of it, but true to *Heroes*, it wasn't.

I got a call four months later from the producers that they had another rewrite and wanted to reshoot my death. Normally it wouldn't have been a problem, but this time it was. In the interim I had been in a terrible accident and had broken my neck. Yes. Thrown from a horse, I broke five vertebrae. I was wearing a hard brace on my neck 24/7. But never let it be said that a near-fatal injury stopped the production of a television show. The assistant director called me at home and said, "Stephen, that sounds pretty bad about the neck and all, but what do you think you could do on camera with the neck brace off?"

"Die," I said.

"Yeah. I mean other than that?" she said.

I told her, "Well, without the brace I can't walk. I can't turn my head. I can't even hold my head up." I thought for a second and said, "Maybe I could sit in a high-backed swivel chair and use the back of the chair to support my head and talk, but no one could touch me. No makeup. No hair. Nothing."

About three weeks later they called back and said they had written a new death scene. I came in with my son Robert to help me with my brace. I rehearsed with the brace on. I removed it when they said "Action" and handed it to Robert, who sat under the camera. When they called "Cut," my son helped me put the brace back on.

Kristen Bell had to discover my dead, brainless body and deliver an emotional monologue. She was terrorized about working with me for fear she would vibrate the chair too much and kill me. I could hear her heartbeat as she stood next to me. Her hands shook as she touched my chair. She saw my head bobble and she started crying. After the shot she knelt down beside me and asked if I was all right. I assured her everything was fine. I guess it was. That was the version of the scene they used: Kristen terrified and me with a broken neck.

As I left the set, Greg Beeman thanked me for coming in and shooting in spite of everything. "Stephen, just because you're dead, remember, this is *Heroes*. Don't be surprised if we call you back for more episodes," he said.

As Robert helped me back to the car, I laughed to myself. Only in Hollywood could they kill you, cut off your head, eat your brains, and tell you with a straight face, "You may be back." And then I thought about it a little more and realized that only in Hollywood was it possible that they could be telling the truth. And at the end of the day, that's what makes it all so wonderful.

17.

THE POLITICS OF ROMANCE

I N THE DEAD of winter in 1974, Beth and I took a once-in-a-lifetime trip to London and Paris. I say "once-in-a-lifetime" be-cause no one can be that stupid more than once and survive. We traveled with seven hundred pounds of luggage and a pillow from home. We traveled with no hotel reservations. We slept in a brothel. We rode in the luggage car of a train (I made this leg of the journey wearing two wet wool suits, covered in table scraps).

On the way home from France, Beth took a detour. She went back to Mississippi to visit family. Mom and Dad picked me up at the airport and drove me back to our home in Oak Cliff, Texas. My childhood home. But something in me had separated from my past. Now I felt like a man. Sort of. My mother still did my laundry, but I could have done it if put to the test. Beth and I had our own apart-ment near the SMU campus. We slept together. We had our own dishes that we bought at the dime store. We gave parties and had our own group of friends. Our futures lay before us—unlike Mom and Dad, who were busy picking me up at the airport.

I told Mom that we'd had a good time in Europe. We saw lots of theater. We saw Laurence Olivier. We saw Buckingham Palace and the Eiffel Tower. I left out the part about Beth and I getting thrown out of our hotel for punching a toilet. It sounded too irresponsible. I did mention Michael, the German art student who vomited on me, because that story not only painted me as a victim but also explained why I needed to get my suits dry-cleaned.

I arrived home. The smell of pot roast filled the air. I took a shower and dressed in some of my high school clothes that were in my closet. Mom unpacked my suitcase to prepare for the massive wash, dry, and fold routine.

Mom always did my laundry, even after I moved in with Beth. Mom would call me at the apartment in the morning and say she would be by to pick up my dirty clothes. She would drive twenty-two miles to our place. She would stand at the bottom of the stairwell and call up that she had arrived. I would bring down a laundry bag. She never came upstairs. She felt the apartment was coated in sin. She would take the clothes and drive back to Oak Cliff. Wash, dry, and fold. Drive back twenty-two miles and leave the sack of clean laundry in the stairwell. Nothing crazy about that. In our defense, I was her little boy, and I was more than happy to accommodate a pathology if it meant clean laundry.

As Mom cooked and washed, I made phone calls. First call was to Sarah. I was going to tell her that I was back in town, and she would have to leave our apartment. Sarah was a fellow student who needed a temporary place to stay over the winter break. Beth had offered our apartment without consulting me first—or ever. It meant that before going to Europe I would have to spend three days alone with Sarah in the apartment while Beth went back to Mississippi to find more clothes to take on the trip.

Sarah was a product of the sixties. She was a natural-fiber, make-love-not-war kind of girl. She was in the drama department. She majored in posture. She was the straightest-walking person I have ever met. Her neck was a foot long.

In our three days alone together I was afraid Sarah would want to engage me in some kind of Tantric yoga sex that would put my morality to the test. That didn't happen. Instead she vanished into the bathroom for hours at a time, putting my bladder to the test. I was embarrassed to ask her why she spent so much time in there. I couldn't imagine an answer that didn't make me cringe. After a couple of days of running to the gas station to use their bathroom, I asked her if she was all right. She smiled and said yes, she was fine. She was using the bathroom to do her yoga meditations as it was so quiet and peaceful in there.

So now three weeks later, I was back in Dallas and she would have to "om" somewhere else. No answer at the apartment phone. I called Beth to see if she had gotten to Mississippi safely. She had. She told me that Sarah sent a message that she had left the apartment a week ago. The bathroom was mine again.

Beth and I chatted about the trip and our respective families. Before we hung up, we picked a good time to look at the stars. This was our custom when we were apart. Operating under the assumption that the night sky would always be the same wherever we were, we would pick an hour when we would both go outside and look up. Using the night sky as a vehicle, we could still be together. The final words of our phone call may have gone like this: "Tonight at nine. I'll start at the Big Dipper. I love you."

Our stargazing was a little like someone who wants to be friends with Madonna in hopes her notoriety would be transferred by proximity—except Beth and I were hanging out with the eternal. Of course, real astronomers will tell you that the stars aren't eternal at all and the Belt of Orion is not a belt. It is just an illusion created by the enormity of time and distance from Earth. But we weren't astronomers, and we weren't that interested in what was actually there. We wanted to create a new reality through the politics of romance.

The next morning bright and early I drove the twenty-two miles from my childhood home to my new home, the one I shared with Beth. On the way, I got a haircut. For all of my bald readers, try to go back to that time when a haircut mattered. I got up from the barber's chair smelling of talc and looked at the world traveler in the mirror. I liked what I saw. I was energized. I made a plan. I would go back and clean up the apartment from Sarah. I would wash the towels and the sheets and prepare for Beth's arrival in a couple of days.

It was January. It was a new year. The air was cold and clear as I parked in our garage. I ran upstairs and opened the door. I felt like I was at home. The only thing amiss was a sour smell in the air. I thought it could be residue from some sort of yoga ritual until I noticed an unusual container in the hallway. It was a cardboard box filled with cat poop. Odd, as we didn't have a cat. I figured it had to be Sarah-related somehow and filed it under the "damn dirty hippie" category in my brain. I took it outside and threw it away. I came back upstairs and opened a window to let in the cold, fresh air when the phone rang. I sat on the daybed and answered it. It was Jac Alder, the managing director of the only real professional theater in Dallas, Theater Three. He was offering me a job! He wanted me to play one of the leads in *The Importance of Being Earnest*. Yes! This was going to be the year of Stephen! I was a graduate. I had a girl. I had access to a credit card (which my parents paid for). My life was beginning. And just when the sounds of my personal triumph were blasting in my head so loud I couldn't hear Jac anymore, my eyes crossed.

Yes. As strange as it sounds, my eyes crossed and my heart fluttered and started racing. I paused to get a breath. Jac asked me what was wrong. I laughed and said, "Jac, I have no idea, just felt funny for a second. Must be a combination of jet lag and getting a real theater job." I looked down my shirt front and straightened it out and saw that I had dark red drops staining my shirt. I looked carefully. It was blood! There was blood on my shirt. Now I couldn't hear Jac at all. I ripped open my shirt. My stomach was wet with blood. I yelled over the phone, "Jac! I'm bleeding, got to hang up now!" Jac yelled into the phone as I hung up, "Call me back!"

I pulled up my undershirt. I was covered with little black dots. I brushed at them with my hand and they started to crawl. Fleas! I was covered in fleas! I undid my belt. There were about a hundred gathered under the elastic waistband of my underwear. I screamed. I was in a Roger Corman movie! I started ripping my clothes off and ran to the bathroom. I turned on the shower and the sink, dropping my clothes in the hot water as I stripped them off. There were fleas on my ankles under my socks. I jumped in the shower. I scratched them off. Piles of black dots went down the drain.

I scrubbed myself until I was confident I was flea-free. As water pounded on my head, I tried to come up with a plan. What. What. Think. Think.

Dad. I could call Dad! He was a doctor over on the SMU campus five minutes away.

I stepped out of the shower and ran wet and dripping down the hardwood hallway. I saw fleas jumping on me from everywhere. I reached for the phone. I transitioned from a Roger Corman movie to a John Carpenter movie. I knocked the phone off of the table. I started to dial. More and more fleas covered me. I couldn't take it anymore. I ran back to the shower. I heard the eerie dial tone and the automated operator's voice in the background: "If you'd like to make a call, please hang up . . ."

Hot and steaming, I watched another pile of fleas go down the drain.

I had to get out. I had clean clothes in the bedroom. I made another dash. Fleas jumped up on me from the floor. I opened my drawer to pull out a shirt. Black specks crawled all over them. My clothes were infested. We moved from a John Carpenter movie to a David Cronenberg movie.

I ran back to the shower to wash off again. Then it happened, I started to run out of hot water. Whatever I was going to come up with, I would have to do it fast. New problem! I had no clothes! Everything in the apartment was infested. The clothes I wore were in the sink. I made a snap decision. Like most snap decisions, it was not good.

I reached for my keys in my soaked, flea-infested pants, and I ran out of the apartment naked.

I ran down the stairs, and across the parking lot and into the garage. I jumped into the Oldsmobile and backed out of the driveway onto McFarlin Boulevard. I felt like the girl at the end of *Texas Chainsaw Massacre* screaming, "I'm alive! I'm alive!"

But, unlike movies, life has no editing room or credits to give one a false sense of conclusion. In life the movie continues. I was naked, in an Oldsmobile, driving around Dallas. I couldn't go to the health center to see Dad. The campus police usually stop the naked people in the lobby. Yeah. That was out. I had two options. I could drive to Midlothian, Texas, stagger into a bait shop, and say I was abducted by aliens, or I could to drive the twenty-two miles back to my childhood home and pray Mom was at the grocery store. Now I was in a Harold Ramis movie.

When you drive naked, you become aware of a whole different set of problems you never even think about when you are a regular, clothed driver. Red lights provide a new horror. You never know who will pull up next to you: a station wagon, a school bus, or a random police car. I managed to avoid any accidental "Naked Man" sightings until I got to the heart of downtown Dallas. At the juncture of Interstate 35, a red dump truck pulled up beside me. I turned to look. This caught the attention of the trucker, who was in his sixties wearing a baseball cap. He turned and met my eye. Then he took in the entire vista. His jaw dropped, his eyes bulged out of his head, and as he silently screamed, "Oh, shit," he swerved off the road onto the shoulder. I hit the freeway with one directive: go as fast as possible without getting pulled over. In Texas, being stopped by police while driving naked could be a life-changing event.

I drove through Oak Cliff. I passed my old elementary school. I passed the minimall where I bought comic books. I saw our driveway dead ahead. Oh dear, Mom's car. I parked in the driveway and ran into the garage. The backdoor was open. I could see Mom through the screen door ironing in the kitchen. My only option was speed. I ran into the kitchen, through the living room, and into the back bathroom where I turned on the hot water to continue purging the remaining fleas. As the water warmed up, I heard a knock on the bathroom door. It was Mom. In a polite but uncertain voice she asked, "Stephen, is that you?"

When I finished my shower, I dressed and explained the horrors on McFarlin. Within minutes Mom and I came up with a plan that in hindsight made no sense at all. By any instrument of measure, it was a bad idea.

We didn't call an exterminator. We didn't call the landlord. We went to Skillern's Drug Store and bought four huge cans of Raid, tucked our pants into our socks, and went back and sprayed the place ourselves.

Mom got at one end of the apartment. I got at the other. We took a deep breath and with a huge can of Raid in each hand, we worked toward the center of the apartment where we met in a big cloud of poison. We sprayed the floors, the doors, the carpets, the walls, the sofa, the bed, the dressers, the kitchen, the phone. Everything. We ran outside for a hit of oxygen and then back until the cans were empty. When we finished, every surface was shellacked in Raid. The air had a sweet, toxic smell about it.

Amazingly we felt this plan had merit. We went back the next morning and hit the place again with four more cans of Raid, and once again that afternoon. In twenty-four hours we had emptied a dozen cans.

I called Beth later that day and told her that the apartment was poisonous. We should avoid the entire block for a while. She said that was okay. She would stay in Mississippi an extra day, or she could stay on a friend's floor, or check into a motel, or dress up like a pirate and sail up and down the Brazos River. Then she asked what time I wanted to look at the stars that night. I told her I was going back home to take a couple more showers to detox and then I would go outside. "Eight p.m.," I said, "and I'll look to the east." She said, "Eight o'clock. I'll look to the west. I love you."

"I love you. Good night."

And as if by magic, I was in a Frank Capra movie.

———

As I suspected, the fleas were an indirect product of Sarah. And perhaps, a direct product of the *Woodstock* album. While Beth and I were in Europe, Sarah decided to save the planet one stray cat at a time. She brought the cats into the apartment and set up a cardboard box of sand to serve as an improvisational latrine area, but for some reason known only to herself and her god, she never threw the litter away. So for three weeks, fleas bred in the cat poop. For the last week with no cats in the house to feed on, they just got angry. When I walked in with my new haircut and sat right in the middle of them, dinner was served.

After two weeks of being displaced, Beth and I came back and scrubbed the apartment down. The fleas never returned. Neither of us grew a second head from all the insecticide. To celebrate we decided to have a special dinner at home. I volunteered to cook, a bold move on my part as I had never cooked in my life. Beth added to the challenge that she wanted me to make a dish that I had "invented." Why not? When you don't know what you're doing, it's easy to come up with something new.

I invented a dish I called Chicken Volcano. It was a sort of casserole that combined undercooked chicken, jalapeño peppers, and grapes. The only thing volcanic about it was the diarrhea afterward. Instead of throwing the rest of the mixture out, we put it in the refrigerator where it could age properly and become a petri dish.

Beth signed up for her final semester. Her acting career at SMU had been unfulfilling. She didn't seem angst-ridden enough to get the big roles. If she got cast at all, it was usually as a child. I shouldn't have been surprised when she came home and told me she had signed up for a playwriting class, but I was. Beth seemed way too impulsive—way too "quixotic" as she put it—to come up with something as disciplined and coherent and unified as a play.

She started walking around with a torn-up spiral notebook. She carried it wherever she went. She took notes at restaurants, in bed, in the car, everywhere. We were all dying to know what this magnum opus would turn out to be. Occasionally, she would say something like, "I think I'm going to name a character Mr. Spoon."

I tried to be encouraging but realistic. I said, "I don't know if that is such a good idea. Mr. Spoon is a strange name."

Beth would smile and say, "That's why I like it." Then she would take more notes.

She enlisted several of us to type the play for her. Her former roommate Louise, our friend Terry, and I each took shifts typing away. Like the blind men and the elephant, none of us had any sense of what the play was about because we kept taking turns. I typed some exchange about a character wanting to put "blue food coloring in her water to make drinking it more exciting." Beth kept joking that she was probably writing "the biggest ptomaine wreck ever to hit the stage." We all laughed, but there was nothing in what we read that gave us any reason to think that it wouldn't be the biggest ptomaine wreck to hit the stage. Louise sat at the typewriter and she said questioningly, "Mr. Spoon?" Beth laughed and said she liked the name. Louise gritted her teeth and kept typing and said under her breath, "Disaster . . ."

When we finished typing the play, Beth sat down to write the title page. She couldn't think of a name quite yet so she just left it blank and wrote underneath on the author's line, "A play—by Amy Peach." I said, "Amy Peach?" She said she had to go incognito so she wouldn't get laughed out of the school. After my recent experience with my professor Joan Potter, I understood all too well the value of a low profile.

As I look back, it was amazing the number of big changes we were going through at that time, unaware. Beth, writing. Me, acting professionally. We, living together as a couple.

Also, for the first time in our lives we had developed friends outside of our circle at school. Alex and Allyn. This was big, but we didn't know it at the time. A widening circle of friends is an invitation to become part of what is known as civilization.

They lived a couple of streets away. They were both actors in the real world. Allyn had sandy hair and a beard and an extremely kind disposition. Alex was from Kentucky and was the niece of character actress Sudie Bond. We were kind of in awe knowing someone related to a true staple in Hollywood. They were a part of an acting troupe known as the Alpha Omega Players.

During the day, I played cribbage with Allyn and listened to Paul Simon's first solo album, speculating as to whether Paul would have a career after Garfunkel. We decided he would. On nights off, Beth and I would go over to Alex and Allyn's apartment and listen to FM radio and eat a pizza. And believe it or not, that was all it took to have a great time. I remember one evening the local radio station was going to premiere Elton John's new album, *Goodbye Yellow Brick Road*. They played it in its entirety, in sequence without commercial interruption. We sat in silence around the radio like those old pictures of a family listening to FDR during World War II. The importance of friendships cannot be underestimated. They are created the same way the Bible describes God's creation of man, with free will. And the exercise of free will is what defines you as a person.

When you watch a movie, a soundtrack guides you. The swelling music tells the audience that a letter you are reading is important or something on the other side of a door is waiting for you. In life we don't get that kind of guidance. You never know when you hear news that will change your life.

I needed that soundtrack for the evening Beth came home, scared and excited. One of the main-stage plays in the school's season had fallen through and the department had decided to fill the spot "from within." Plays by SMU playwrights past and present could be submitted to a committee. Beth's playwriting teacher, Biff Leonard, had submitted an untitled play by someone called Amy Peach.

After a week or so of deliberations, a simple notice was thumbtacked to the call-board in the green room. The committee selected the play by Amy Peach to finish off the subscription season.

We were screaming. We were flabbergasted. Beth's play—the one Louise and Terry and I typed—the one we never read and all made fun of—had won!

The entire school was caught up in the mystery of who was Amy Peach. No one suspected Beth. Some thought Amy Peach was a man. Some thought it was a professor in disguise. Some thought it was one of the amazing talents who were past or present students in the department like Kathy Bates or Powers Boothe or James McLure. Tony Graham-White, our Theater History teacher, joked that he "wanted to take a bite out of Ima Peach."

Once the director was selected, the identity of Amy was revealed. No one knew what to make of it because I don't think anyone had a clear opinion of Beth. She was the odd, cute girl who didn't get cast much.

Beth ended up calling the play *Am I Blue* because she loved Billie Holiday's version of the song. The play went into immediate rehearsal. For the next few weeks Beth and I were in different worlds. I was playing my first leading role in a professional production. Beth was attending rehearsals as a first-time playwright. There was something unreal about the changes in our circumstances. Not in terms of money—we were still broke—but in terms of notoriety. I was learning what it was to leave the cocoon of anonymity.

After I graduated, I noticed the one thing all acting majors had in common: frustration. When you don't get auditions and don't get acting jobs, it is easy to hide behind the persona of someone with enormous talent that the blind, underachieving world has overlooked. But when you get the job, those excuses vanish. You are no longer a genius in waiting. Your name is in the program. You have to deliver. And there's almost nothing more frightening than being judged on your own work.

Beth and I would have to face the critics. What if we were sliced and diced? What if the *Dallas Morning News* made a meal out of Mr. Spoon? What if our parents had to watch our public humiliation?

Beth told me she wanted me there opening night. We asked Alex and Allyn to join us for moral support. We sat together with friends and family. We laughed and made small talk, but the level of chatter and anxiety rose as the Margo Jones Theatre filled to capacity. I saw critics from the newspapers pull out notepads. The house lights started to go down. It hit me how huge this was in human terms, and what would be left of Beth if this play was an embarrassment.

We sat in the dark. Beth squeezed my hand until my circulation stopped. Lights came up onstage. There was a young girl, sixteen, wearing pieces of different outfits—reminiscent of Beth's long-underwear/miniskirt look. The play got a little laugh right away. I breathed easier. The girl appeared to be a street urchin with no home.

She meets our leading man, a lonely, fat boy of seventeen. He's been given an all-night pass to a whorehouse as a fraternity hazing. He's a virgin. And he's terrified. She has nowhere to go. They decide to spend the night together.

As the play proceeded, laugh followed laugh. There was a certain wacky reality, but underneath it all there was terror and hurt. To Beth's credit, after about ten minutes, I wasn't thinking about her at all. I was captivated. In the middle of the hilarity, our young heroine gets a phone call from her drunken father. The laughs in the theater stopped in a heartbeat. Everyone was silent. Tears burned down my cheeks—not just because of the play—but because of Beth. This play was not just good. It was one of the best things I had ever seen. And, remember, we had just seen Laurence Olivier and John Gielgud in London. Rather than answer any questions I may have had about Miss Hard to Get, now I had more questions than ever. Who was this girl sitting beside me? What was her talent?

The play ended with a thunderous ovation. Beth was brought up onstage. She took a bow. We were on the mountaintop called triumph. We celebrated with an impromptu party at our apartment. Everyone came. It was interesting to watch our friends relate to Beth in a different way. She was no longer anonymous. Her work set her apart from everyone. In the room that night you could have observed on a microscopic level the seeds of fame: the busy, joyous, noisy form of isolation.

The drinking started, reefers were lit, chaos reigned in a tame imitation of a future party we would have in the Hollywood Hills a little over a decade from now. I checked on the status of the kitchen. Everything in our home had been eaten, including the remains of the Chicken Volcano. I grabbed Beth and showed her the empty dish in the fridge. She made a face of mock horror, laughed, and then mimed slitting her throat with her index finger. In that moment I realized the two great qualities of actors: they'll eat anything and they'll take advantage of any opportunity to celebrate. Not a bad road to walk in this world.

As Beth and I cleaned up from the party, our spirits were soaring.

Our lives had changed since we got back from Europe. We had a handle on things. But in truth, we had no idea what was coming our way. And even if we did, we would not have had the foresight to know what it would mean. We had no defining soundtrack.

Within a few weeks, Beth would be in despair working as a waitress in a Mexican restaurant. Our friend Alex would call us in tears to tell us that Allyn had vanished without a trace. And instead of pursuing our careers in New York or Los Angeles as we had planned, we were heading to Illinois to be students again.

18.

—

DATING TIPS FOR ACTORS

VALENTINE'S DAY HAS been accused of being a made-up holiday, a holiday invented by candy salesmen and flower shops. I have known women who get livid around this time of year, saying the holiday is designed to make single people feel inadequate. I have also known men who start to get the sweats around mid-January, fearful of getting the wrong present, again.

Regardless of what you think about Valentine's Day, it does tend to make you think about relationships. Relationships have always proved the simplest and most complex of human endeavors. Even though people talk about relationships all the time, it is hard to make any headway. It is difficult to define what men look for in women and what women look for in men. One thing is for certain: it's not the same thing.

A group of sociologists performed an experiment in which they took the silhouettes of forty women's bodies (tall, short, fat, thin) and pasted the shapes on a poster. Then they traveled all over the world and had men pick which one they found the most appealing. From Berlin, to New York, to the Outback, to the Amazon jungle, to nomads in the Sahara desert, interestingly, men everywhere picked the same shape as the most desirable: the silhouette of Marilyn Monroe.

Obviously, not everyone can have Marilyn Monroe. Even Joe DiMaggio, who had Marilyn Monroe, found out that having Marilyn Monroe wasn't what he thought it would be.

Because relationships are so difficult to make and keep, people always try to simplify them, codify them, and crystallize them into something understandable. One popular form of the canon is found in dating tips.

I am always interested in dating tips, and I believe them all. I remember one I heard from the nineteenth century: a woman could tell everything she needs to know about a man from his shoes. Does he work hard, is he vain, does he travel a lot? That morphed into the early-twentieth-century advice that you can always tell how a man will treat you by the way he treats his mother. Yikes.

When I was in New York a few years ago, a woman told me that she looked for potential men to date in sports bars. She said she would get there early and sit next to a big-screen television so she would be noticed. She figured if a man was there to watch the game, he was probably straight. If she could divert his attention from the TV for eight straight seconds, he was dating material. Thirty straight seconds, we're talking marriage.

Online, they recently had an expert say that the three things that will doom you on a date are bad posture, dirty fingernails, and cat hair on your clothes. When I read this article I was sitting in my office chair, with a cat on my lap, right after I cleaned the rabbit cage.

I have boiled down my view of relationships over the years. I've made peace with the idea that most men are looking for a woman to deliver the three L's: Laundry, Lunch, and Lovin'. Some may call that crass. I look at it as simplicity itself.

Women are much more complicated. They are like walking, talking dramas looking for the type of movie they want to be. The man provides the genre: family film, horror, comedy. Many relationships end up as film noir.

I conducted my own sociological experiment on a trip to New York several years ago to see if I could understand what women look for in a man. Recalling the study with the silhouettes of women shown around the world, I went to three bars with my friend Greg and told three different stories to see what a woman would respond to. I wanted to know, if this were a real-world situation, could I have gotten a date?

Bar number one was the famous White Horse Tavern on Hudson Street. Dylan Thomas drank himself to death there. Greg and I sidled up to the bar and found two available-looking women. We said hello, offered to buy drinks, and then I hit them with story number one. I said I was a dermatologist. I lived in New Jersey and was having the time of my life coming to Manhattan. Business was so good I decided to cut down my practice in Newark to only two days a week and open up an office in Greenwich Village. I'd work one day a week in Manhattan, take in some shows, go to the symphony, eat food—basically, have some fun.

Without even a casual glance at my shoes or a question about my mother, the woman took out her card and wrote her phone number on it. She said that it sounded exciting and if I needed a "guide" around town to give her a call. Her eyes lit up as she asked me how I liked dermatology. I told her I loved it, except for lupus and melanoma. Otherwise, it was all rashes and acne. Within five seconds I knew whether to moisten it or dry it up.

Bar number two was McHale's Sports Bar. We found two unsuspecting subjects. Greg and I walked up and offered to buy them drinks. I started story number two. I told the woman that today was the happiest day of my life. I paid off my bicycle *and* I got put on the night shift at the delivery service where I worked. This meant I could continue to take acting classes during the day and start to earn money to get my pictures and résumé together—and then, hopefully, get an agent. She didn't check my shoes, either. She just excused herself to go to the ladies' room and never returned.

Bar number three was McAleer's Pub on Amsterdam. Same drill. Greg and I walked in. We went up to the bar. We met two women. We bought drinks. I started story number three—the unadorned truth—that I was a successful actor in films and television and was having a great time visiting friends in Manhattan before I had to go back to L.A. and start my next movie. The girl put her drink on the bar untouched and said with a certain degree of hostility, "Why do I meet all the fuckin' nuts?" And then she left. So for all you guys out there looking for the three Ls, I would go with dermatology.

Of course this experiment had way too many variables to be validated scientifically, but it does illustrate two points of irony. One, in all three stories it was the happiest day of my life and that didn't seem to affect the outcome at all. Two, honesty, it would seem, was not the best policy.

I have never seen honesty mentioned in any online dating tips. From shoes to cat hair, no one mentions honesty. Maybe we all know honesty is essential, and we don't have to restate the obvious. Or we know the hopelessness of being honest, so why should we depress ourselves further?

I've taught improvisation for the last seven years in Los Angeles. I do an exercise the first session of every class where we end up getting down to the basics of what matters most to us on a human level. Ninety-eight percent of the women and ninety-five percent of the men say quickly and with a complete sense of assurity that the most important part of a relationship is honesty. And number two is finding someone with a positive attitude.

The human interaction most like dating or starting a relationship is an actor auditioning for a part. Actors are perpetual teenagers on a first date. They pick out their outfits and dress up to make the right impression. They practice their lines in the shower. They study themselves in the mirror to see which is their best side, and if their flaws are suitably covered.

When I first started out in Hollywood, I used to practice shaking hands—with myself—to see how I came across. I concluded that my handshake was so clammy and invasive I had to retire it in favor of the fraternity boy head-nod and a "Howdy. How ya doin'. Good to see ya." All of this in hopes of getting lucky, which in an actor's case is getting a callback.

Instead of the padded bra, the actor relies on the padded résumé to get attention. It is hard on young actors. Unless you were Mickey

Rooney you don't have a lot of credits from your teen years. I used to take a scene I did in acting class and put it on my résumé as if I had done the entire play at some made-up theater: Tom in *The Glass Menagerie* at the Meadowlark Dinner Theater. Over the years I didn't get more parts, but I did get better at making up credits.

You have to get the knack of making up names that sound like real theaters. You can try this technique at home. Pick a geographical entity—say, the Great Plains or Cripple Creek or the Grand Canyon—and then add the words "Playhouse" or "Dinner Theater" to it. It will sound real. You can also pick a name from the phone book like Kevin Montgomery or Sally Daniels and add "Playhouse" or "Dinner Theater." It will sound real. Or you can take locations from the back of cereal boxes: Battle Creek Dinner Theater or the Quaker Oats Playhouse. It's a little like having a fake ID to buy beer. It all smacks of desperation, but as actors we are all nerds trying to date the head cheerleader.

Things got better for me when I stopped thinking that I was trying to get the part but, rather, seeing if I wanted to start a relationship. I quit worrying about what I wore. I stopped making up phony rave reviews of when I played Hap Loman in *Death of a Salesman* at the Cream of Wheat Playhouse. I started focusing on the one thing the producers and I had in common—the project.

So my dating advice for actors is the opposite of cruising the bars of New York. Be prepared. As impossible as it seems, be honest. And make sure you're not covered in cat hair.

I HAD JUST finished reshooting my death scene in *Heroes* with a broken neck. My manager, Steven Levy, sent me a script for a new show called *Glee*. I was anxious and excited. I hadn't had an audition in about seven months.

My troubles had started earlier in the year when I had lost my voice. I had a ruptured vocal cord. In the end I needed surgery and two months of silence to recover. I was told I couldn't whisper, let alone audition. When I recovered from the surgery, the doctor told me to take a trip where I could remain quiet and not use my voice. I went fishing. It seemed like a good idea. It wasn't. The first thing you do when you catch a fish is scream. After that, my wife suggested that we go horseback riding in Iceland. That seemed peaceful enough until the third day of our trek. We were riding single file along the side of an active volcano when a freak wind lifted me and my horse off the ground and threw us onto a lava flow. I broke my neck in five places. It was a yin-yang sort of thing. Now I could talk. I just couldn't move. I had a neck brace on day and night. I couldn't drive. I couldn't get socks out of my drawer. I had to sleep vertically for three months. And I couldn't audition.

So here I was in my neck brace, reading a script for a show called *Glee*. It seemed to be a musical about high school with lots of show tunes and good humor. But there was a difference. A note to young actors out there: the first reading of a script is important. It is pure. It can tell you how you feel about a project. It is a good indicator of how the public will feel about it as well. You should never read a script for the first time in a hurry or with the television on. Read it in silence so you can hear your instincts.

When I read *Glee*, I felt heartened. Even though it had all of the familiar high school symbology, it made me feel good about humankind, not an easy task these days. I couldn't pinpoint the ingredients that made me feel good. To be honest, everything in the show had been seen before: the high school setting, the sincere teacher, the mean teacher, the mean cheerleaders, the cute football player with the heart of gold, the singing pedophile—all familiar characters in high school comedies. But there was a tangible positiveness in its wacky humor and music that made me want to audition.

They wanted me to read for the role of Sandy Ryerson. I thought that was a good sign. The Ryerson name had served me well in *Groundhog Day*. I had four scenes to prepare and about five days to work on them, which by Hollywood standards is a lot of time. As I worked on the part, I didn't feel more confident. I felt greater and greater pressure. It had been so long since I had auditioned, it was like dating again after a breakup. What if I did poorly? What would it say to my agents and my manager? What kind of blow would it deliver to my self-confidence?

I knew from the *Heroes* reshoot just a few weeks earlier how diminished my physical condition was post-injury. I didn't have the strength to hold my head up. I couldn't walk without the brace or turn my head. The neck doctor told me I would be healed after three months. My audition for *Glee* was set for three months and ten days after the catastrophe in Iceland. I was terrified to take off my brace.

My wife, Ann, drove me over the hill for the audition Tuesday afternoon at rush hour. She waited in the car as I made my way through security and found the *Nip/Tuck* offices where the audition would take place. I walked in and was surprised. The room was empty except for a nice young man minding the phones. He asked if he could help me. I told him I was reading for *Glee*. He furrowed his brow and said, "Really?"

I said, "Yes." I showed him my audition sheet: four p.m. Tuesday. He saw my brace and asked if I was all right. I told him I was thrown from a horse and had a broken neck but in theory I should be fine. He looked concerned and said he didn't know anything about the audition, but he would look into it.

Oh dear. Things like this don't happen often, but when they do, there is almost a 100 percent chance something is wrong. I sat alone in the waiting room. Alone with my script. Instead of running over my lines, I imagined meeting the producers. Like any young man going to pick up a girl for the first time, I started to get clammy.

I haven't had to mislead anyone about my résumé for years. I have lots of legitimate credits now, but the pressure I felt over being honest about a different issue surprised me: Should I wear my neck brace on the audition? Should I tell them about my accident? Would it scare them away from hiring me?

I took the brace off and put it on the floor beside the couch. My neck felt fine, but I felt creepy, like I was on a date and didn't tell the woman I had two children from a previous marriage. I put the brace back on. The young man returned looking mortified. He told me there had been a terrible mistake. There were no auditions for *Glee* today. Someone gave me the wrong information. The auditions were tomorrow at the same time—four p.m. He hoped I wasn't too angry.

That word got to me. "Angry." Funny, I felt relieved. Not because I was unprepared, but because I had not resolved the neck brace issue. I smiled. I realized there was a time in my career when I would have been angry. I would have been put out for the waste of time.

In the true regret of that young man's face, I understood I had received a gift. A new perspective. I said, "Don't worry about it. Do you know how lucky I am just to be sitting in this room on the wrong day? There are millions of actors around the country who would love the opportunity to sit on this couch on the wrong day, to have a script of *Glee* in their hands. I took a nice drive with my wife. She's lovely and a good companion, and, now, I will get the opportunity to have another nice ride with her tomorrow. I figure I am the luckiest guy on earth." His furrowed brow vanished. He smiled and walked away.

I showed up the next day at four p.m. It was a different scene. The waiting room was packed. Now I was nervous for all the regular reasons, and I still hadn't decided what to do about my brace. After about a twenty-minute wait, they called my name to go in the room. I made a decision. A decision is different from a choice. We make a choice to get through a crisis. We make a decision to indicate a life path we hope to follow. I made a decision to wear my brace into the room.

All the guys were there—Ryan, Brad, Ian, Dante—a roomful of executive producers. I came in with my brace on and got some raised eyebrows. "Hello," I said.

They all smiled and said hello back. Ryan said, "I heard you were the happiest man on earth to be in the wrong place at the wrong time?" Everyone laughed.

"Yes. You can't beat it. I'm livin' the dream."

Ryan continued, "I heard you had a problem with a horse?" I said, "Yes, I broke my neck." The vibe in the room changed. I continued, "No, no, I should be just fine. But yesterday I was debating whether

I should come in with the brace or without it. I have to tell you the whole neck brace thing is giving me a lot of stress. So I decided we should do this together."

(Cut to a shot of the producers with a look of horror as if I just told them I had genital herpes.)

"I'm going to take my brace off now and do the scenes. I haven't auditioned in a while as I'm sure you have figured out, and frankly, I don't know if I can do this. If I can't, I'll just put the brace back on and leave the room—no harm, no foul. But if I can, you and I will both know I'm fine, and I can do this job. I love *Glee* too much to lie about the neck thing. If I am lucky enough to move forward in the casting process, I want you to have the confidence that I am not damaged goods. So shall we do it?"

Silence. I took my brace off.

(Cut to a shot of the producers looking like I was about to show them traffic safety films.)

I did all four scenes. Ryan directed me. And they laughed. It worked, and I left.

Three weeks later I found out I got the part. I was thrilled. I was proud. Surprisingly, not so much for getting the role of Sandy, but that I didn't lie on the first date.

19.

THE UNCERTAINTY PRINCIPLE

BETH'S TRIUMPH WITH *Am I Blue* happened in May near the end of the school year. It took about two weeks for the excitement to turn into "So, now what are you going to do with your life?" It was crazy enough to be an acting major in college, but to be a writing major made as much sense as studying to be a rodeo clown. As college students, we knew firsthand that nobody read books anymore. At least *we* didn't.

For many fine arts majors, graduation is a time of celebration, a short celebration—say, about two days tops. Then comes the realization that they may have to turn to Plan B: desperation. A large percentage of the crème de la crème of the SMU drama majors were now applying for jobs selling shoes or installing air conditioning.

Beth's friend and director, Jill Peters, got her an interview at Pepe Gonzalez Mexican Restaurant to be a waitress. The advantage Pepe Gonzalez had over its rival, Pedro's, was that they didn't serve dog food in the enchiladas. The disadvantage was that it wasn't a buffet so the waitresses had to carry gigantic trays with huge plates of refried beans, and chips, and mile-high margaritas.

The fall from your dream into reality is especially hard when you've seen that you can fly.

I appeared to be doing better careerwise than Beth. Emphasis on "appeared." I was starring as Jesus in a successful production of *Godspell*. Teenage girls would surround me at the laundromat asking for my autograph and wondering what it felt like to perform miracles. The only miracle I needed was to get paid.

Even though *Godspell* was a hit, the theater had a policy of asking the actors to give most of their salary back to the front office or they wouldn't get cast in the next show. The only real income I had was from my assorted day jobs. I was doing sketch comedy for a couple of producers who paid me in Chinese food. I also was making twenty dollars an hour reading a dirty book to an eighty-year-old woman. That was bad. What was worse—it was her autobiography. The only time I was upwardly mobile was when I climbed the stairs to our apartment.

Burnet Hobgood, a.k.a. Hob, the head of the SMU Theater Department, announced one day that he was leaving. He was starting a brand-new masters program at the University of Illinois at Champaign-Urbana. He asked if Beth and I wanted to come with him and enroll as students, sort of like test pilots. I reminded him I had barely survived my undergraduate career. Beth and I had planned on going to New York to be Babes on Broadway like in the Busby Berkeley movies. The idea of doing more class scenes, more essays on eighteenth-century drama, more potential run-ins with difficult teachers made me ill. Hob laughed and said he understood, but this time we would be the teachers. Beth and I would be paid to teach Beginning Acting and Voice, and the university would cover our tuition. I told him thanks, but no thanks. I was done with school for this lifetime.

Back at the apartment, Beth was trying on her Mexican waitress outfit. It was one of those green and red and white striped skirt-vest combos with the white, scoop-necked blouse and the big puffy sleeves. It was ghastly. She had trained for two hours. Tomorrow would be her first day. She looked at me with sad eyes. She had a casual despair you only see in Diane Arbus photographs. I told her she looked cute. She almost burst into tears, murmuring that she looked like a vomitorium.

The next day, Saturday, Beth started work at eleven a.m. I had two shows. I was nervous. It wasn't the matinee of *Godspell* that had my stomach churning. I wondered how Beth would fare on the weekend lunch shift.

When she left, I gave her a kiss. I headed for the theater. As I put on my Jesus costume, which was a pair of denim overalls, I looked at the clock. It was noon. Beth was working. I decided that she'd be fine. She was smart and resourceful. She would triumph.

I was wrong.

An hour later Beth came running through the back door of the theater in her waitress outfit. She was crying so hard her body shook. She ran into my arms, and I held her. We slid to the floor backstage. I rocked her behind the curtains until she could talk. "It was horrible, horrible. The people were mean. I can't take it. I can't take it anymore," she said.

I shushed her. "There, there, now. It'll be okay. Just catch your breath." I could hear the audience entering the theater on the other side of the curtain. "Hang out here until you get a second wind and things will go better tonight," I told her.

Beth's head almost spun around like the little girl in *The Exorcist*. "Tonight? Are you out of your mind? I quit. I was fired. I dropped a tray. I can't do this." She burst into tears again. "I'm never going back. Never, never, never, never going back."

"Okay. Okay. You don't have to go back."

We sat rocking for a few minutes. The stage manager called out, "Fifteen minutes," on the backstage PA. The band started tuning up.

"It'll be all right," I whispered.

Beth sniffled and looked at me as if the pit of hell had opened up in front of her. In a small, plaintive voice, she asked, "What are we gonna do? What are we gonna do?"

I scanned my universe of no options and said, "What do you think about going to Illinois?"

I ARRIVED IN Champaign-Urbana in August before the school year started so I could find a place for us to stay. There weren't a lot of options on our budget. I ended up renting a couple of rooms in a pre–Civil War house within walking distance of the drama school. That was good. The rent would be only $150 a month. That was great. The only problem was that the two rooms weren't connected. They weren't even related. That's not entirely true. They both were on the second floor. We had a living room and kitchen on one side of the public hallway—and a bedroom and bathroom a few paces down on the other side. Every time you wanted a beer or needed to go to the bathroom, you had to cross the hall.

This is how I met Helen.

Helen lived in the apartment at the end of the second floor. One morning she ran into me crossing in my bathrobe. She laughed and said, "I guess they finally unloaded the split apartment." I grinned like the chump I was. "Yeah. I guess they did," I replied. She said they offered it to her but she thought it was unsafe. "You could be sound asleep in the bedroom while I was being robbed in the living room or you could have people over for dinner in the living room while I was being raped in the bedroom. No one would ever know," she said.

I said that I hadn't thought of that, but that was a definite downside.

Helen was a foreign-language major, specializing in Asiatic languages. She had mastered seven so far. Impressed, I mentioned that Beth and I were new to the university and were in the masters program in acting. She found that exciting. She invited us over for dinner when Beth came into town. I accepted.

When Beth arrived I showed her our new digs. She liked the look of the old house but was perturbed about the split arrangement of the rooms. "You could be in the living room reading and you would never know someone was attacking me in the bedroom," she said. I nodded in recognition of my error. "We'll just have to lock the doors," I said. She unpacked and we set out to explore our new world.

We walked across campus. It had two defining elements. It was huge. Whereas SMU only had around five thousand students, the University of Illinois had thirty-five thousand. I also noticed the entire campus smelled like doo-doo. As Beth and I walked, taking in the enormity of the place, she looked at me, squinched up her face, and said, "This place stinks."

"I know, I know." We both stopped and looked at the bottom of our shoes. Nothing. We walked over to the brand-new Krannert Center for the Performing Arts where we would be teaching and hopefully acting in plays. It was amazing. It was a palace. There were beautiful theaters, an outdoor amphitheater, and gigantic dance studios.

We met John Ahart, the tall, sweet, affable head of the directing curriculum. He shook my hand and then Beth's. "So, here are Hob's Chosen Ones. Nice to meet you two. I think you'll be happy here. We're certainly happy to have you."

I nodded. "Yes, it's all a little overwhelming."

John laughed. "The new building? Or the smell?"

"Well—"

"Yeah, this time of year the university smells like shit. It's pretty interesting. It's the trees. The entire campus was planted with ginkgo trees. They're prehistoric. They predate the evolution of pollination by bees. They use flies. So the smell is an ingenious biological mechanism of attraction. Amazing, huh?"

"Yeah. In a way it's proof there's a God. How long does this smell last?"

"Six weeks."

"Well, they sure don't mention that in the brochure."

We ran into Hob walking down the hall with his beret at a fetching angle, smoking a pipe. He threw up his arms, ran over, and gave us a hug. He asked if we had settled in. I started to go into enormous detail about our split-room apartment. He nodded, not hearing a word, and told us secretly that as graduate student teachers, we were invited to a special party for the faculty.

That evening we followed Hob's directions to a building on the edge of campus. The party was held in what looked like some kind of basement. A Peter Frampton album played in the background. There was a table with pretzel sticks, salami, and a cheese log. The only difference between this and our graduation party in sixth grade was the tin washtub filled with beer.

I looked for a place to gravitate toward. Not knowing anyone, I made up my own zones of safety. I avoided men with beards. I avoided men wearing ties and corduroy jackets. I avoided women eating salami. I saw a man in his early thirties standing alone looking uncomfortable. He was wearing faded blue jeans and drinking a Coors. Coors was the international symbol of approachability. I walked over and introduced myself and Beth. I asked him what he taught. He said his specialty was physics and math. I was impressed. I told him I liked science a lot. I asked if there was a facet that interested him in particular. "Yes, the behavior of subatomic particles," he said. "I was part of the team that just won the Nobel Prize."

Pause.

"Really?" I asked.

He grinned shyly and said, "Yeah. It was a surprise, but it was pretty cool."

"I'll say. I guess you're done padding your résumé. If I may ask, what did you win for?"

"We won for developing a mathematical theorem proving the Uncertainty Principle."

I confessed I didn't know what that was.

My ignorance excited him. He launched into an explanation. "The Uncertainty Principle states that nothing can really be known. We came up with a constant that proved that the closer you get to the truth, the more incorrect your findings will be. And when you are standing right on top of the truth itself, the fact that you are standing there will make your observations one hundred percent wrong."

In that one moment, he made me feel both foolish for having read Voltaire, and insightful for watching cartoons. He said the theorem originated from a study of subatomic particles. The electronic equipment used to study mesons and pi-mesons affected their behavior. The closer you observed the particles, the more they diverged from their normal behavior. His team developed a universal constant that the truth is proportionately hidden from close observation.

I mentioned that coming up with a proof that truth can never be known at a university was like biting the hand that feeds you. It was the essence of comedy. He laughed and said, "Yeah. And the school even paid us to figure it out."

I told him it was a pleasure to meet him. I finally found someone who made me feel good about being an actor. He chuckled and said, "How so?"

"If what you say is true, it sounds like we'll always need art: to understand truth from a safe distance."

We clinked our beer bottles in a toast. We exchanged names and numbers as we parted. "See you around," he said. We never did. It's not surprising when you consider a university of thirty-five thousand people multiplied by the distance between science and art.

After the party Beth and I walked around the campus. I had never experienced an Indian summer before. The stars had a different sort of light. They seemed closer and clearer. At the center of campus, we came upon a bronze sculpture of various angels and people reaching forward to embrace us. I stopped and looked at the inscription: "To thy happy children of the future, those of the past send greetings."

I looked into those unseeing bronze faces and outstretched arms and knew at that moment, somehow, I was in the right place. Unified, not by anyone who had answers, but by generations of others who stood right where I was standing with nothing but questions. Then I had a pang of fear. I thought about how far away Beth and I were from where we thought we'd be at this time in our lives. It was the Uncertainty Principle. Could it be possible that distance was a friend to truth?

Beth looked at me with unexpected joy. She walked forward and touched one of the bronze faces. "I love this statue," she said. "This is how angels really look."

"How do you know?" I asked.

"'Cause I see them in my dreams."

And I thought of my friend at the party with his shy smile and Coors beer. Maybe he was onto something.

———

THE SCHOOL YEAR started. Beth and I were teaching. We were taking Modern Dance, Acting, and a class in Shakespearean Verse taught by Hob. I was amazed. All of this time I had only known Hob as a sort of academe to the third power: a man who would never call a spade a spade when he could call it a partially conical metal digging implement used primarily in recreational agriculture. Now I was seeing a totally different Hob, a great teacher—who wore a beret.

I was going to be in Tom Stoppard's *Jumpers*, playing an old man. Beth was going to be in Thornton Wilder's *The Skin of Our Teeth*, playing a child. We were slowly creeping up on parts our own age. As a fitting climax to this whirlwind first week, we went to our neighbor Helen's apartment for dinner. She told us she was cooking Italian. All we had to do was bring ourselves.

More than flowers, more than children, cooking makes a house come alive. My grandparents' house always smelled of lima beans and vanilla cookies, and when Mom was alive, our home in Dallas always held the traces of Betty Crocker cakes and pot roast. When the cooking leaves, an emptiness takes its place.

As we walked up the spiral staircase of our new, old residence, Helen was in her kitchen. The tomato and oregano and garlic were working their way through every board and beam.

She met us at the door. She looked put together in her powder-blue sweater and brown plaid skirt. Her apartment was big and airy and had huge windows with old, old glass facing the street, making the outside world seem like an impressionistic painting of a rainy day.

We sat down and feasted on salad and spaghetti and sponge cake and wine. As we munched on garlic bread, I told all the old stories about how Beth and I met, and Van Cliburn, and Joan Potter, and

Am I Blue. We were finishing our wine when Helen started looking at me across the table. Something in her look was odd and put me on edge. Beth and I were such a cute couple, she said. She poured herself another glass of wine. I cut off some more sponge cake and asked if she was seeing anyone. She said she had a boyfriend who was going to Southern Illinois, but she didn't get to see him much. She couldn't visit him on the weekends because she had so much work to do for her language major. For whatever reason, he couldn't get up to see her.

At a certain point of mild intoxication, Beth and I called it a night. As we walked down the few feet of hallway to our bedroom, I looked back. Helen was still looking at us through her opened door. She stared for a moment and then disappeared inside her apartment. I heard her door lock.

Over the next week or two, Beth and I fell into the rabbit hole of study and teaching and work on our respective plays. It was an exhausting routine fueled by pizza and beer. One night I had rehearsal at the Krannert Center. Beth had the night off. She was going to stay in the apartment and catch up on her Shakespearean Verse homework.

On my way to rehearsal that night, I thought my biggest problem was learning the five-page monologue that opened our play. I was wrong. Around ten p.m. Beth came running into the theater in a panic. Rehearsal stopped. I ran over to see what was up and to calm her down. She said she couldn't stay in the apartment anymore. It was haunted.

I stared at her, searching for something comforting to say that didn't use the words "hallucinating" or "crazy."

"Listen to me," she said. "I was in bed, reading, and I heard a scream." I told her it was probably the television in someone else's apartment. Maybe it was some noise coming from Helen's place. "No. It was in our bedroom. It was a ghost, and I'm not going back there alone." I rubbed my forehead. I was starting to get my "Beth headache." I got this headache when I confronted something in Beth's reality that didn't fit into my understanding of the planet

Earth. There was the time in upstate New York when she went running into the woods because, as she told me later, insects from Mars were trying to get into her brain. Or the time when she scolded me for kicking mushrooms along the side of the road because those were the houses where the fairies lived. It was a Beth headache.

After rehearsal we went back to the apartment. And no. There was no ghost. Big surprise.

During my play rehearsals we had a run-in over my hair. The director wanted me to wear a gray wig. They picked a sort of gray bun and stuck it on my head. I sat in front of the mirror. When they were done brushing and combing, I looked like a gigantic Granny Clampett. I asked why couldn't I do it "au naturel." That way the audience wouldn't have to confront the huge lie of my wig every time I went onstage. The director said that I was playing an *old* philosopher with a young wife. It was intrinsic to the story that I be *old*. I admitted, in theory, that he had a point. But in reality, why pick a play where a twenty-four-year-old plays an eighty-four-year-old? The answer is not to put the twenty-four-year-old in a gray bun. Maybe it could be just as poignant if the philosopher were young but more in love with his ideas than with his wife. At some point, I reasoned, we were going to ruin this play. I suggested it would be better to risk ruining it with bad acting than with bad hair.

I went home in a huff and took a shower to cool off. Beth was still at her dress rehearsal. I put on my jammies and settled in for a favorite guilty pleasure—watching reruns of *Ironside* with Raymond Burr. *Ironside* was not just a television show in Urbana, it was the centerpiece of popular culture. It was on three times a day. Raymond Burr was always in a wheelchair except for the flashback episode where he stands and walks for about sixty seconds before he gets shot. I was lying in bed drinking a Rolling Rock thinking how brilliant Raymond Burr was for coming up with an idea where he didn't even have to stand up when he went to work—except on break.

And then it happened.

I heard a shriek that made me choke on my beer. I sat up in terror. I heard it again, an eerie, high-pitched wail. I jumped out of bed and turned off the TV. It was a ghost! My heart flip-flopped in my chest. The hair on the back of my neck stood at attention. The only thing worse than a Beth headache was when Beth was right!

It had to be the wind. That was it, the wind. Or a branch scraping on the roof. And there it was again! Somewhere above me. I walked around the room looking for the source. It seemed louder over by the closet. The closet door was closed. I grabbed one of my Frye boots to use as a weapon. I opened the door. Silence. I started looking through the clothes. Nothing. I heard the shriek again. I ran out of the closet and slammed the door. I dashed across the hallway to the living room/kitchen and grabbed our flashlight. I came back and pointed it to the roof of the closet. I had never looked up there before. It was not solid but just slats of wood. I tried to focus the beam of light on the darkness between the slats. Everything was quiet until a blood-curdling scream ripped through the room. A hand slapped the ceiling of the closet. And then I saw a finger! Oh my God! The ghost! I ran out of the apartment in my pajamas, down the stairs, and out to the street.

Beth came home and saw me shivering in the front yard. She asked me what was going on. I told her about the shriek and the hand. She nodded. "It's probably a ghost from the Civil War. Someone murdered for money for trading slaves. We'll have to move," she said. I realized Beth was probably right. As I started coming up with a story to get out of our lease, out of the corner of my eye I saw movement on the roof of the house. We turned to see our ghost—or ghosts, as it turned out. It was a mother raccoon and three babies waddling out of a hole in the roof and down the big tree beside the house and then waddling away in single file. "Aww. So cute," Beth cooed. "We'll have to put out bananas for them during the winter."

The next month our plays both opened with success. Beth was beautiful as the little girl. I ended up compromising with the director over my hair. Instead of a wig I let them spray my head with silver Streaks 'N Tips. It was also a terrible choice, but it only made me look like a bad high school actor instead of an old transvestite.

After two weeks I finished my run in *Jumpers* and got another leading role in a new play to close out the semester. I felt the first flush of success in Illinois. I walked home after that final matinee, jumped in the shower to wash off my old-age makeup and remove the Streaks 'N Tips for the last time when, to my horror, a huge chunk of hair fell from my head. I couldn't believe it. I rinsed the shampoo out and another handful fell out. And then another. And another.

I lost my hair that afternoon in the shower. Not all of it, but enough to where I looked like I was "balding." From that day on, my chances of playing a young romantic lead were over. From that day on, whenever a woman or a casting director met me, her eyes would dart to my hairline.

It was far more traumatic than I ever admitted to myself. All of the Tobolowsky men were bald, but all of the men in my mother's family kept their hair. I always hoped that I favored her side. It was not to be. The closing day of *Jumpers* was the last day I looked like a young man.

It was around this time we met Claudia Reilly. Claudia was the only student in the playwriting curriculum and she looked the part. She had sharply cut short blond hair with bangs, and big intelligent eyes. Like Hob, she wore a beret, black turtleneck sweaters, and smoked cigarettes. She had the magnetic quality of appearing jaded and innocent at the same time. She had just written a new play and asked Beth and me to read some roles in it at its first public presentation.

There were about forty people in attendance. All of the actors sat in a semicircle at one end of the room. Claudia made a short speech beforehand. Her cheeks flushed with excitement and terror. We commenced.

The play was witty and had interesting characters. Claudia had written the only student play I had seen, other than *Am I Blue*, that didn't make you want to step in front of a bus. The evening was a great success for Claudia. It was also a great success for the school, for turning out a playwriting student who actually wrote a play.

After some champagne with Claudia and her friends, Beth and I walked home in silence. There was an unspoken tension between us. It was another one of those moments when I needed a defining soundtrack. When we got to the living room/kitchen side of our apartment, Beth walked around the room nervously and then she turned to me and said, "That was so brave of Claudia."

Being clueless, I asked, "What was brave?"

"Writing a play. Being a woman and writing a play."

"I don't know how brave it was. She is a student in school. She wanted to write so she took a playwriting course."

"But she is the only playwriting student. Think of that. Wanting to do something so badly that you are willing to be the only one. The only one in the class. The only one to write a play. And to be a woman. There was a time when they didn't even let women own pencils."

"Yeah. But that was a long time ago. Women own pencils now. They own all sorts of things. It's a whole new world. Women can be cowboys. Men can be strippers. Times have changed."

I still had no idea where this conversation was going. Beth looked out our window onto Green Street. "If Claudia can do it, I can do it. I want to be a writer."

Without the orchestra in the background, I was unaware of what movie I was in. Beth was making a declaration of purpose while I was wondering if it was too late to watch the eleven p.m. episode of *Ironside*. Casually, I said, "I think that's great. *Am I Blue* was great. You should be a writer if you want." The conversation ended. I went to get a Rolling Rock.

Indian summer is a strange phenomenon. Periods of fall are interspersed with periods of warm, springlike weather all the way up until winter hits like a runaway snowplow. It was the beginning of December and we had a short, unexpected warm day. At breakfast I had a certain sensation—and it wasn't good. The smell of the ginkgo trees had long since passed, but now there was a new smell. It was the smell of rot and decay. I checked the refrigerator, the rat trap behind the couch, the bathroom. Nothing.

Beth woke up and shuffled into the breakfast nook. She looked around and made a face. "I know," I said. "It stinks."

Beth said, "It's probably Helen."

Helen.

I hadn't thought about Helen or her look across the table for months. I hadn't seen Helen since she watched us walk down the hall after dinner at the beginning of school.

"Beth, have you seen Helen?"

Beth thought for a second. "No. She's probably a murderer and killed her boyfriend and he's rotting in the bathtub."

We both sipped coffee. "Seriously," I said. "Have you seen her?"

"No. Not since we had dinner over there."

"Neither have I."

Beth took another sip of coffee. "I'm telling you, she's a murderer and there's a body in the bathtub. That explains the smell."

A Beth headache started.

Over the next couple of days, with the warmer weather, the smell got worse. Lying in bed I asked Beth if I should go over there. Beth told me not to, that I didn't want to see what was in that room. The weather turned cold. Winter arrived. The smell didn't abate. Now the thought of Helen and that apartment became a fixation. I had to go over and see if Helen was still there. Maybe she smelled the rotting mess, too. I thought of a ruse to cover my investigation.

I bought a bottle of wine. I could knock on the door. Offer her the wine as a much belated thank-you for the dinner party, have a quick peek at the apartment. If it seemed appropriate, I would mention the stench of decay and then leave.

I walked down the hallway with my bottle of Lancers. I knocked on the door. Nothing. A couple of hours later, I wandered over again and knocked, again nothing. I had a new sense of dread. That look Helen gave me. The talk of what a cute couple Beth and I were; her mention of her boyfriend who never found the time to visit her; the stress of being an Asian-language major. What if she killed herself? What if she was dead in the bathtub?

I ran back to our apartment. I told Beth my theory. She didn't look up from her notebook. She just muttered, "There's no suicide. Not the type. She's a murderer."

I had trouble sleeping that night. I lay awake running possible equations of time, smell, and disappearance—the physics of it all was not hopeful. Then, I heard a noise on the floorboards outside our bedroom door. I got out of bed. I turned the knob slowly and silently and opened the door a crack. It was a stray yellow cat. The cat looked back at me and then wandered up to Helen's door and meowed. It turned and sprayed pee all over the bottom of her door and wandered back down the hallway and down the stairs.

I had no idea what this meant in the cat world, but I was sure it was bad. I left our bedroom and crept over toward Helen's door. I thought I heard the faint sound of a radio coming from inside. I knocked quietly. If she was asleep she couldn't have heard it, but if she was up I could tell her about the cat. And the pee. Give her the bottle of Lancers. She never came to the door, but the sound of the radio stopped. I told Beth about the cat and the radio. I decided we had to call the landlord the next day. He could come by with a passkey and confront whatever was behind the door.

The next morning I got up early and headed across the hall to make some coffee. I loaded the pot up and headed back over to the bedroom to get dressed. As I crossed the hallway I noticed Helen's door was opened a crack. I stopped and looked down the hallway. There was no one around. The only sound was the early-winter wind cutting through the trees. I had to look. I crept down the hallway, floorboards creaking under my weight. I got to Helen's door and tried to look inside. No movement or sound anywhere. I pushed the door open with my finger no more than an inch. I stuck my eye up to the crack. I tried to peek inside without my nose pushing the door open any farther.

I couldn't believe what I saw. Through the opening I could see into Helen's apartment and her kitchen table. There, on the table, were the remains of our dinner! Untouched! The three place settings and our dishes with uneaten spaghetti all covered with mold. The Italian salad, the partially eaten garlic bread, the bottle of wine where we had left it months earlier. There was mold on the remains of the sponge cake dripping onto the floor. And there was no trace of Helen.

I ran back and woke Beth up and told her. I thought it was probably her boyfriend who came up the same night we had dinner. He killed Helen and drove her body back to Southern Illinois in his pickup truck. Beth shook her head no. It was someone from the language department insane with jealousy. But we would never find her body.

Now we would have to go to the police. Beth got up and got dressed and we ran down the staircase. Going out the front door we ran into Helen. She was in her plaid skirt and blue sweater. "Hi, guys. I haven't seen you in forever. What are you doing up so early?"

"Nothing, Helen. Rehearsal. For a scene, you know, before class starts. What are you up to?"

"Just been busy. My parents are coming in to see me today so I'm just cleaning up a little."

"Well, that's nice. Have a good visit. Maybe we'll see you later."

That afternoon I ran into Helen's parents coming out of her apartment. The smell was gone. Every trace of our dinner was gone. The dishes were washed. The floor was scrubbed. The bed was made. No one would ever have known what was there only a few hours before.

What I saw on that kitchen table through the crack of Helen's front door was worse than a body in the bathtub. It was the difference between illusion and reality, between safety and danger mixed gently with a powder-blue sweater. At close distances the human eye cannot discern between the two.

I was relieved no harm had befallen Helen, but now I had a constant dread of what lay beyond the door at the end of the hall. I had never been so uncertain of the world around me. Lying in bed that night, each sound posed a question. Was it a warning, was it the wind, or was it just the Ghost of Green Street looking for her three children?

20.

—

WITHOUT A HANDLE

A S ONE OF my dear, departed companions once said, "The reason you can't get a handle on life is because it's not a bucket." And he was right. It's not a bucket. And yes, he drank a lot. But the idea that life was not a bucket was more perfect than he imagined. There was no single thing to grab on to.

Beth and I were deep into our first year at Illinois. We alternately felt successful and foolish. We were doing well, but we were still in school. We were making good grades, but who cares. We still wanted to be Babes on Broadway, but we were nowhere. One of the pitches the University used in its brochure was that the school was within a three-hour drive of Chicago, Indianapolis, or St. Louis. We were the very definition of being in the middle of nowhere, and the University thought it was a selling point.

In retrospect, we were victims of the "yeah, but" syndrome. The "yeah, but" is a mental disorder that has affected everyone I have ever known in varying degrees. Actors get it all the time.

Here is an example of how it manifests itself: a case study. Someone says, "What are you working on?"

"I'm playing Hamlet in a new production."

"Wow, that's great," he or she says.

"Yeah, but we're performing in a parking garage."

"Well, that's interesting."

"Yeah, but we're not getting paid. We even have to pay for parking."

"At least you get to work on that great play."

"Yeah, but the play has been cut to one act with five characters and we have to dress up like cats."

"Well, at least you'll get home in time to see *Ironside*."

"Yeah, but I've seen all the episodes—twice."

The "yeah, but" is the way we have developed to diminish our own lives into footnotes. To demoralize, trivialize, and squander the greatest gift we have been given—the joy of watching the sun rise for another day, even if it is only to have the opportunity to fail.

You would think there would be massive campaigns to eliminate the "yeah, buts." There aren't. People who use "yeah, buts" frequently are considered measured and intelligent. Many go into politics.

One of the oddities I lugged to Illinois was a gigantic, white family Bible I bought when I was playing Jesus in *Godspell*. The musical is based on the book of Matthew. I bought the Bible for research. I had never read it before. It wasn't for lack of interest. It was just too daunting. The problem with most Bibles is that the font they use is too tiny. You had to go blind to read a book meant to give you vision. Not so with this white Bible. It was huge. And it had pictures. And maps. I would like to say that after I brought it to Illinois, I started to read it in earnest. I didn't. I am embarrassed to admit that I used it to hold up the window in the bedroom so we could get fresh air. I guess that is one step above using it as a doorstop.

Occasionally on a lazy Saturday or Sunday morning, I would pull that Bible out of the window and read some part of it to see if I could make sense of it. I never could. Like life, I often found that I needed a handle. Every time I read a story or part of a story, the meaning kept shifting, or I would see something in the story I never saw before. I could never get a grip on it. Back then I thought all of the ironies and inconsistencies in the Bible were a sign of age and the need for a rewrite. Now I understand these incongruities were the calling cards of the book's greatness.

I was always partial to the stories of Joseph. Easy to understand, right? Dramatic. Even Andrew Lloyd Webber found them so. The Hebrew word used to describe Joseph is not used to describe anyone else in the Bible. It is the word *matzliach*. It is an unusual word and it is translated as "successful." Joseph is characterized as being "successful." Not Moses, not Abraham, none of the other prophets—just Joseph.

Now here is a guy who was spoiled by his father, tattled on his brothers. He was beaten by them, almost murdered, sold into slavery, ended up in an Egyptian prison. Those who promised to help him forgot him. I know. It sounds like Hollywood. But Joseph is called "successful." Why? Either the book is wrong or it's using a set of priorities we aren't used to thinking about.

Joseph was able to "read dreams." He had ESP, second sight, whatever you want to call it. He foretold a worldwide famine and saved Egypt. He made Pharaoh a wealthy man. Is the Bible saying that unless you're psychic you can't succeed? If not, what is the yardstick being used to measure "success"? For Joseph it was not peace of mind or an easy path.

Whatever you think about the Bible—if you see it as a divine text, a spotty piece of history, or a dangerous collection of children's stories—this narrative is a powerful lesson that you can never be certain if you are in a good or a bad situation. The yardstick we should be measuring success by may not be related to what the eye can see.

We all take stock of our prospects, and get alternately excited or depressed by them. But our vision is never 20/20. Just when you thought you had a career in Dallas, you're off to Illinois. Just when you thought you had Helen, the great Italian cook, as your neighbor, a door opens a crack and you discover you're living next to the Texas Chain Saw Massacre.

As a rule in life, if you want to feel thin, hang out with fat people. If you want to feel better about your prospects, talk to friends who are worse off than you. Throughout the first months in Illinois, we kept contact with our friend Alex Winslow in Dallas. At the end of the summer she called to tell us her husband, Allyn, had vanished.

Then events separated us. Beth and I left town. We called regularly to see how she was doing and if there was any news. Over the weeks, her tears gave way to depression that gave way to rumors that Allyn had resurfaced—somewhere. He was alive. She told us that he had misgivings about his life. He felt lost. He had gone crazy. It all seemed like science fiction to me. Allyn was one of the sweetest and smartest guys I had known. But then I thought of Helen, and maybe I just hadn't had a peek behind Allyn's door. Perhaps my vision was not 20/20.

There is almost nothing more powerful than the current of unhappiness. It can carry you far away. It can separate friends and family. It can even separate you from yourself. We left Alex behind on a different shore and went on with the little dramas of our own lives.

Classes seemed to take on artificial importance. We were instructed to do acting scenes on one foot to see how it would affect our performance. Our teacher chastised me for not taking the exercise seriously. I wasn't a flamingo, I told her.

In Modern Dance class, our teacher was also a grad student on scholarship. Her name was Blake Atherton. Every straight guy in the drama department took her class and fought to be in the front row. Our interest was not related to the love of dance, but to Blake Atherton. She was the 1975 version of Viagra.

I was now in rehearsal for one of the biggest parts in my life—not the best, but by far the biggest. It was a new play written for the upcoming Bicentennial called *'76 Town Hall*, or as we dubbed it, *76 Pound Turkey*. It was three hours and twenty minutes long. It ended with me delivering a forty-minute monologue dressed up like Uncle Sam, in a red, white, and blue sequined costume, with a white beard and top hat.

The play was a scathing criticism of how commercial America had become. Of course the playwright hoped that he might be the beneficiary of some of that same disgusting commercialism. But he was safe. His play was to theater what the root canal is to dentistry.

My character was called "Narrator," already a bad sign. But that didn't keep the other acting students in the department from envying me, partially because my role was so huge. Just like in porno, young actors believe that size matters.

It's also understandable for other reasons. It all smacked of favoritism. Hob brought me in, and I got the lead in *Jumpers*. It was a gigantic role. I played an old man that delivered long, incomprehensible monologues on physics to an occasionally sleeping audience. Then, in a move of almost De Niro–like transformation, I lose my hair in the shower and get cast in the largest part in the longest play ever written, where I got to deliver another set of huge, incomprehensible monologues. I was becoming the school's "go-to guy" for unwatchable theater.

I mentioned to Hob that I talked for a long time at the end of the play and had no idea what I was saying. Hob smiled and said not to worry. He was going to run a slideshow behind me during the speech with images of American iconography like Superman, and Kent State, and Gumby. This is one of the primary directing techniques of modern theater—when in doubt, cover the incomprehensible with the inexplicable. The audience will just think you're smarter than they are.

Oh, and did I mention the play was going to be directed by Hob? With Hob at the helm, I knew I was going over Niagara Falls in a thespian barrel. Survival was possible, but not likely.

Beth was not cast in the play. The children's parts were being played by other children. She started carrying her tattered notebook around with her again. She would jot down a word or sentence. Sometimes I would look over her shoulder and see she had doodled the picture of a woman holding a baby who had the head of a dog. I was once again getting that Mr. Spoon feeling in my stomach.

The school brought in a professional acting coach to handle the new master class. His name was Ed Kaye-Martin, a handsome middle-aged man who always wore blue jeans and flannel shirts. He was gay. But not just gay. He was mean-gay, like on the Bravo channel. I had never encountered anything like it. He could cut you to ribbons with any of six lethal disparaging glances, and that was before he opened his mouth to tell you that you were hopeless and should get out of acting—and going home and committing suicide would be an option except you were too worthless to waste the sleeping pills on.

Ed batted me around the head and shoulders a little but never went for the jugular, primarily, I suspect, because I possessed a penis. But the women in our class were drawn and quartered. And sadly, the brunt of his wrath fell on Beth. Every time she got onstage, he attacked her. He would mock every choice she made. He made fun of her voice, of the way she dressed. It was painful. She was falling into the same position I had been in with Joan Potter.

Ed made the mistake many people did in dealing with Beth. He thought she was what she appeared to be, a sorority girl gone astray. But he had not looked behind her door. He didn't recognize that she possessed a unique blend of Southern charm and nihilism. She was not to be shaken or stirred. She had the ability to break him into pieces if he pushed her too far.

I did what I could to protect Beth and support her outside of class. But I was afraid for both of them if a showdown occurred. Ed wrote up evaluations for everyone and handed them out in envelopes. Teachers like Ed survive this way. They do their damage in sealed envelopes. Beth never opened hers. We went to Burger Chef that afternoon. I offered to open her envelope for her and read it. But she snatched it from my hands and flicked it into the trash. "What's the point," she said.

The next class she had to perform her final scene. It was something from a play that's not done anymore, *The Days and Nights of BeeBee Fenstermaker*. Beth was brilliant. She was passionate and tough. She was funny in an offhanded way. The class was silent. I was screaming inside, "That's my girl. Yes! You show 'em."

Ed sat there in silence. The class waited for his slights and his condescension. They waited. The slights didn't come. Ed, who was so quick to shoot down a dream, kept sitting there and said nothing. A tension built in the room. Finally he asked, "Why have you done this?"

"Excuse me?" Beth said.

"Why have you done this now? Why at the end of the session?

Your work was flawless. It was beautiful. If I were doing a production of this today, I would cast you in a second. Why did you wait until now to show me you could act?"

Beth gave Ed one of her looks. Her eyes were whirlpools of emptiness and anger. She said, "Ed, I don't know what you mean." Ed was silent. Regaining his composure, he said, "I want to apologize for what I wrote in your evaluation. I was wrong, and I'm sorry if it hurt you." Beth, who had been staring at Ed the entire time without changing her gaze, said, "Oh, Ed, I never read that. I threw it in the trash at the Burger Chef."

Ed again took a breath and then raised his arms to the ceiling and yelled, "Bravo! Bravo to you! Ladies and gentlemen, this is the real actress. To act you must be strong. You must have autonomy. Beth, I salute you."

And I salute Ed Kaye-Martin. In that small classroom of a dozen students, he put truth before pride. That takes a special sort of person. And on a side note, it made the entire day so much more pleasant.

I WAS REHEARSING '76 *Town Hall* on the stage of the big eight-hundred-seat theater at the Krannert Center. The time had come for me to work on my concluding forty-five-minute monologue with Hob. The problem with writing a forty-five-minute monologue is that no one (except one of the mothers at our preschool) ever talks that much. It's unnatural. It's almost as long as an NBA game. It's exactly as long as an entire one-hour episode of *Ironside* without the commercials. It's longer than it takes to barbecue a two-pound tri-tip. Even if it is written brilliantly, it means you have too much to say and you're in the wrong profession.

It's hard to learn something that long. Many actors have asked me for pointers on how to memorize lines. I have two general tips. Tip one is to break down whatever you are learning into three acts, per Aristotle's suggestion. Every speech, no matter how long or short, has an introduction where the geography of ideas is laid out; a

conflict (usually the subject of the speech); and a climax where resolution occurs. You will then have an internal landscape that makes
the ideas easier to follow and consequently easier to learn.

Tip two is that all language has meaning and order. If you think
about the meaning of what you are saying and the order in which it
is revealed, you will be able to memorize anything. The secret is specific thinking, and not rote memorization.

I was alone onstage performing the first half of my monologue for
Hob and our stage manager when a crowd of students came in and
sat at the back of the theater. They were all taking notes. Hob noticed
them and called out to me, "Okay, Tobo. Let's take it from the top."
I started the speech again and got through about ten minutes of it
when Hob called out, "Tobo! Tobo! Hold it right there."

Hob sidled out of the row where he was sitting and made the
long walk onto the stage. He came up to me and in a secretive tone
said, "Tobo, Jane and I are having some people over this weekend for
hamburgers. You eat meat, right?"

I nodded. "Yes, Hob. I eat meat."

"How about Beth? She eat meat?"

"Yes, Hob. She's a meat-eater, too."

"Why don't the two of you come over for dinner?"

"Sure."

"Come over at about seven."

"Okay."

Then Hob turned and in a loud voice, "Once again from the top!"
Hob started to walk off the stage and then he stopped. "Wait. Tobo?
Tobo?"

"Yes, Hob?"

He came back over and whispered, "You and Beth haven't been to
the house, have you?"

"Ah, no, Hob."

"Then why don't you come by at six thirty and we'll show you
around."

"Sure."

He turned once more to the huge empty theater and called out majestically, "Okay. One more time from the top."

I went through the entire speech. We took a break. I went over to my little corner and continued looking over my lines while drinking some hot tea. One of the students approached me clutching her notebook. The girl introduced herself as Randi, a directing major. Hob had assigned them all to observe his directorial techniques. She wanted to know what he told me onstage because after he talked to me, my entire performance changed. I told her I couldn't discuss it because it was a deep part of my process, and I didn't want to blow my subtext. But it did have to do with Americana as we know it. Hamburgers and chili fries—that sort of thing. She nodded, wrote some notes, and gave me my space.

At the end of the evening, Hob came up to me and said, "Tobo, I have a great idea. What do you think about starting the final monologue inside a giant casaba melon? And then jump out and we'll start the slideshow."

Pause.

There have been times in my life when I had no idea what someone just said to me. If you were to do a pie chart, probably 90 percent of the time it was because I didn't hear what was said. 9.999999 percent of the time, confusion occurred because I was talking to Beth and I didn't grasp the concept. And now I could say that 0.000001 percent of the time, it was because someone told me that I was going to jump out of a giant casaba melon.

It was a statistical anomaly. It short-circuited my brain. Like most terrible ideas, I didn't have to use my brain, I could just use my nose. I knew this idea stunk but I tried to remain civil and keep my response in the realm of artistic babble. I said, "Yeah, but I am already dressed up like Uncle Sam. Aren't we mixing metaphors?"

Hob said, "Even better."

"Yeah, but, how will people hear the beginning of the speech if I am inside the melon?"

"You'll be miked."

"Yeah, but, we just staged the speech running all over the place, what will happen to the mike cord?"

"We'll get someone on the crew to wrangle the cord."

"Yeah, but—should Beth and I bring anything for dinner?"

"No. Just bring yourselves."

So they built a giant casaba melon and mounted it on train tracks. Backstage, dressers got me into my Uncle Sam outfit. For speed, they decided to remake the red, white, and blue sequined suit with Velcro. I would start the speech offstage on a lavaliere microphone while finishing the costume change, then climb into the melon. At the appropriate time, the melon would roll onto the stage, and I would jump through the paper side like a football team making an entrance at a Bowl game. I land onstage as Uncle Sam, hold for applause, then I start my forty-five-minute monologue with slides of Gumby and whatever running over my head.

That was the theory. Of course we never got to practice it completely. The Uncle Sam costume wasn't finished, they never had paper for me to jump through in rehearsal, and they never had the real microphone or the cord wrangler.

Opening night arrived. In the dressing room, Hob gave us a pep talk. He told us we were going to show this audience something they had never seen before. He smiled and said, "Good work. Now let's go give 'em a show!" Everybody clapped. Hob pointed to me. "Tobo, one thing."

"Yes, Hob."

"I think we should change your makeup a little. I had an idea."

I felt a little vomit in the back of my throat. I wasn't sick. It was just a Pavlovian response to Hob's ideas.

"Sure, what?"

Hob got a wicked smile on his face and said, "Have a seat."

I sat and faced Hob. He grabbed my eyebrow pencil and spit in his hand. He started smooshing my eyebrow pencil in his concoction of Hobgoodian saliva. When the tip was slimy enough, he started drawing gigantic eyebrows on my face. When he finished I looked in the mirror. I was horrified. I looked like a young, balding Brooke Shields. The stage manager called places.

I peeked through the curtain. The audience was huge—several hundred people. The house lights dimmed. There was the expectant hush. The stage lights came up. The play began. The audience was suitably entertained for the first, oh, ninety seconds. Then they started getting restless. "Oh dear. Only three hours and twenty minutes to go," I thought.

On my first entrance I could have sworn I heard gasps when they saw my makeup. There's nothing like bad makeup to make a sort of fatalism descend on an audience. But just like life during wartime, audience members hardened themselves to trials and privations. They bore up bravely. Most stayed through intermission. We slogged our way through act two. I finished my last little bit before the big finale. I ran offstage and the fast change began. I was throwing on my Uncle Sam outfit. My two dressers were slapping the Velcro together. Velcro pants. Velcro vest. The white beard was hung over my ears like glasses. The soundman attached the mike to my spangled vest as my cue approached. I started the speech offstage and continued as I climbed into the giant melon. Right on cue the melon rolled onto the stage where it was received with perplexed silence.

The moment came to leap onto the stage through the front of the melon. That's when we ran out of luck. My mike wrangler was a smoker. No one told her she shouldn't light up in the melon. But she did. I jumped through the paper at the exact moment when she was busy flicking her Bic. She took her first big drag instead of feeding my mike cord.

The net result was a near strangulation and garroting of Uncle Sam in midair. The cord snapped tight and stopped me in midflight. I crashed down onto the stage. The audience gasped. But it didn't stop there. The stage had been rebuilt to slant downward toward the audience. So I started to roll. On my way toward the front row, I heard all of the Velcro on my costume separating. *Rip, rip, rip, rip, rip.* I stopped rolling before I landed in a patron's lap. I looked around. My

Uncle Sam hat was up by the melon. My white beard was hanging from one ear. My vest came undone, along with my mike. When I stood up, my pants fell off. Then, the slides started.

I stood in my jockey shorts with dangling Uncle Sam beard in front of several hundred people. I had forgotten my entire speech, rendering this endless play literally without an end. On a bright note, we finally had the audience's full attention.

What many in the audience never realize is that while you feel that you are anonymous, sitting in the dark, actors on the stage can see all of your faces lit by the stage lights. I saw several hundred expressions frozen in horror, wonder, and amusement as slides of Kent State, Monticello, and Mickey Mouse started changing above me.

I gathered my wits and yelled up at the control booth, "You can turn off the slides. Yeah. Just turn 'em off."

They did. I gave the booth a thumbs-up. "Thank you." I picked up my fallen mike and blew in it. It was still on. So I stared walking aimlessly around the stage in my underwear and my huge painted eyebrows speaking extemporaneously.

"Wow. That was something. And you know what? I have no idea what my last speech is." The audience was transfixed. "This speech is supposed to end the play. But here I am. I guess none of us knew we were going to see anything like this tonight. I sure didn't."

The audience was still in shock. I continued. "Before we started the play, Dr. Hobgood, Hob, our director, gave us a pep talk and told us to get out on that stage and show you something you've never seen before. We have succeeded beyond our wildest dreams. When I woke up this morning, I had pancakes. I had no idea my day was going to end this way. And neither did you. That's the great thing about theater, you just never know. Do you? It is about 'now.' And here we are. For better or worse this is what we have tonight." I looked up to the booth and yelled out, "You can start the slides up again." The play ended and we took a bow.

After the curtain call, I climbed the fire ladder backstage. I scurried up a hundred feet into the flies and sat on the catwalk. Too humiliated to go to the dressing room and change, I waited in the darkness for about twenty minutes before I climbed down. The dressing room was empty. I looked at my gigantic, smeared eyebrows in the mirror. I washed my face and got dressed. I snuck out of the Krannert Center.

On my way down the steps, there were two audience members discussing the play. I eavesdropped.

"Man, what did you think of that play?"

"I don't know. What did you think about the guy with the brows?"

They just shook their heads.

I got home and opened a Rolling Rock or three and snuggled into bed. I turned on the TV. It was the late weather report. A series of severe fronts were heading into the Urbana area. I didn't care. My mind was still numb. My cheeks burned with failure.

I can look back now and think of how close the handle to some sort of comfort was that night. It was wedged in the window, letting in the cold night air—that big, white family Bible right where I had left off in the story of Joseph and the meaning of success. I didn't know this then, but the name "Joseph" comes from a three-letter Hebrew root—*yod, samech, pey*—that means to carry on, to do again, to continue.

And maybe an underrated element of success is *joseph*, the ability to keep going. I went back to class the next day and faced my smiling schoolmates. I played Uncle Sam again that night, this time without incident if you don't count the toxic boredom. I never realized I had achieved one of the biggest markers on the yardstick of success. I made it to tomorrow.

21.

A SEASON OF MISDIRECTION

S ITTING IN THE bedroom-bathroom half of our Illinois apartment, I was feeling like it was time to pull out that big, white family Bible again. Not out of the zeal to get in touch with the spiritual side of my life. Outside the icicles were melting, the land was thawing, and it was time to prop open the bedroom window again.

Winter was ending. Whoever conceived of the idea that hell was hot never visited Illinois in January. The best part of the subzero temperatures was that it froze the sheep and cow dung that seemed to be stored on our end of the campus.

I had survived the long, dark months like a bear. I built up a layer of protective fat from a diet of Rolling Rock beer and something called Ireland's steak and biscuits. I had never heard of a steak and biscuit. It was a local delicacy that I'm sure contributed to any spike of coronary heart disease in the area. They combined a buttermilk biscuit, a pat of butter, and a slice of salty meat. If it wasn't in the Garden of Eden, it should have been. You could order them by the dozen. And I did.

Now that the ice was melting, I heard the frantic footsteps of the Ghost of Green Street in the attic above me. Momma Raccoon survived the winter. One morning I saw the footprints of Momma and her troop of youngsters in the snow on our balcony. That alone made me feel unbearably happy.

The first semester was over. I had developed the reputation of being one of the brightest lights on the Krannert stage. Don't ask me how. I'm not talking myself down, but the body of my work consisted of two main achievements. I had played an old man who talked with a phony British accent for twenty minutes at a time about Bertrand Russell and the theorem of the limiting curve. I talked audiences into the sort of numbness you get on a long subway ride. My second effort was even more remarkable. I ended up in my jockey shorts after a mishap with a gigantic papier-mâché casaba melon.

My career at the Krannert made me remember the line from *King Lear*: "Who is't can say, 'I am at the worst'?" It was Shakespeare's way of saying that when it comes to bad, there is no bottom.

Beth kept writing notes in her spirals but hadn't begun to turn them into a play, yet. She was a Taurus and, as she liked to remind me, a Taurus moves slowly.

We both got to act off campus in a production of *Story Theatre* in an old train station aptly named the Station Theatre. Even though the station was no longer used for trains, the tracks next to the theater were. It was not uncommon to have a play interrupted by a mile-long cattle train. You would hear it at a distance, a low rumbling noise that would vibrate your rectum. The theater would start to shake, and then the whistle would blow. The actors would speed up their performances, knowing that they had to get to a good stopping place before the train got too close.

One of the best train-related theatrical moments came in the Station Theatre's production of *Godspell*. The actors were getting near the end of the play when you could first feel the vibrations of the coming train. A new sense of urgency descended in the middle of singing the final number. The cast sped up their choreography. They lifted Jesus on their shoulders and started running around the stage. As the rumbling came closer, a little boy in the audience yelled, "Momma, are they puttin' Jesus on the train?"

In school, I was taking a class Hob had invented called Visual-

ization. If it accomplished nothing else, we learned the seemingly infi-
nite variety of ways there are to waste time. I was also taking Modern
Dance with the lithe and lovely Blake Atherton.

All of the straight guys in the drama department took her class.
It was not out of newfound love for dance, but was more out of the
timeless love men have had for women in dance clothing. We were
developing strong preferences for various leotards Blake wore. I liked
the royal blue. It suited her with her short reddish-blond hair. Others
preferred a dark leotard with light pastel tights. Others went for the
leopard-skin pattern, which I thought was too obvious.

It became the subject of conversation in the hallways. Vic Poda-
grosi would come up to me and whisper out of the side of his mouth,
as if we were making a drug deal, "Hey, Tobo, blue. She's wearing
blue today."

I'd say, "Yeah, I know. Richter told me already." We would exchange a look, the visual expression of "hubba, hubba," and then go
about our day. On one hand it seems disgustingly male and awful,
but on the other it bears testimony as to how far we have come since
the Ice Age. No one was killed. Blake hadn't been dragged off by her
hair to a cave. That's progress.

Beth and I adapted to a new routine of meaningless endeavors.
We did scenes from sixteenth-century Spanish plays. We pretended
to teach our own classes of freshman students. We played pinball.
We drank beer. I was introduced to hashish and was encouraged to
smoke it regularly to lose consciousness more efficiently. Beth and
I functioned well as a couple. We kept each other amused and supported each other's fiction about how our lives would turn out.

We divided up the chores on what we did best. I would drive, answer the phone, and pick up take-out food. Beth would write, listen
to Billie Holiday records, and hang spoons off of her nose. I always
volunteered to do the laundry. I enjoyed it. It was perfect for people-
watching. I would pack sacks of clothes into the car and drive to
Do-Duds, about five minutes away. I'd pull out a roll of quarters and
a book and vegetate.

On one such afternoon I had just loaded a bank of five washers with every scrap of clothing we owned, from whites to delicates. I poured in the Cheer and popped in the quarters. I heard the satisfying sound of running water and settled in for a good read when the television program playing in the background was interrupted by the venerable Mr. Roberts, the ancient local weatherman. Mr. Roberts was never lighthearted, but this afternoon he was particularly grim. He announced a severe weather system was heading for Champaign-Urbana. Seven tornadoes were converging on the area. We had fifteen minutes to get to a shelter.

What! Seven tornadoes? Converging? And what was that thing he said about fifteen minutes?

Now I got it. That's why they call it Tornado Alley. They have tornadoes here. Too bad I hadn't thought about it until this second. First I froze. My brain stopped. I looked out the window. It had gotten dark outside. The next thing I thought of was Beth. Did she know? Was she still at home? Was she safe?

And then I thought about the laundry. It was in the middle of the wash cycle. If I believed what I just heard, I would have to take all of the soaking-wet, dirty, soapy clothes, and dump them back into the car. It would be terribly nasty and take up a definite chunk of the fifteen minutes I had to get to where? Oh right—a shelter. What was that? Where was that? I had no idea.

I sat like a lump for about fifteen seconds and then I screamed to myself, "Move it!" I looked at the clock. Thirteen minutes left. It was a five-minute drive home. I ran to the washers, pulling my clothes out by the armful. I didn't have to worry about getting wet from the clothes. As soon as I walked outside with the first armload, I ran into a thunderstorm. I was drenched. The water poured into the open trunk. I ran back and forth from Do-Duds to my car, throwing the clothes into the open trunk. I was just finishing when the first hail hit. I jumped into the car when what is scientifically referred to as "marble-sized" hail pelted the windshield.

I headed home as fast as I could. I figured I had eight to ten minutes left, tops. I could hardly see the road through the rain and the hail. It dawned on me that there was a chance that I would never make it back, that I would never see Beth again, that I would have to rely on the last refuge of the unprepared: dumb luck.

Then as fast as the rain and hail started, it stopped. I turned down Green Street and saw Beth's car. She was home! Thank God. I parked on the dirt driveway and ran upstairs. Beth was watching Mr. Roberts. The seven tornadoes were five minutes from Champaign. Five minutes.

Beth and I looked at each other. In a panic we ran downstairs and out into the street. The air was becoming warm and thick. A bank of heavy, low clouds moved around us and everything started turning green. I heard a distant roar like the sound of an approaching train— like during a performance at the Station Theatre. We ran around our house looking for something to hide in, a box, a fallout shelter, an old bumper from a car, anything.

We ran back upstairs. We crawled under the kitchen table. Beth said this probably wasn't safe anyway because we were on the second floor. She was probably right. We ran to the bedroom to check out Mr. Roberts. He was looking as grim as ever, saying that the tornadoes were moving into the city. Everyone should be underground. Underground? How do I get underground?

We ran outside again. I didn't know what to do. I decided to crawl under my car. Beth didn't. She leaned down and asked what if the tornado picked me and the car up and carried us both away? Beth was probably right. I crawled out from under the car.

I remembered something about what to do in case of an emergency. It involved lying facedown in the street next to the curb. Something like that. Maybe that was for a nuclear blast. Maybe I just made it up. I couldn't remember, but this was no time for indecision. I ran out to Green Street and lay facedown next to the curb with my hands folded over the back of my neck. Beth didn't. She just bent down, and said that it didn't make a lot of sense. I could still get sucked up by the tornado, plus now, I could also get run over by a car or hit by a falling tree or electrocuted with falling power lines. Beth was probably right.

I got out of the road. I was now wet, covered with oil from the street, dirt from hiding under the car, and All-Temperature Cheer from the laundry. I looked at Beth. She looked at me. There was a special moment. It wasn't the look of two lovers saying their final farewells, but two people thinking that they had been running around for a lot longer than five minutes. We ran upstairs. Mr. Roberts reported that Champaign was all clear. Apparently tornadoes gravitate toward higher ground. Because Champaign was built on a swamp, the twisters circled the city and headed for the nearest, highest spot in the area. Homer, Illinois.

That afternoon Homer, Illinois, was leveled by the converging storms. I drank a beer and headed back to Do-Duds to redo my wash.

THERE WAS ANOTHER element of the Bible I found perplexing. It seemed littered with sudden shifts from one story to the next with no warning and seemingly no context.

Joseph, stripped of his coat of many colors, is thrown into a pit by his jealous brothers where he is to be murdered. One of his brothers argues that he should be spared, and as a compromise he is sold into slavery. You know you are in a terrible place in your life when being sold into slavery is the "good option." Joseph ends up in an Egyptian prison. Here is where the story gets interesting. Joseph's ability to read dreams allows him to see the future. This ability at first leads to his survival, then to his fame, and his rise to power. He becomes second-in-command to Pharaoh himself. We'll jump ahead to somewhere in act two.

Joseph, according to some scholars, is now is his thirties, even though the Bible is never good at counting. A famine devastates the world, except for Egypt. Joseph's ESP has saved Egypt and made Pharaoh wealthy and powerful. Joseph's brothers, back at home, are now in a dire situation, and make the journey to Egypt to find food.

They come to the palace and don't recognize Joseph. But Joseph recognizes them. What follows is a series of scenes that are some of the most heartbreaking and dramatic in the Bible. Will Joseph reveal himself? How will he reveal himself? Will he seek revenge? In the end, he can't take it anymore. He sends his servants and guards out of the chamber and breaks into tears. His weeping is so overwhelming that "all of Egypt hears." He reveals himself to his brothers. He hugs them and in an amazing preemptive strike begs them not to reproach themselves for what they did to him. Their selling him into slavery led the way for him to arrive in Egypt, which enabled him to foresee the famine and to save the Egyptians' lives. Joseph calls himself the instrument of "astonishing deliverance."

At this point in the story, we are either moved by Joseph's largesse or we feel he is a little too good to be true. Swept away by emotion, the reader often overlooks five verses of legalese that occur shortly thereafter. In Genesis 47:20–25, Joseph changes the property ownership laws of Egypt. In the middle of all of the drama, we hit this obtuse section that states that in time of crisis—which could be declared by the Pharaoh—Pharaoh owns everything, eliminating personal property and self-determination. It's a paragraph that would never find its way into the Lifetime movie version of the story.

What was the reason for the strange juxtaposition? Even in the beauty of forgiveness, of brothers and fathers and sons reuniting, even with the phrase "astonishing deliverance" still ringing in our ears, it was Joseph who, with the best of intentions, passed the laws that would be used to make the Jews slaves for over two hundred years. Joseph, not the pharaoh. Joseph. And remember, he was the one with ESP!

So the question is: Is this a story about the end of bitterness or the beginning of bitterness? Is Joseph the hero of this story for forgiving his brothers and reuniting his family, or the villain for creating the legal machinery for the near annihilation of his people?

I don't intend this question just for people who like the Bible. It's a question of simple logic. In this story, was Joseph the architect of the end or the beginning of a chain of events? I think the answer is both. And like a braided rope, it is very difficult to untangle.

Another element that this portion of the Joseph story illustrates for me—and I'll admit, it's a bit of a stretch—I think the structure of the story demonstrates misdirection. Like a magician, life draws our attention to the right hand—to family and tears and union. Then the left hand slips in a couple of laws and the history of civilization changes. I would offer that misdirection is not a plan gone wrong, but is part of the plan itself.

A classic example of misdirection was in the Battle of Cowpens in the Revolutionary War. The American militiamen were so scared and so ill-equipped that their commander feared they would just run away in the face of the superior British forces. They had done so in the past. So the commander, Daniel Morgan, told his men to "Fire three shots and you're home free." Meaning: I don't want much. You don't even have to aim. Just fire the gun three times and then you can run like hell. Some stood, most ran. Eventually, they all ran. Amused, the British rushed forward and attacked the main American forces with abandon.

But the escaping militiamen couldn't cross the river to get out of the battle zone. They kept running through the trees, trying to find a way out, and ended up running onto the back of the battlefield behind the British forces. The British felt as though they had fallen into an amazingly clever trap. They were surrounded. They surrendered. Misdirection led to an American victory and snowballed into the final victory over the British and the beginning of the United States of America.

Beth and I felt being in Illinois was a misdirection from the start. But we were unaware of the real forces at work in our lives. The seeds for all of our future successes and heartbreaks were being laid, every day, while we blinded ourselves with pizza, pot, beer, and schoolwork.

Take Hob's Visualization class. It was a two-hour class that met every Tuesday and Thursday. On Thursday we were subjected to a work of art, be it a movie, or symphony, or poem, or play. Over the weekend we had to "translate" that work into another art form and perform it on Tuesday. Sounds cool, I know. It looks impressive in the brochure, but it is impossible to do, impossible to grade, and is absolutely meaningless.

It was meaningless because none of us were going to read *King Lear* over the weekend and then write a symphony that captured the essence of the play. None of us were going to hear Beethoven's *Eroica* and then go out and buy a set of oil paints and an easel and translate it into a still life with pears and a curious cat. In reality, we came up with what could be described as bullshit in hopes of misdirecting Hob into thinking we were wildly creative.

Some class visualizations: One Thursday we read *Philoctetes* by Sophocles. On Tuesday one student stripped down to a jockey strap and fired arrows into the wall over our heads. One Thursday, we saw *Who's Afraid of Virginia Woolf?*, and on Tuesday, a class member came wearing an apron and served up hot chocolate with whipped cream and cookies—which we ate and drank while chatting about the play. After a few minutes the student performing the visualization announced that he had put a vomit-inducing drug in one of our cocoas. Gary Genard ended up puking an hour later.

On one Thursday, we took a field trip to the art museum where we saw Zen paintings of a lone monk on a mountain smiling with an enormous empty sky above him. I was first up on Tuesday with my visualization. I came to class holding a brown paper bag. I told Hob that he and the class would have to wait down the hall in the little coffee area while I set up the room for my presentation. Everybody left giggling with anticipation.

After they rounded the bend, I took off all my clothes and set them up in my seat as if my body had vanished. I put my socks in my shoes and my underwear in my jeans. I wrote on a piece of paper, "This too will pass." I placed the note on my desk with the pencil beside my fallen shirtsleeve. Out of my brown paper bag, I pulled out a bathrobe. I put it on and snuck out of the room. I went down three flights of stairs to the theater dressing room where I had stashed another set of clothes. I got dressed. With a sort of smug abandon, I walked home and watched television.

I heard from Beth that the class waited for twenty minutes before Hob got the first twinges that my setup was "taking too long." After forty-five minutes I heard that Hob began fuming and marched the class back to the room. He knocked on the door and yelled that I had been preparing long enough and now I "was wasting everybody's time." When he got no response, he barged into the room and surprise! No one there! They saw my vanished presence and read: "This too will pass." How Zen.

That morning I was only trying to punk Hob and the class. I never realized that in that perfect expression of how I felt about Illinois, I had punked myself. I never saw that, in truth, my "visualization" didn't end when I left the class and walked home. It continued. It became a living poem of my escape into another escape: from wasting my life in school to wasting my life at home. My visualization illustrated that my life had become a misdirection.

In the next few weeks I got cast in another big Krannert production. I would play Sparkish in a Restoration comedy, *The Country Wife*. Once again I had the opportunity to appear in a play that no one would understand. Even our director, Clara Behringer, professor, scholar, and alcoholic, recognized that no one born after 1740 could follow the play. Her technique for rehearsing was less Stanislavski and more *The Dog Whisperer*.

Clara would shout: "Enter." "Stand." "Speak." Whenever we had an incomprehensible laugh line—for example, "Doctor, there are Quacks in love as well as physic, who get but the fewer and worse patients for their boasting"—Clara would ring a little bell that meant we should stop talking and hold. She would press the button on a little cassette player she brought with her, and we would hear a recording of people laughing. At the suitable moment she would press the stop button and call out, "You may continue."

Sometimes, when she was drunk during rehearsal, she would press the laugh button and accidentally pass out for a couple of minutes. We would just stand onstage looking at each other, waiting for the huge laugh to end. We should have enjoyed it. It was the most laughter we got during the entire run.

One of the high points of rehearsal was when the stage crew was working on the set and had not finished the floor. Clara entered with her bell and tape recorder, stepped into a hole, and vanished. It was a win-win situation. The high amount of intoxication kept Clara loose and safe from injury, and the fall itself sobered her up. We ended up having one of the most constructive rehearsals we ever had.

I was costumed in pink and had a long curly blond wig. I marveled in the dressing room mirror that, at this moment in time, I looked more like a French poodle than I would ever look again.

After the run of the play, Hob ran into Beth and me on our way to acting class. He was in a jovial mood. He walked with us for a bit. He asked how we liked Urbana and we both expressed how much fun we were having. Hob was pleased and then dropped that they were still evaluating the masters program in acting as to whether it should be a two- or a three-year program. In that brief walk, without sharing a glance or a word, Beth and I both realized we were done with school. I was twenty-five and losing my hair. If I stayed in Illinois until I was twenty-seven, I might as well buy a beret and become Hob.

Beth was more eager than I ever imagined for a change. She said she was going to write a screenplay. That was brave. We didn't know any filmmakers and we didn't have ten million dollars. *Am I Blue* was a short two-person play. It was easy to see your work realized. When you write a screenplay, all of your efforts may be wasted. It seemed to me that the screenplay was a misdirection, but again, I was unable to see beyond my limited horizon.

Almost more than any time in my past, I can turn and point to this season of misdirection as the braided rope: every choice I made was an end—and a beginning.

I had blocked out some time in the dance studio to work on my final project. Blake wanted each student to choreograph and perform an original dance. Not being a dancer, I knew I could never rely on skill. I had to hope for another tornado to destroy the building. I did come up with a dance (and I use the term loosely) that would contrast motion with lack of motion—similar to my time in Illinois. I would start on the ground in a fetal position (a favorite among dancers) and transition into a horizontal position on the floor (reminiscent of a man watching television). I would slowly rise to my feet extending my arms to the sky (like a man finishing the final swallow of a Rolling Rock), and then I would move across the floor in a series of leaps (demonstrating my desire to get out of school). While I was plotting it out, I heard an unexpected voice. It was Blake. "Good to see you're working hard." She ambled into the studio in preparation for another class.

"Well," I smiled, "hard work is Plan B for the ungifted."

Blake laughed. "What's Plan A?"

"Complete avoidance."

She laughed and shook her head. "Not necessarily. Hard work means you care."

I looked at Blake. I suddenly found myself in a time machine deposited back into fourth grade. I got nervous and stammered, "I don't know. I think I'm just allergic to failure. At least I want to give the final my best shot."

Blake looked off as if she were grasping some unexpected memory. "Believe me, just spending the time puts you way ahead of the game. And besides, I think you have talent. I liked you in *The Country Wife*."

I blushed. "Well, thank you. I did as well as I could, considering I looked like a poodle."

Blake nodded and laughed a little. "I thought that was the point."

"I'm thrilled you saw a point. And I'm glad you like dogs."

Blake's entire face lit up. "Well, I'll let you finish," she said. Blake walked back into her office.

I continued to rehearse. With a renewed fervor and intensity. Never underestimate the power of an erection. It built the pyramids. I was never so happy to have been wearing a dance belt.

Let me be clear, I had never seen Blake as anything other than a teacher, albeit an attractive teacher, before that moment. I never imagined there being any other life than one with Beth. But in an exchange of a few words, I saw that the world was not comprised of the stable elements I thought. I recognized the possibility of other lives, other loves, other paths. It was not a good thing. It scared me. I was not comforted by a world of multiple choice.

On the day of the dance final, I wanted to do well. Not just get by. I wanted to impress Blake. She called on each student, one by one. It was my turn. I looked to Blake, who was looking like an angel in her royal blue leotard, my favorite. The music started. I tried to embody every move. I felt it. I came up from the ground like a tree yearning for the sun, I slowly came to life like the world at dawn, and then I exploded in movement. I never felt so much like a dancer. I felt at one with the ground and the space above it.

I was on my final leap on my final time across the floor, and I extended as I never had done in my life. I landed on my right foot, and I heard a loud crack almost like an explosion. Unexpectedly I crumpled to the floor. I was dazed, but I wasn't hurt. The first twinges of embarrassment started creeping in when I realized I couldn't move. Blake called out, "Stephen, are you all right?" I laughed and said, "Yes! I just thought I could fly for a second." The class laughed.

I tried to get up. And I couldn't. I looked down. My big toe of my right foot was turned backward. It was twisted in a horrible way, dangling from my foot. It looked like something in a zombie movie. A flood of adrenaline got me to my feet. I started hopping to the men's dressing room, with Blake yelling after me, "Stephen, Stephen, are you all right?"

"No. Not really," I yelled back. "Please go away." I got to the men's bathroom and put my foot in the sink and started running cold water on my toe. It was numb and was starting to turn black. The bathroom door blasted open behind me. It was Blake. I tried to cover my toe with my hands. She rushed to the sink and pulled my hands away. She saw my foot. She never said a word. Without a second's hesitation, Blake lifted me up in her arms, turned, and kicked the bathroom door open. That five-foot-five girl ran with all six-feet-three of me down the hallways of the Krannert Center, out through the side door, and into the parking lot. Without stopping she carried me through rows of parked cars to her VW bug. She put me in the front seat and floored it to the hospital. "I had no idea you were that strong," I said. She looked over at me and with a trace of a smile said, "I'm a dancer. I work hard."

Blake took me to the emergency room. She kept me good company. She left phone messages for Beth as to what happened and where to come. Blake talked to doctors and nurses to get them to hurry up and help me. She was my advocate. She sat with me for two hours. She told me she had to get back and give another final exam. She apologized for having to leave. I told her no apology was necessary.

Beth drove to the hospital as fast as she could. She ran to me just as I was sent to X-ray. My big toe was broken in four places and dislocated. A doctor came in and rolled up his sleeves. He was there to "set" the break. He reached into what seemed like a set of tools you would use for taking an engine block out of a car. He grabbed a three-foot pair of pliers. I couldn't watch the process, but I could tell from Beth's expression it must have been like a scene from Brueghel's painting of hell. A nurse misread the orders and put two full casts on my foot. Beth thought it wasn't a bad mistake. It just made me look like Fred Flintstone.

I got home that evening with my gigantic cast on my foot and went to bed. Around eight p.m. there was an unexpected knock on my bedroom door. It was Blake Atherton with a container of soup. She sat on the edge of the bed and asked if I was all right. I nodded and thanked her. She said it was her last day of teaching. She was leaving campus the next morning. She said she guessed she would see me again next year. I told her I doubted it. I thought Beth and I were going to leave. Actors needed a master's degree about as much as professional bass fishermen did. She looked at me. She smiled in a way that seemed to say, "Have a nice life." It was a silent moment of misdirection.

I did see Blake again. In 2002, I was on Broadway in *Morning's at Seven*. Blake drove three and a half hours from upstate New York to see the show and meet me afterward. She could only stay a minute because she had to make the long drive back. But I got a chance to thank her again for that afternoon twenty-seven years before.

I have mentioned that Harold Ramis during *Groundhog Day* told me, "It is impossible to succeed in show business without the help of at least four heroes." The same thing has to apply to life. All of us require angels to get us through unexpected and perilous turns we encounter.

Blake Atherton was one of my angels. Once upon a time in an empty dance studio I had a moment where I saw her as a romantic figure. But I was mistaken. She was a heroic figure who taught me through a chance moment of misdirection that one should never underestimate the lasting power of kindness.

22.

THE WORLD'S NOT WHAT IT USED TO BE

WHEN I WAS in grade school, I used to see an advertisement everywhere that read, "Join the Army and See the World." The allure of the ad, of course, had nothing to do with the drawing power of the Army, but had everything to do with the romance of the world. I know the world isn't what it used to be. A lot has happened since the fourth grade to kill the romance.

Among the culprits, and in no particular order, are: the twenty-four-hour news cycle, terrorism, AIDS, flying coach, and the Hallmark Channel. I don't mean to pick on the Hallmark Channel. It is the last vestige of programming aimed at the romantic. But several years ago even they gave up on our current world and resigned themselves to produce made-for-TV movies that take place in the Old West—or Canada. While most people look toward a nuclear Iran or melting ice caps to get a heads-up on the end of the world, I train my eye on the programming of the Hallmark Channel. The more modern the time frame and the more cynical the casting, the closer we are to the end of the world. For example, if you see a Hallmark movie entitled *The Search for Mrs. Santa* starring Liza Minnelli and Simon Cowell, consider it one of the seven signs of the Apocalypse.

In spite of everything that has happened in the last few years to our poor old world, I do think the lure of travel is still alive and well in the entertainment industry. Lots of youngsters wanting to be in show business look at Brad Pitt and Angelina Jolie flying off to Namibia to have a baby as an adventure.

When I shot my opening scene of the second season of *Heroes*, meeting Dr. Suresh at a hotel in Cairo, I had many young fans swooning over the idea that they flew Sendhil and me to Egypt to shoot at a café in front of the pyramids. In reality we shot in East L.A. at an abandoned hotel in front of a green screen.

My focus here is not that we shot in front of a green screen and added Egypt in later, which frankly I prefer. But I realize that in those young fans' hearts and minds, they still thought flying to Cairo for a day's work would be something to put in the "wonderful" column of the Chinese dinner menu of life. The romance of travel still burns.

I remember one of my first jobs out of town. I was cast in a TV movie called *Last Flight Out* with an absolutely incredible cast: James Earl Jones, Richard Crenna, Eric Bogosian, Arliss Howard, and the great Haing Ngor. The movie was about the last flight out of Vietnam at the end of that war. We were shooting in Thailand.

The production flew me to Bangkok first class on Northwest Orient, which was as luxurious as you can make sitting in one place for twenty-two hours. The head cartoonist for the *Garfield* comic strip in Asia sat beside me. Behind me a beautiful Asian woman was curled up in her seat like a cat, reading a movie script. To hell with the mixed nuts, we drank martinis and ate three kinds of appetizers before we even took off. They gave us massages midflight. Only Humphrey Bogart flying the plane could have made this flight more exotic.

When we arrived in Bangkok, hundreds of screaming fans awaited us. They weren't there to greet any of the American cast on the plane. They wanted to catch a glimpse of the Asian woman curled up in the seat behind me. She was the biggest star in Vietnam. Her name was Kieu Chinh. In America you have seen her work in *The Joy Luck Club*. She played a woman who had to give up her two infant children during the war. If you haven't seen the movie, rent it and keep a box of Kleenex nearby.

When we left the plane, the screaming started. She was like Elvis. We needed police protection to get through customs. In the car on the way to our hotel, she told me that she had lived in Vietnam. Now she had a place in Studio City, California, as it turned out, about four blocks from my house. She told me she had seen me several times shopping at Gelson's. I found this amazing. One of the great actresses of the world shopping at the grocery store with me, squeezing peaches, checking heads of lettuce, and I was unaware. I think one of the things we hope to find in travel is confirmation that people are the same everywhere. I never expected this to include the produce section.

We arrived at our hotel in the heart of Bangkok. You want luxury? This was luxury. Our hotel had a gigantic live elephant covered with Christmas lights standing by the front doors. We walked past the elephant where a gentleman from the hotel greeted us, bowed to us, and led us to a couch in the lobby. He told us to sit and relax and have a drink on the house. We had been through enough stress for one day. He would check us in and handle our luggage.

I had a gin and tonic and took in the wild orchids and waterfall in the lobby. It was stunning. The man returned and said, "Stephen, follow me." He took me up in the elevator and down a hallway. He was quiet and not chatty. He just mentioned that he could provide me with anything I needed or anything I had forgotten to pack. I wanted to marry this man.

We walked down exquisite mahogany hardwood to my room where I was instructed to remove my shoes and leave them outside the door. He joked that no one would steal them. He showed me to a chair in my suite. As he left, a beautiful woman in a full Thai ornamental gown and headdress came into the room. She brought in a plate of fresh Thai fruits. She washed my hands in rose water. She pulled back the covers of my bed and tossed gardenia blossoms on the sheets and pillows. The room exploded in the scent of perfume. Then for the final touch she pulled out a remote control! God had sent me an angel! She asked which I preferred, CNN or ESPN. I like easy questions. She turned on the game and instructed me to eat some fruit and drink the water she placed by my bed and then go to sleep. I would feel better in the morning, she told me. I wanted to marry her, too.

We spent three days in Bangkok. One night Eric Bogosian and I walked down to the infamous sex district, Patpong. One morning I shared some tea with a shopkeeper and bought a ruby and a sapphire for Ann. One afternoon some monks kidnapped me. They took me to a temple, and beat me with sticks. They gave me a necklace with a picture of the reclining Buddha on it and returned me to my hotel. Then it was time to leave for our shooting location about three hours away in the jungles near Rayong.

We arrived at our new digs, a place called the Rayong Resort. We were on the ocean on a corner of land carved out of the jungle. Instead of mahogany, the rooms had concrete floors with a drain in the middle. This was an important architectural feature as the rooms were cleaned by hosing them out. We were told not to drink the water and take short showers because the water had diphtheria in it. Too much exposure could be fatal.

The woman at the front desk warned me to be careful walking on the beach. That was where the medical waste washed ashore. Since AIDS was rampant, a prick from a buried syringe could prove disastrous. We were told only to eat food that was boiled, not to go outside early in the morning or at dusk because of malaria mosquitoes, and by all means not to drink tea with shopkeepers.

One afternoon I had some time off. I looked out at the jungle surrounding the hotel, with the wild orchids growing out of the trees. I had to take a stroll to get a better look at this amazing part of the world. Our hostess at the desk stopped me and asked me where I was going. I said I was going to look at the orchids. She smiled and responded, "Well, mind the cobras."

My experience in Thailand had danger, drama, and a cornucopia of things I had never imagined. Somehow the chemistry of all of these elements, both the good and the bad, created what I would call romance—the exotic possibilities of life on Earth.

Yet drama, danger, and novelty alone do not necessarily create the world of wonder. "Stunning" and "stupid" are sometimes next-door neighbors. You can take the same three ingredients, shake them out a different way, and you get my experience in Mobile, Alabama.

I flew coach to Mobile to shoot the film *Love Liza*. We arrived at the airport and were taken to the Lamplighter Inn along the juncture of Interstates 10 and 65. There were no elephants out front, but I did notice two things that made the Lamplighter unique. It was the only hotel I have ever seen in my life that advertised "heated hallways." The second was that the restaurant at the Lamplighter was closed. Let me be more specific, not closed but closed down: locked, bolted, chained shut with tables and chairs stacked to the ceiling inside.

I mentioned at the desk that we were going to be here for a few days and needed a place to eat. The desk clerk told me there was a coffeemaker in the room. I explained that I liked a good cup of coffee as much as the next guy, but I would need solid food as well. She told me that Schlotzsky's delicatessen was across the freeway.

"You have a delicatessen in Alabama?" I asked in amazement.

She shrugged and said, "Well, we got Schlotzsky's."

I told her I didn't have a car. She told me that I "didn't need no car. It's right across the interstate." She pointed out the front window and there was the Schlotzsky's sign, across the six lanes of seventy-five-mile-an-hour interstate traffic.

I took my bags up to my room. It was nasty but gigantic. I have no idea what this room was before it was converted to a hotel bedroom, but I could have taught a yoga class in there. On one end there was a bed and a dresser with a small TV sitting perched on the dresser. An expanse of about twenty yards of industrial carpet reached the bathroom and closet on the other end. There was a dressing table and mirror outside the bathroom and on the dressing table was the aforementioned coffeemaker with Styrofoam cups and packages of Sweet'N Low, sugar, and stirrers. The other remarkable feature of this room was a large dark stain on the rug outside the bathroom. It looked like someone had been stabbed to death on it.

I got my *Love Liza* script and studied it that afternoon in preparation for the next day's work. Around evening time I was getting a little peckish and wondered if I dared try to make it to Schlotzsky's deli. With script in hand I walked to the edge of the hotel property and looked down across the interstate. When you're standing near a freeway, the cars seem to go a lot faster than you imagined. But the traffic was light. I decided to go for it.

I headed down the grassy embankment to the interstate's edge. I looked to the south. The cars seemed to be a quarter of a mile away. I hitched up my pants and ran like a mo-fo. I got across three lanes before any cars were even close and climbed over the median railing that divided northbound from southbound. I looked north. It seemed that there was a sufficient margin of safety. I took a breath and dashed across the remaining three lanes to the grassy bank on the other side. I trudged up the embankment to the deli's parking lot.

Deli food is never a great choice after vigorous exercise. I was finishing my turkey and cheese with Russian dressing and a bag of Miss Vickie's jalapeño potato chips when it occurred to me that I would now have to run back across the freeway—on a full stomach—at night.

It wasn't as bad as I thought. The advantage of running across an interstate at night is the headlights. You have a much greater sense of depth perception and speed. I huffed and wheezed my way between a variety of rapidly moving pickup trucks, like a high-stakes game of Frogger.

I had an uneasy sleep that night, nervous over the start of filming and burping up Miss Vickie's potato chips. I awoke at dawn and remembered my coffeepot. Of all the luxuries in all the years I have spent on the road, the most useful perk is not the free massage, or the free tickets to the basketball game, or the first-class seats on the plane. It is a coffeepot in your room.

I brewed a small carafe of coffee and poured myself a cup. I took a sip unaware that the little machine made coffee hotter than the surface of the sun. I not only spit out the coffee, but dropped the whole Styrofoam cup. Coffee splattered everywhere, and then I noticed the spill pattern of the coffee matched the large dark stain on the carpet. The mystery was solved. I slept easier that night knowing that no one had been murdered in my room. The next night, instead of Schlotzsky's, I ordered a pizza. It was delivered to my door. That's the first rule of the road: we live and learn.

——————

I WAS AT a party for CBS when Steve Miner, a major bon vivant, good guy, and absolutely great director, asked me if I wanted to do a movie with Gérard Depardieu. I almost dropped my cocktail weenie. Gérard Depardieu has always been one of my favorite actors. Steve saw the glimmer in my eye and hit from all sides. He said they were doing a remake of a French film, *My Father the Hero*, for Disney. He had this great young actress, Katherine Heigl (sixteen years old at the time) for the lead. We'd shoot in the Bahamas. He said that there was a part for my wife, Ann—to play my wife! He said the production would put us up in a suite at Merv Griffin's Resort on Paradise Island. And he'd even throw in an extra suite for me to bring a nanny to watch our young four-year-old, Robert.

Was there any answer other than yes? Yes! Yes! A resounding yes! I mean, come on. Every angle was covered. It sounded like an actor's dream come true. What could possibly go wrong?

Pause for dramatic effect.

The trip began great. Robert slept through most of the five-hour flight from Los Angeles to Miami. Our first trial was a three-hour layover. Robert woke up. Waiting has never been his strong suit. It also wasn't the strong suit of the nanny we brought to watch him. She left to buy some gum and a magazine.

After waiting for two hours and not hearing our flight called, I was anxious. I heard a couple of guys sitting near us saying that there was a big tropical storm moving into the area. Out of my growing concern, I went to check with the desk agent. That's when we hit a pothole. She told me that our flight was scheduled to leave in an hour, but we didn't have seats. I showed her my tickets. She told me that what I had were "reservations" for the flight, but not "seats." I felt like I had fallen into an episode of *Seinfeld*. I asked her what she thought a reservation meant, if we didn't have seats? She said it meant we were entitled to get seats, but as it stood, the flight was full. I asked her when the next flight was. She said it was being delayed by the weather. It may not leave at all. I came back to face Ann.

As I walked back to the waiting area, Robert was screaming that he wanted to go home. Carla, the nanny, was reading a magazine because she "wasn't on the clock yet." I told Ann the news. Maybe we were stuck here overnight. Ann didn't move. She just stared straight ahead and blinked twice. In a Clive Owen fashion, she stood up and said blankly, "Give me the baby. Give me the tickets." I passed her the screaming child. She walked up to the ticket counter and plopped Robert in front of the agent. "I heard you bumped us from our flight. You can watch him until we leave," she said. With that Ann left. The desk agent found four seats for us on the flight. We left in an hour.

We arrived in the Bahamas in a blinding rainstorm. That wouldn't have mattered except the luggage handlers left our bags on the runway. I pointed out our four bags sitting on the tarmac. A man driving a cart told me not to worry. He would get them on his next run.

We got to Merv Griffin's Resort Casino Hotel with our soaked clothes and ruined luggage at one a.m. Our son was still screaming. We were told that our room wasn't ready yet because a man had killed himself on our floor. The police had closed the area off. They were just starting to let housekeeping up there, so if we could just wait a little longer our room would be cleaned. He suggested we grab a bite at the Casino Café. It shouldn't be too long.

There was nothing edible on the menu that was one a.m.–appropriate. Spicy clams, onion rings, jerk chicken. I asked the waitress if they had a children's menu. "Not in the casino in the middle of the night, sir." I considered just getting Robert a martini and a pack of cigarettes to hold him over until morning. Instead I ordered him a ten-dollar hot dog.

Everybody was cranky. And you can't blame them. It had been a long day of travel, none of us were used to being up this late, let alone eating this late. We shouldn't have been surprised when Robert announced he had to throw up. But we were. I said, "Carla?" Which in nanny short-speak meant, "Take him away somewhere and let him erp." She just looked at me with that "no way" look that only an off-the-clock twenty-year-old can muster.

I went back to the desk with Robert in my arms and said, "Excuse me, sir, we have to get upstairs to our room. The maid can clean it tomorrow, first thing, but we have to go to sleep." The desk clerk was starting to shake his head "no" when I pulled an Ann. I set Robert in front of him and said, "Look, this boy is about to vomit. I'll leave him here until you give me a room key."

With key in hand, we got off the elevator on the ninth floor. Our room was a disaster area. There was the smell of mildew everywhere. Tiny bottles of Johnnie Walker from the minibar littered the bedside table and dresser. There was black mold dripping from the air conditioner vents. The "sanitized for your protection" ring was gone from the toilet. Ann started crying, Robert kept crying, we all crawled into one unmade bed where perhaps a dead man had just slept. It was the longest two minutes of my life. That's when I decided to leave Ann and Robert crying in the room and go downstairs to look at the casino.

Here's the story I got. Merv Griffin's Resort Casino Hotel had fallen into bankruptcy six months earlier, which is why the hotel had gotten so nasty and also why the film company got such a great deal housing the entire production there. Gérard and Katie stayed in Thailandlike tranquility at the exclusive Ocean Club Hotel down the road.

As it turned out, Ann was eight weeks pregnant, so now she was crying for two. We didn't want to tell anyone because we were afraid the producers would say it violated the insurance for the movie and fire her.

We started shooting our first scenes the next day. We had no idea that Paradise Island in the Bahamas was so far from paradise. There are no natural resources so everything has to be shipped in, making the prices sky-high. There was a lot of unemployment, making armed robbery a popular career path. The AIDS rate was rampant at something like 30 percent, making health care a large part of the gross national product. And to cap it off, the termites were swarming. This was not like termites swarming in Southern California. It was like something from *Starship Troopers*. The moment you walked outside after dark, two-inch-long flying bugs would land in your ears or try to lay eggs up your nose. It was ghastly.

In spite of the nightmarish living conditions, the shooting of the movie was going well, thanks to Gérard, Katie, and Steve Miner. I remember a night shoot at the Ocean Club where we pretended we were at a swanky tropical party with occasional bugs flying into our drinks. It was fun to hear Gérard swear in French. There was a grand piano in the scene. During breaks I would go up and play. I had learned a Mozart piece used in one of Gérard's films, *Germinal*. As I played, Gérard came up and asked me, "What is that song?"

"Mozart's Fantasie in A Minor. It was the theme of your last movie," I told him. He laughed and said he thought it sounded familiar.

We took a break at about three a.m. Everybody left the set. I had the night sky, the ocean, and a few minutes alone. I sat down at the piano and started playing the "Moonlight Sonata." I sensed someone behind me. It was a Bahamian man who was an extra that night, playing a waiter in the background of the scene. He came around and leaned on the piano and listened. The song wound to its unrelenting conclusion. At the end the man stood and wiped the tears from his eyes and asked me what the song was. I told him it was the "Moonlight Sonata" by Beethoven. He said it was the most beautiful song he had ever heard. He asked me if there was a recording of it. I told him there were—lots of them. He gave me a piece of paper and asked me to write down the name so he could remember it. As I wrote it down, he told me he was getting married in two weeks. He wanted to find this song and have it played for his wife. She deserved something this beautiful. He said at the ceremony he would swear before God that he would try to make every day for her as beautiful as this song.

If Beethoven could come back and read all of the writings by musicologists, all the reviews of his works, I would put money down that he would be more pleased by this one man's pledge to his bride.

We shot for a month. During that time I was so worried about

Ann and so worried about Robert, I had not taken any Stephen-time to enjoy myself. It had been too hot to go outside without risking a stroke. I was too afraid of being raped or robbed to go shopping, so I lived in the hotel room or I went to the set and worked.

I had a day off and I decided enough was enough. It was my life. It was my time here on earth and I was going to enjoy it. I exploded out of the hotel. The beach was amazingly empty. It was like a dream. I had the entire blue Caribbean to myself.

I put on my mask and flippers and dove into the warm, beautifully clear ocean. I was one with the waves as I started to swim toward the horizon. I made it past the first line of breakers, and as I came up for air, out of the corner of my eye I saw a man dressed in white on the beach waving at me. I kept swimming and I waved back. He kept waving and yelling something like "Come back, come back." I couldn't quite make it out, I just kept swimming and I yelled back when I came up for air, "Yeah, I'm a-swimmin'! I'm a-swimmin' and loving it!" and as I looked under the water with my mask, I saw with a new clarity that I was in the middle of what looked like a lot of trash. And then I thought back to the woman years ago in Thailand telling me to be careful not to swim in the ocean. That was where they dumped all the medical waste. What was this? It seemed like hundreds of clear Baggies floating in the water. I looked closer and I could see they weren't exactly Baggies. They seemed to move on their own—and they had tails! Oh God! Jellyfish! I was in a swarm of jellyfish!

I turned around and started swimming for my life. I felt the jellyfish cluster around me, swiping me with their tentacles. I was getting stung on my neck and across my chest. Oh God, oh God, get me out of here. I tore through the water like a sputtering motorboat. When I reached shore I headed for the man dressed in white. I fell down on the beach. I had red whip marks on my upper body. The man came up to me. He was the big black man who put deck chairs out by the swimming pool. He bent down and looked over my wounds. He shook his head. "Jellyfish. No good. Very poisonous," he said.

"It's bad?"

The man nodded. "It's very bad. Very, very bad. You could die."

I started to panic. I said, "You're kidding."

"No kidding. Jellyfish bad."

"Is there anything I can do? Go to the doctor?"

"No, man. Doctor not gonna help you now. Only one thing can stop the poison. You need to pee on it."

I stared at the big man. He stared at me.

Pause for reflection.

I have learned that certain pieces of advice can change the way one views the world. Going to Illinois was a big example. It didn't seem like the right thing to do at the time. But I took Hob's advice, I went, and it changed my life. Conversely, the counsel I have given myself over the years has, on occasion, been suspect. Covered with fleas, I decided to drive through downtown Dallas naked during rush hour. That was not a wise choice. Now I stood at another crossroads. Would I take the advice of the Big Man, as curious and hideous as it seemed, and in doing so—choose life? Or would I just blow it off, and perhaps choose death?

The red welts were starting to burn. I was paralyzed by fear, pain, and stupidity all at once. And now, in this diminished capacity, I had to find someone to pee on me.

At first I thought if I could get behind the deck chair hut, I could pull my trunks down and try to get an arc of urine going and pee on my own chest. Then I noticed hotel guests moving down to the pool area. I would probably get arrested.

Then I thought I could run up to the room and get Ann to pee on me. But she was a woman, and I needed accuracy. I could ask Robert to pee on Daddy, but then I thought about all of the psychiatry bills I would have to spring for later in his life. Then I looked back at the Big Man. Maybe I could just pay him five dollars to pee on me and call it a business expense.

In the end, I chose death. I ran back up to my room and made an appointment with the doctor on call for the movie.

The Big Man was right. The doctor didn't help me much. She looked over the red welts on my chest and told me to stay indoors out of the sun. I asked her if it would help to get my wife or son to pee on me. The doctor stopped and stared at me for a long moment and asked, "Why?"

"I heard that peeing on the sting will take the poison out," I said.

She laughed and said, "No. That only works for sea urchins."

The day was already looking up. I had avoided paying the Big Man five dollars to pee on me for no reason. The doctor said you can get your wife to pee on you if you want but if it were me, I'd just take a couple of Tylenol and rest.

I HAVE MENTIONED that movie companies are notorious for shooting in any locale where they can save on living expenses. Cheap rooms, cheap food, cheap non-union crews are always at the top of any producer's list. The ultimate find for any producer is a casino. Casinos love to get seventy or more people far from home with cash per diem in their pockets.

I have a natural antipathy toward gambling. I have never liked it. I never am happy when I win and I hate it when I lose. I told Ann she would never have to worry about me sneaking off to the casino when she was asleep. I hated the thought of losing all my money in one of these places, especially with another baby on the way.

One of our first days on the set, our director, Steve Miner, cajoled one of our actors, Mike, to tell us about his experiences in the casino the night before. Mike was a funny guy, New York through and through. He just shrugged and said, "Well, I went to the casino and picked up three grand." Wow. There were shouts of amazement, congratulations, and pats on the back. Mike shrugged it off and said it was nothing. Someone suggested evilly that I should go with Mike that night and play some blackjack. "You wanna come?" Mike asked.

"No. I don't do gambling," I said.

"I understand, from your point of view. But what I do isn't gambling. I treat it like a business. I won $3,000 last night. I take $1,500 of it and put it in the sock. The sock remains under the bed. I do not touch the sock. The sock is inviolate."

"I got it. You leave the money in the sock," I said.

"The sock is never touched except to put money *into* the sock."

"Got it."

"So tonight, I will take the $1,500, and say I don't win so much, say I only win $500. $250 goes into the sock."

"Which you never touch," I said.

"Right," Mike said. "The sock is sacred. You don't mess with the sock. Then I take the remaining $1,750 and play, and so on and so forth. They paid me ten grand to do this movie. If I play my cards right," Mike laughed and continued, "Yeah, yeah, the play on words was intentional." (Which it wasn't.) "Anyway, if I play my cards right, I could leave with maybe an extra fifteen grand in the sock."

His strategy amazed me. It seemed so simple, so perfect. Four weeks later I asked Mike how he was doing. He grimaced and said he had had a setback. He had lost all of the money in the sock and lost his entire salary of ten grand playing blackjack. I was horrified. "How was that possible?" I asked.

Mike shook his head and said, "I touched the sock, Stephen. Never touch the sock."

"I won't, Mike. I won't."

But I did.

On the last day of the movie, on my way out of the hotel, I put a quarter in a video poker machine and pushed the button. I got a royal flush. I made twelve dollars on my twenty-five-cent bet. I told Mike about it on the way to the airport to go home. He laughed and said, "Hey, look at Mr. I-Don't-Gamble. You beat me out by twelve dollars." Of course, I was thinking I beat him out by $10,012—but who's counting?

As I headed to the airport, I carried a collection of thoughts for the long flight home. Only a few of them had to do with having been on location. I was worried about our son Robert. He had his fourth birthday in the Bahamas. He swam with dolphins. He caught a crab and brought it to our bathroom. We christened him Mr. Jones before we released him back into the ocean. But most of Robert's time there was not happy. For several days in a row he pretended he was a king snake and crawled into a closet where he stayed for hours. He said he didn't want to come out because it was his "nest." He hated the food. All he ate for a month were hot dogs. He begged to go home. He cried so long and so hard, we sent him back with the somewhat ineffective nanny, Carla, who was also crying. She got her phone bill. She had been talking nonstop to her new boyfriend in the States. Communication at the beginning of a relationship is always difficult, especially when there are roaming charges.

Ann was pregnant with our second child. Our lives were about to change again. That was far more present in my mind than the images of girls with the cornrow hairdos, calypso music, or jerk chicken.

To be honest, as I got on the plane to go home, the main recollection I had wasn't the swarming termites, or swimming with jellyfish, or even whether I would heed the Big Man's advice—but was remembering one afternoon when a series of storms were heading in from the open ocean. From our hotel room we could see the curve of the earth and what Herman Melville called "the watery part of the world." Ann and I looked out at the darkness that seemed on the edge of nowhere and watched the silent, tiny lightning strikes headed our way.

As the plane flew back to Miami, I recognized that the real romance of travel isn't travel at all, but the act of putting yourself in a position to be surprised. The key was surprise, not geography. As long as you keep that precious commodity, life becomes a romance. As we flew, I dug in my carry-on, and I found the case of CDs I had brought to listen to on the set—which I never did. I was too busy playing Tetris. In the small collection were two discs by Beethoven: one of the "Tempest Sonata," the other, the "Moonlight Sonata."

My mind went back to the night by the ocean and meeting the young Bahamian man. I had forgotten about his wedding. It must have been two weeks ago. I wondered if he found the "Moonlight Sonata"? Did it play as his bride-to-be walked down the aisle? Did she know he picked the song for her, to honor her life with beauty? I was happy that one of my souvenirs of this trip was something I left behind.

23.

HEART. BROKEN.

I WENT ON a Boy Scout hike one weekend with my then eleven-year-old son, Robert, in the San Gabriel Mountains. We were hiking to a place called the Bridge to Nowhere. It was a bridge built during FDR's first term when the government made up all sorts of projects to get Americans back on the job. They built things all over the country, but few are as beautiful as this bridge. The problem was that they never got around to building the roads to or from the bridge, so consequently you have to hike a day into the mountains to find it.

We saw it eventually. We didn't see it that day. Our fellow Scouts were into competing with one another in hiking fast. Robert and I fell behind. Somewhere we must have made a wrong turn. No one looked back. And we ended up lost. Lost in the mountains. Lost in the mountains, alone, with about three more hours of daylight.

It was a terrifying day, but a revealing one. I learned what is so awful about being lost isn't really "where you were" but "when you were." It is an issue of time more than location.

The thought keeps coming back into your mind, "*When* did I make the wrong turn? If I can only get back to the spot where I went right instead of left, I'd be happy." But you can't. And the reason you can't is that you don't know how long you've been lost. A minute?

Five minutes? An hour? Were you ever on the right path from the beginning? Without time as a frame of reference, your strategy can only be to wander.

And after an hour of trekking through mountain brush with no path, you give up on that question and settle for the follow-up: "Okay, I don't need to know how long I've been lost. Just please, make me found."

While lost, you look for all sorts of signs that you're not conscious of in regular day-to-day life. You look for signs that others may have come your way. And failing that, you look to see if you can survive here on your own.

I knew in the early eighties that I was lost. My life with Beth had become unrecognizable. Over the past decades my mind has sifted through clues, looked for bent twigs and footprints that could have shown me the first misstep. I keep coming back to that year in Illinois. Was it the night Beth and I read Claudia Reilly's play, and we walked home in silence? That night when Beth made a declaration in our living room that she wanted to be a writer? I heard her words and supported her, but at that moment I felt that wanting to be a writer was like wanting to be an actor. No matter how much you want to do it, you become one when someone else hires you and says that's what you are. Was that the first wrong step off the trail? My disconnect with Beth's passion?

Or was it the summer before Illinois, when Beth had the success of *Am I Blue* followed by graduation, followed by a large expanse of nothing, until out of desperation she got a job as a waitress at Pepe Gonzalez Mexican Restaurant? The net result of that endeavor was that, for the two hours she had the job, she got to wear an outfit that made her look like a farm girl on a chili pepper jar.

Was it her crying in my arms that afternoon before my matinee of *Godspell*, when she looked up at me with a soul full of despair and said, "What are we gonna do? What are we gonna do?"

Or was it a dream she had one night a couple of years earlier? She woke up screaming. She sat up in bed crying so hard it scared me. She stumbled to the bathroom sobbing. I followed her and asked what was wrong. Through her tears she just choked out mysteriously, "It's too late. Too late. Nothing will ever be the same again. Nothing."

I remember a moment when I first felt our relationship tear. It's a trivial moment, almost invisible. But I still remember it, almost thirty-five years later. Beth and I had just moved in together into the apartment on McFarlin in Dallas, the one with the fleas. We were playing cards on the living room floor. Nothing serious. Just something like Go Fish—and not for money, just killing time. Beth wanted a Coke, so I offered to get it for her in the kitchen. Beth wasn't aware that on the wall of the kitchen was a picture covered with a glass frame. It acted like a mirror. I could see Beth around the corner sitting in the living room as I got her Coke. In the reflection, while in the kitchen, I saw her pick up my hand and look at my cards, and then look through the deck to put a card she wanted on top of the deck.

I giggled in the kitchen as I put ice in her glass, figuring she was about to pull one of those Beth jokes on me that was nutty and dear at the same time. I came back from the kitchen waiting for the punch line. But she never said a thing. She asked for a card from me. I didn't have it. I said, "Go Fish." She drew from the deck, and whala! She had the winning hand. I stared at her, waiting, but there was no joke. She was just cheating at cards, with me, for no other reason than the thrill of it all.

I never said a word. At first because I was waiting for the joke. Then because the timing was wrong and I didn't want to embarrass her. I thought I was overreacting; after all, we were just playing cards. Then, I was embarrassed for myself—for conspiring with her to allow her to believe she had cheated me, to say nothing of forever ruining the integrity of the game Go Fish.

I look back at my silence in the living room as one of the profound mistakes in my life. I see it as one of the wrong turns I made in our relationship.

In that one little game of cards, the trained eye of a seasoned gambler could have marked the psychological "tells" in the ways Beth and I both dealt with life. It demonstrated Beth's desire to knock down barriers, and it showed my reluctance to deal with unpleasant truth. My weapon of choice was silence. Just like lying, silence is a form of altering reality.

It's easy to tell this story and portray myself as the victim, but a true reading of events will reveal that we both cheated. People cheat in two main ways. They cheat to try to make themselves look better. Or they cheat to make themselves look worse. Make no mistake about it; both are driven by ego and the desire to control the way you are viewed by the world. There are clearly more disadvantages to the first, cheating to make yourself look better. If you cheat to win, people will expect more of you than you can deliver. You will always feel their disappointment and the pressure to continue cheating to succeed.

When you cheat to make yourself appear worse than you are, you may feel the rush of amazement and surprise from others when you do well, but it becomes irritating when people think you are always lucky when you succeed, and not talented. The only compensation is that feigning incompetence is often confused with courtesy.

I don't want to offend any atheist readers, so feel free to substitute any noun here, but I think people want to show that in their life somehow, in some way, they are touched by God. They cheat because they're afraid that they're not. The one common tragedy I have seen woven throughout my life and the lives of others is that we can't feel the miracle of our own lives.

It was the summer of 1976. Beth and I were finishing our first and only year as graduate students at the University of Illinois. John Ahart, the head of the directing program, offered Beth and me acting jobs for the summer working in Springfield writing and performing a show on the life of Lincoln. Beth accepted. I declined. The obvious reason was that I had just broken my toe and was in a gigantic plaster-of-paris cast. I thought it would be a little anachronistic for me to portray Ulysses S. Grant in a walking cast with autographs on it. I had already provided the theatergoers of Central Illinois with enough unintentional comedy that season.

Another reason, and probably the real reason I turned the Lincoln show down, was that I was done with act one. The act one of my life.

Act two had to begin, becoming an actor and making movies. I told Beth I would head out to L.A. and get a place for us, try to lay the groundwork, get a job, get an agent, or whatever a life in show business required.

I could tell Beth was reticent, but I never asked why. We never had a discussion about it. It was another unfortunate use of silence. I could never see any life for myself other than a life with Beth. Likewise, I could never see any other path for myself than one that led to Los Angeles or New York. I was determined. Determination is often mistaken for purpose. Usually it is only a sign of a lack of imagination.

I packed up my Oldsmobile with books and clothes and various odds and ends I collected during the school year. It's amazing how many keepsakes one can gather from a part of life considered merely a detour. The oddest things I packed up for transport were three rocks I found in front of our house. I had kicked them down to Green Street on my walk home from the Theater Department one day. When I saw that they were still on the curb a couple of days later, I picked them up. I liked the way they fit into my hand. "What if I kept these rocks for the rest of my life?" I said to myself. I thought just the act of possession might make them magical. Maybe like my relationship with Beth. Maybe that's why I was determined to stay silent. I didn't want to break any accidental spell that had been cast to grace us.

I headed south for Dallas for a few weeks of recovery and to have my cast removed before my journey west began. Beth packed up her car and headed for Springfield. We were still a couple. We still talked about the future. And it's true we had more adventures ahead of us than we ever could have imagined.

The three rocks are still on my shelf. If they became magical in the past decades, I haven't been aware of the transformation.

My first prayer of knowing when I was lost has never been answered. Fortunately the second one has been. I was found. And as for my many varied memories of my final years with Beth, they were also like that sunny afternoon on the mountain when, without a path, I saw the beautiful bridge to nowhere.

———

As I HAVE gotten older, I have recognized that there is a difference between an event and a process. An event is like turning on a light. You do it and it's done. A process is not so easy to describe. It has a beginning, middle, and an end, if you're lucky.

Among the greatest wrongs movies have perpetrated on us is the false impression that relationships are some kind of event. There are movies where people fall in love and kiss, there's music, and—it's over. Or the girl runs out to the bad boy in his Mustang. They drive off—and it's over. Or even more to my point, someone says, "It's over," and—it's over. To quote Yogi Berra, "It ain't over till it's over."

A broken heart is not an event. It is a process. The reason is that a relationship is not a singular thing. It is a multiheaded beast. It's like playing football—completely different at different times in your life.

I started to play tackle football in the sixth grade. My position was the kid on the bottom of the pile. Back then, all of the plays were runs up the middle followed by the inevitable, ineffectual punt. The games were usually decided by fumbles, or when too many players on one side were crying and couldn't tackle the runner on the other team. As you get older, the game evolves. It becomes trickier. There are buttonhook passes and double reverses. There are pulling guards and stunts on the line of scrimmage. Plays up the middle become more rare. Plays down the sidelines become more frequent. Both sides test the boundary lines for the big gains.

In a long relationship it is simple to end up with one person still playing by peewee rules on a sixty-yard field while the other person decides to switch over to Canadian football on a business trip to New York. The boundaries aren't the same. The invisible agreement has changed from love, honor, and cherish to pretending we're still playing by the same rules.

One of the first symptoms of a broken heart usually happens before a relationship ends. The therapists call it "drawing a line in the sand." One partner tells the other partner that things have to change.

Translation: the other partner has to go back to the way they were when you thought you were happy. But the line in the sand is just as symbolic as the punts in peewee football. They're just a gesture to say the game will continue even though no one knows how to play.

The brokenhearted draw lines in the sand over many things, from the obvious (money, drugs, infidelity) to the obscure (cats, coffee, dry cleaning). I talked to one woman who said she got a divorce because she couldn't stand the way her husband made eggs for her.

The partner who is "drawing a line" is really saying: "We need to change things to protect what is mutually valuable."

The brokenhearted often focus on the first part of that phrase, "We need to change things." But the real heartbreak rests in the last few words: "to protect what is mutually valuable." At the end of a relationship, as much as people want to have discussions on changing the behavior of their partner, the hard truth is understanding that the relationship, the thing you felt was constant, is no longer mutually valuable.

This is a hard truth to accept. It requires awareness, self-reflection, and the courage to own your part of the breakup. Since no one can do this, we generally try to get through the pain by alternating varying amounts of tequila and psychiatry. The results are often that we end up just as miserable but with a new appreciation for country music.

I had never been to a psychiatrist before I broke up with Beth. It's hard to find a good one. There are so many bad ones, and to get the name of a good one you have to ask friends who go to psychiatrists and they're usually crazy.

I got the name of Joan from a theater friend of mine who had been subsidizing the mental health industry in Southern California for years. I asked if she was good. He started laughing and exclaimed that he was still "mad as a hatter," but he gave Joan credit for keeping him from "flying off into space." See, that's what I mean. It's hard to tell if that is a good recommendation.

I decided to pay $160 for fifty minutes and see what this psychiatry thing was all about. I sat in Joan's waiting room as her assistant gave me a mountain of paperwork to fill out on my personal history.

It was like the SAT, but all of the questions were about me. I was terrified I wouldn't pass.

I walked into Joan's inner sanctum and my first impression was that she collected clocks. But then I realized from their unusual placement in the room that they were all functioning and set strategically to allow Joan to appear to be deep in thought while she fixated on how many more minutes were in my session.

She slid a box of Kleenex in my direction before we started. I found this intimidating. I wasn't going to cry. I don't think she thought I was going to cry. I think she just thought, "If he's paying full fare, I have to give him the whole show." I began to talk. I focused on the first year of my relationship with Beth and the last year, hoping to show the juxtaposition of love and loss, hope and despair. Joan called time at forty-nine minutes and fifty-three seconds.

The next day she called me up and told me that she didn't think she wanted me as a patient anymore, but she asked for Beth's phone number. She gave me a recommendation to talk to her colleague Jack over in the Wilshire district. She said a man would be better suited for me. I wasn't sure if she was a sexist or had just slept through the sixties, but I agreed to move on to Jack. The next day I sat in Jack's waiting room. His assistant gave me a huge mountain of paperwork to fill out. Another SAT. Therapy, I realized, was as bad as dating. You always had to tell the same story over and over again. When they called my name I walked into the private office. Jack was lying on a couch smoking a pipe. An empty metal folding chair awaited me in the middle of the room.

Jack languidly blew pipe smoke in my direction, explaining he needed the couch. I would be in and out in an hour, but he had to listen to people all day long. I told Jack he should spring for two couches. We could pretend we were bunkmates at YMCA summer camp. He was not amused. I noticed Jack had four clocks positioned around the room. Multiple clocks were just part of the cost of doing business.

I got through session one with Jack where I retold the stories of Van Cliburn and looking at the stars at night, followed by an angry

Lifetime channel version of the Go Fish card game and a laundry list of the abuses I suffered in the last few years.

Jack refilled his pipe and told me that I needed a lot of help. He recommended I come twice a week for the next few months. I don't think Jack thought I was coming unhinged. I think he just realized he hit the mother lode: someone who could tell stories for an hour straight and didn't care if he smoked.

I went back to Jack later that week. I hit him with episode two of my life story: "Beth and I Start Living Together." Jack never said a word until the end of the session. He then gave me his first piece of advice. He said, "Stephen, I think you're going to find that being a single, heterosexual man, being tall, in your thirties, with a good income, is a good thing. I think you'll find that women will be throwing themselves at you. I want you to play the field, Stephen. Go out and have as many varied experiences as you can and come back and tell me about them."

I was shocked. I said, "Jack, maybe I should be charging you. What are you talking about? I can't go on a date. I'm heartbroken. And what do you mean 'play the field,' have you seen the field lately? There are a lot of broken bottles and old tires in the field these days. The field ain't what it used to be, Jack. Every woman I'm going to meet in their thirties is either single for a reason or has been dumped and hates men."

"Angry sex isn't necessarily bad sex," Jack said.

"Jack! That's not why I'm here. I'm here because I feel like I'm dying every minute of every day. I can't see tomorrow. It hurts to breathe. I can't sleep. I can't eat."

"Well, that's normal. That's just how you're going to feel. Can't do anything about that. That's how people feel after a breakup."

Wow. In that one moment, Jack earned his money. "That's just how you're gonna feel." And my mind went back to the first time I rode a horse at Claire Richards's birthday party in fourth grade. My horse, Big Gray, wouldn't move. The other kids wandered down the trail, but I was still outside the barn furiously jumping around in the saddle, kicking him in the sides saying "Hiya! Giddyup! Go! Go!

Go, Big Gray!" No dice. Big Gray had been down that road around the barn too many times. He wasn't going to go this morning. The skinny, mean man in the blue jeans who saddled us up came over to me and said, "What? He ain't a-goin'?"

"No, sir."

The skinny man picked up a fallen tree branch from the ground and walloped Big Gray in the head. Big Gray took off as though he were in the Kentucky Derby. Skinny Man laughed, calling out to me, "Well, he's a-goin' now." The simplicity of Skinny Man's methodology impressed me. That's what I needed now. I didn't need Jack or any other psychiatrist. I needed to be my own Skinny Man and wallop myself in the head.

I decided I would change my life. I moved out of the house and rented another place. I needed furniture. A bachelor friend of mine winked at me and said the first item I needed was a bed. And make sure it's a soft bed but a strong bed, if you know what I mean.

That afternoon I bought the first bed I had ever bought as a single man. It was a futon. And my friend was right. The bed was so important. It was much better having a soft place to cry. In the previous few weeks I would cry unexpectedly. I would lose strength in my knees and fall on the floor. It not only hurt, but you realize floors are a lot dirtier than you imagined—even if you're a relatively clean person. When you're crying facedown on a floor you see all sorts of clumps of dust, and bits of food, and ballpoint pens under the tables and chairs.

If I started crying, I found it better to go outside before collapsing. The ground was much softer than the kitchen floor. But it was dirty, too. It was actual dirt. Having a soft but strong bed to cry on was a revelation. It was clean and usually a remote control was nearby.

Several of my guy friends saw my being single as a green light to party. My rented house had a swimming pool, and it was Los Angeles. They suggested I throw a pool party where they could introduce me to some of the women they knew. My buddy Mike assured me I wouldn't be rejected. These women not only set the bar low, several of them had no bar at all. I thanked him for his help, but I told him

I was not in a party mood. I preferred to be alone. If I needed company, I could always buy a cheesecake.

Another friend of mine, Jeff, who was a road manager for rock bands, called me up and asked me how I was doing. I told him that I recognized that being heartbroken was just about the same as being jet-lagged except for the suicidal tendencies. I couldn't eat at mealtimes, but then I would wake up at three in the morning and have a king-sized bag of Fritos. I lay awake all night and would sleep during the day, except for watching *Unsolved Mysteries*.

Unexpected events made me cry uncontrollably. I went to the movies and broke down at the end of *Star Trek III: The Search for Spock*. An usher told me if I couldn't control myself, I would have to leave the theater. To this day, I can't think of Spock's death without tearing up. Another night, I stopped by Greenblatt's Delicatessen to get a sandwich. I noticed a lone roasted chicken turning on a rotisserie. I broke down in sobs and had to leave.

I explained to Jeff that when a rotating chicken brings you to tears, you know you're not operating on all cylinders. He said I needed a normal night out. He invited me over for dinner and then to hear some music afterward. I thought that sounded safe.

I showed up that night with a bottle of wine. Jeff and his girlfriend were there. The table was set for four. Oh dear.

I heard his bathroom door open and the sound of high heels on the hardwood floor. It had to be a woman. It was a single, very attractive woman in her late thirties. She had her black hair up in a sophisticated twist. She wore a crisp white blouse and a tight black skirt. She reminded me of one of those movies where a mannequin in a department store comes to life and you end up dating her. The first sign of danger was that her blouse was unbuttoned to reveal the top of her bra.

Jeff jumped in and made introductions. Janet was an old friend of his girlfriend's. She needed a mental health break, too. She had just gotten divorced after a long marriage.

I smiled at Janet and extended my hand. She smiled at me as her eyes made a quick Terminator scan of the weaknesses in my DNA:

balding, double chin, belt not matching shoes. A slam-dunk no-go from the start.

We sat down. Jeff asked if I wanted wine. There are several good things about saying yes to wine when you are heartbroken. When you hold a wine glass you always look like a coping adult. Also, scientifically, I'm not sure if it is the color of the wine or the shape of the glass, but it's harder for people to track your refills.

At dinner Janet looked at me and said, "I heard you're single again. So how long were you together?"

"Sixteen years or so."

"Oh, that's awful. That's like forever. And Jeff said you were never married?"

"No," I said. "She didn't believe in marriage. She said she didn't want to wake up when she was forty and realize she wasn't in love and tied down by a piece of paper. She wanted to be able to walk away. No strings."

"So she walked away?"

"No. I guess I did. I moved out. But there are still strings. The strings are killing me. I think it would have been easier if we were married. Then you have a judge say, 'It's over.' There's paperwork involved. It's more clear. I can't imagine an actual divorce would hurt more than this."

Janet looked at me and said, "Don't kid yourself, Stephen. A divorce isn't easy. We were married. Twelve years. Twelve years of being with the man who was going to take care of me and love me for the rest of my life, the man who was going to be the father of my children. Now the clock is ticking and I have no children and he ran off with his secretary. His secretary. He didn't just cheat on me. He stole my life."

Well, this was going well. Three minutes into dinner and I was on my second glass of wine. Janet was a delight. I hoped Jeff had checked her for weapons at the door. We finished dinner. Jeff announced we were all going out dancing. Dancing? I mentioned that he said we were going to listen to music. He said what do you think they play when people dance? It's called music. Jeff said he would drive over to the club. We could follow. Janet added she was going to take her own car, in case she wanted to "leave early."

At the club, Janet disappeared into the ladies' room. She came out five minutes later with a new look. She had let her hair down and was wearing a different bra. I knew she had changed bras because it was a different color. She revealed it by unbuttoning a couple of more buttons, letting the world know she was available to anyone—except me.

The music started. Jeff and his girlfriend and Janet vanished into the pulsing throng of miserable humanity. That was the last time that evening I saw them. Maybe Janet had to get back to the store window before midnight, I don't know. I sat at the table, alone, drinking more wine while being driven into the ground by the sledgehammer of mediocre eurotrash dance music. The air was thick with the mix of a hundred different perfumes and human pheromones. I finished my drink and left. Outside, the night air was cold. The moon was beautiful. I felt better. Until I got to my car. I had been robbed. Someone smashed my windows and stole my radio.

I drove home in silence. The cold wind chilled me, but there was nothing I could do about it but enjoy the cold. Then it hit me. That was it. That was the satori: Yes, I had things taken from me. Yes, I was sad and sick from the loss. But I still had the choice to enjoy the cold.

Thereafter I started a new regimen to heal my heart. It was a program that didn't involve intoxication or psychiatry. Life was short enough without the fifty-minute hour at the therapist's office. I came up with a program on my own.

I decided to invest my time pursuing what I loved instead of what I feared. I started taking piano lessons again. I picked out a type of music I had never listened to, and I gave it a try. It happened to be modern, atonal music. Something I never imagined I would care for. I went to concerts of Steve Reich and Ligeti in warehouses and at community colleges. It was quite wonderful in its own weird way.

I started to focus on getting healthy. I went to the gym. I took walks. I went to art museums to be inspired by beauty.

And it started to work. I left the city whenever I could to be in nature. It's amazing how comforting the simple things were—like trees, or a mountain, or snow. When I turned my attention from my own pain to look at the amazing world around me, I started feeling better. I was rediscovering the miracle of my own life.

It happened that one day, simple sunshine gave me comfort. I was genuinely happy again. But don't be deceived. I never got over my broken heart. Now almost three decades later, I'm still not over it completely, but maybe that's a good thing. What good is a journey if you can't remember where you've been?

24.

—

THE LIGHT OF THE FIRST DAY

WHEN MY SON William was four he asked me what's the difference between a person and a cat. I told him blue jeans and a license to drive. That's an oversimplification, I know. There are other differences. Climbing the drapes. Drinking out of the toilet. But taking a true sounding of the depth of his question, I think William was trying to ask what separates mankind from the rest of the animals.

I thought about it carefully. I have considered lots of different answers over the years. There is the classic: man is the only animal that uses language.

I wasn't sure about that one anymore after listening to a mockingbird outside our house imitating everything in the neighborhood—including a car alarm. I read in the bird book a mockingbird does this for two reasons: to secure its territory and for mating. Tough talk and sweet talk. That is a pretty good working definition of language, as far as I could figure out.

I read an article about an experiment in North Carolina with baby birds. They put a nest of hatchlings in a soundproof room to see if they could still sing. And they couldn't. Apparently their song had to be learned. This finding was further corroborated when the baby birds were released and finally learned they had a melody.

Another answer I could have given William was that man is the only animal that creates tools. This is different than monkeys finding sticks to eat termites. Man can invent air conditioning if he lives in a place that's too hot or build winter homes in Florida if he lives in a place that's too cold. Not only can man make different tools, he can build machines to make the tools for him.

In the end I backed away from those definitions and just told William that man was the only animal that asks why he's different from other animals. That answer has worked so far.

Last summer I visited friends in Maine. To get the cheap fares we had to buy the plane tickets way in advance and ended up vacationing during the end of a hurricane. We sat inside the kitchen sipping coffee while half of the state remained without electricity. My friend mentioned how astonishing the rain had been. She said that the power of the wind had uprooted trees and flooded some communities. "It was amazing," she said.

And then William's question came back to me. I had a new answer. What separates man from all of the animals is our ability to be inspired. You could argue that my cats are inspired by food, sleep, and occasionally toes under the covers. Humans can be inspired by anything. And that inspiration is boundless. Inspiration can take the ocean and turn it into a poem. It can take the life of a man and turn it into a philosophy. It can take the wind of a hurricane and turn it into entertainment on the news channels, a charity for those who had lost their homes, or just a sense of awe while sipping coffee in a kitchen.

Inspiration is only half of the equation of what makes man unique. It is the invisible half. Its visual counterpart is creativity. The two go together. All humans have the potential to feel inspiration and to react creatively. But like the baby birds in North Carolina, we only learn it when we're released into the world.

I remember with fondness one of my first bursts of creativity. I was in fifth grade and Mrs. Middleton, our teacher, had assigned a report on the new state of Alaska.

I was still on the fence about Alaska. I was excited about the idea that the United States could just keep growing by adding new states, but I wasn't excited if it meant that I would have to do more homework writing papers about them.

I decided I would give Alaska a chance and commit myself to the report. The report was not so much the creative part of the project. Back then it was not uncommon to copy your reports directly from the *World Book Encyclopedia.* The students who did the best were not so much good writers as good scribes with the patience to copy paragraph after paragraph from the *World Book.*

The year before we did reports on Kansas. Our fourth-grade teacher, Mrs. Norton, asked us to read our papers out loud. The first three students got up and read identical reports. By the time the third student got up and read about the brave man who survived the tornado in Wichita, the entire class could recite by heart how he was "carried for a half a mile and put down safely in the middle of a cornfield."

I was not a particularly good student in grammar school. I never had the patience to copy my reports from the World Book. Usually, I just made them up.

I was especially proud of my fourth-grade report on Texas pioneer Moses Austin. I didn't feel the need to crack a reference book at all. I just made up his life story out of whole cloth. I had to read this report in front of our school on parent-teacher day.

I based my paper about his life on my family and some of my favorite episodes of *Walt Disney's Wonderful World of Color.* I said that Moses Austin was born outside of Scranton. Just like my mother. His family was poor but he loved to read. Just like my mother. Like Davy Crockett, he wanted to head south for Texas. Eventually, Moses Austin led two hundred settlers from the Scranton-Wilkes-Barre area to Texas. Who knows, maybe he did. But while I was reading the report at the assembly, I felt like the part of the story with the settlers needed more *oomph.* On the spot I extemporized that Moses Austin led ten thousand settlers from Scranton to Texas. Thank God I didn't have a chance for another rewrite, or he might have ended up like a different Moses altogether. Let my people go—to Waxahachie.

In the car on the way home, Mom asked me where I got my information on Moses Austin. Keep in mind this was around 1960. There was no Internet. There were no computers. We didn't even have computers in our science fiction movies. There were only three channels on television, four if you count the one that showed *The Three Stooges* and cartoons. I was stuck.

"I think some man told me," I said innocently. Mom looked over at me and said, "Do you know what man?" I said, "I'm not really sure." Mom looked straight ahead at the road and gently suggested, "In the future, Stepidoors, before you do a report, you always should know who the man is that tells you things."

I told Mom next time I would use an encyclopedia.

When Mrs. Middleton assigned the Alaska report it was my chance to redeem myself. Like so many others, I was inspired not by achievement, but by atonement. I would use the *World Book* just like all of the girls in my class who got Ones on their report card. In Texas at that time, the prevailing grade scale was One to Four. One for very good. Four for absolute failure.

I got home and pulled out the *World Book* marked *A*. I turned to "Alaska" and started writing. I copied paragraphs on Alaska's population, noting population density of several key cities. I copied the paragraph on the location of Alaska's mineral deposits. The fire of plagiarism burned brightly. It was wonderful. I had never written this well in my life. I kept copying. In the end, I had a fifty-five page report. It was massive. This report was much more extensive than the ones on Kansas the girls copied last year. I had trouble putting it in one of the standard-sized folders we bought at Skillern's Drug Store.

I wrestled my report into a yellow folder and bent down the brads. This was my way of saying "Done," as it was hard to unbend the brads, add pages, and bend them again. I placed the finished work on the center of my desk and stood back to admire it. It was truly an achievement. I still wasn't exactly sure who the man was who told me what to write, but I knew *World Book* knew, and that was good enough for me.

But as I stared at the tome I felt a vague sense of dissatisfaction. It didn't have a real cover, a title, and introduction that announced, "This is a monumental work." I didn't want to just freehand the title with my name as I usually did. This report was special. It required a stencil.

I carefully measured the front of my folder. I used pencil to sketch out the block letters "ALASKA." I stood back and looked at the penciled lettering and thought I was ready for phase two: Magic Marker. Back then Magic Markers were not something everyone had access to. They didn't come in a twenty-pack in a variety of colors at the Office Depot. They only came in black. And only the teachers or occasionally truly exceptional students like Claire Richards were allowed to use them. And then, only with the windows opened because of the fumes. I begged Mom to get me a Magic Marker for my report. She looked at me and without saying a word stopped our family's dinner preparations and made a special trip to Skillern's. When I heard her car driving into the garage, I ran into the kitchen. She handed me a small bag. I looked inside. Could it be possible? A Magic Marker of my own.

I ran to my room. I closed my door for privacy. I opened my windows so I wouldn't be asphyxiated and removed the top of the marker. I held my breath and started to fill in the stencil very carefully. You couldn't make a mistake with Magic Markers. When I finished I stood back. There was my yellow folder with black, block capital letters: **ALASKA.** But there was still something wrong. The word looked so unattached and barren on the cover. It needed more. I grabbed my stencil and checked it out. Yes! There were lowercase letters as well.

I went to work with my pencil and then with the Magic Marker. Mom was calling me into dinner. I yelled that I was almost done. I stood back and saw the results of my labor. The report now said: **ALASKA—the 49th state.**

I went to eat dinner. When our family moved into our house when I was four, Mom and Dad hired a handyman to open up a portal from the kitchen to the den. This way we could watch television at dinnertime and not have to speak to one another. But tonight I was not interested in Steve McQueen or Johnny Yuma, the Rebel. I was ruminating on my report. The cover was still wrong. I got an idea. It was bold. It was a type of inspiration I had never had before. A great report required a great cover. Words alone could not tell a story as big as Alaska. I needed art.

After dinner, I copied the outline of a map of Alaska from the encyclopedia onto tracing paper. I transferred it to the cover of my report. I outlined the state in Magic Marker and then used colored pencils to draw in mountains and forests. Looking back, here is probably where the train first came off the tracks.

I used my "Moses Austin approach" as to where I thought mountains and forests were. I just drew them in where it seemed like they should be. I mixed it together with random patches of yellow to signify ice. The results were disastrous. My picture was unrecognizable. Because Alaska is not symmetrical it looked as though I had drawn a liver on the front of my report.

I panicked. To indicate what the map was supposed to be, I drew a picture of a ptarmigan on the cover, Alaska's state bird. The bird didn't help. Through the unfortunate mixing of metaphors, the bird was way too big beside the mountains. It looked like Rodan, the giant pteranodon from the Japanese monster movies, was flying over Fairbanks.

I needed something on the other side of the cover for balance. I decided to freehand a picture of William Seward, who purchased Alaska in 1867. I was not a good artist so I just made sure he had a jaw and eyes. I covered the rest in hair and put him in a black suit. Since he was unrecognizable as a human being, I had to write "William Seward" under his picture. For balance, I had to write "Ptarmigan" under the bird.

I stood back to view what I had done. The cover of my once-great report looked like a vegetarian pizza. I figured I was in for a penny in for a pound, so I finished the cover by writing "Alaska" under the map of Alaska I had drawn.

I went to show my brother, Paul, who was busy doing his homework. I asked him what he thought of the cover. He looked it over, looked at me, and said, "Stevie, you have a lot going on here. Maybe it would be better if it were a little less."

I was embarrassed. He was right. There was no excuse. My brother told me in arithmetic that anything multiplied by zero is still zero. My Alaska report would always be a zero even if I had the best cover in the world. I had spent most of the night foolishly trying to decorate the void. It was too late now to get another folder.

I sat in class the next day with the yellow folder on my desk hidden under my textbook. I decided to show it to Claire Richards who sat in front of me. She looked at it and politely raised her eyebrows and nodded and said, "It's big." Mrs. Middleton called for the reports. We handed them forward. My cheeks burned as I watched the folders go to Mrs. Middleton. She casually looked through them and stopped at mine. She looked at the cover. Then she turned it sideways and looked at it a second time. Mrs. Middleton noted its heft in her hands. She looked over at me—and smiled.

I don't remember much about Alaska but that day I did learn why grown-ups were the only ones who handled the Magic Markers. They were aware of the dangers of a permanent mistake.

A week later I got my report back. I opened my folder. I got a One. Mrs. Middleton wrote: "Good work, Stephen." That is when I learned my second lesson: redemption isn't always based on merit.

———

THERE WAS A third lesson in my misguided Alaska project. Creativity is not the same as beauty. The process is different from the result. It can be messy. Ask any obstetrician.

When we listen to the opening of Beethoven's Ninth Symphony we hear the pure sounds of what could be the beginning of time and space. We hear vastness and majesty, fear and beauty. However, we almost never connect the rapture of "Ode to Joy" with the fact that

Beethoven was a pathological slob. From looking at letters written by his contemporaries, he was a candidate for a segment of *Hoarders*. He was lucky in that he had some money so whenever one of his residences got overwhelmed with trash he just moved into another one. During the course of his life in Bonn, Germany, Beethoven left a string of deserted apartments filled with uneaten food, stacks of music manuscript paper, spilled ink, melted candles, dirty clothes, and abused pianos.

The mangled pianos were not because of his temper. It was not because of any lack of care he had toward the instrument he helped to define. It was part of the mess of creation. Because he was deaf, Beethoven had to come up with unique methods of composing. By the looks of many of his abandoned pianos, his "go-to" technique was to bite into the wood above the keyboard so he could feel the vibrations of the notes through his skull. Occasionally, he would remove the legs from his piano and place the keybed on the floor. That way he could lie on his stomach and feel what he was writing through his body.

I'm not saying that you have to chew on your pianos to be a genius or be a hoarder to be Tennessee Williams. That's how art gets a terrible reputation—by people affecting the appearance of creativity without delivering the product of it. Creativity is sneaky. It rarely comes in the package we envision.

I guess the most famous story of creativity is the beginning of Genesis. Everyone knows that one. It's the story of how God created the world in six days and took the seventh day off. It was one of the first stories I learned when I went to Sunday school.

When I was little, I imagined that when God said, "Let there be light!" the sun was created. I never thought about it much after that. Until a few years ago. In Hebrew class we were slogging our way through the first chapters of the Bible and I realized something that anyone who knows the Bible already knows. When "Let there be light" is pronounced, God is not referring to the creation of the sun, moon, or stars. They were created on the fourth day. So what was the light created on day one?

The answer is not apparent. It is as hard to grasp as the scientific questions relating to the first moments of the young universe. It is as perplexing as what existed before the Big Bang. The question of the light of the first day has been the subject of commentaries, poetry, and is a cornerstone of a branch of Jewish mysticism called the Kabbalah.

The Kabbalah was born from a different sort of battle between religion and science. In the Middle Ages, just about every discipline was based on Aristotle's teachings from almost a thousand years earlier in about 350 BC. Aristotle shaped many of the ideas of the Western world for two reasons. First, he was Alexander the Great's teacher. Everywhere Alexander conquered was exposed to Aristotle. His teachings were everywhere. He was the ancient version of the Internet. Second, Aristotle was smart. At a time when most people knew nothing, Aristotle appeared to understand everything. Entire nations deferred to him on subjects from plants and animals to physics and religion.

Ancient scholars used his methods of examination to parse every idea. Back in the twelfth century, a great Jewish writer and philosopher, Rabbi Moshe ben-Maimon, or Maimonides for short, felt that he could use Aristotelian reasoning to explain all the truths of the Torah.

Another group of rabbis thought this approach to religion was destructive. If you could explain everything in the Bible as a set of easy-to-grasp, sciencelike facts, there would be no mystery. Spiritual truth is like a first date. It works best by candlelight. Shadows are an important part of beauty. They came up with a set of writings called the Zohar. The Zohar reaffirmed the questions of the Bible instead of trying to find answers.

The Zohar tells the story of the light of the first day in mystical terms so ineffable, perhaps it could only be understood by Stephen Hawking. It describes the moment of creation as "a blinding spark of darkness." The initial burst of the creative was so overwhelming it could not be seen.

"Out of chaos He formed substance, making what is not into what is. He has hewed enormous pillars out of ether that cannot be grasped." Rabbi Eleazer's description of the light of the first day of "making what is not into what is" could also be a perfect description of any play I have worked on. It describes the process of making a film or television show and more. It could be a good working definition of all creative efforts.

The singular most creative moment of my life happened when I least expected it. It wasn't my opening night on Broadway. It wasn't running to meet Bill Murray the first day we were shooting *Groundhog Day*. It had nothing to do with my career.

I was twenty-four. I was living in Dallas with Beth. It was late afternoon and she had sent me to the grocery store to buy the fixings for dinner. I bought chicken breasts, Italian Swiss Colony wine, and some mangoes. Mangoes were a new fruit back then. People didn't quite know what to do with them. I had no idea how to tell if a mango was ripe. As I held it in my hand and started shaking it to see if it rattled or sloshed, an older man wearing blue jeans and a black short-sleeved shirt came up to me and put his hand on the front of my cart. That was odd. I grew up believing that someone else's grocery cart was sacrosanct. It's like someone else's belt. You don't touch it except by invitation.

He looked into my cart and admired my cargo. "I see you have mangoes," he said. I tried to press onward but he wouldn't move from in front of my cart. He looked at me steadily and said, "Mangoes are from South America. I have always thought of them as the most exotic of fruits." With that he started to cry. I thought, this is not good. I knew that there could be hundreds of good reasons to cry on any given day but mangoes would never be one of them. I figured he was senile and maybe would go away if I gave him a mango. I reached down into the cart. That's when I saw that he was holding a .45-caliber handgun behind his back.

In a single moment my brain and heart and soul went blank. I knew I was dead.

I stood up with the mango in my hands. He looked into my eyes. He must have seen the emptiness. In my expression of nothing, he knew I knew. He whipped the .45 around and put it in the middle of my forehead. With tears running down his face, he spoke to me with a strange mixture of grief, self-pity, and satanic possession. The man sobbed and said, "I don't know why I picked you today, I don't know why. I contracted brucellosis, a cattle disease in South America. It leads to suicide—or homicide."

Just my luck. Today it had to be homicide.

I looked beyond him. For the first time I noticed that the entire store was empty! Empty! I must have been too busy shaking the damn mangoes to have noticed the mass exodus when the crazy guy with the gun came in.

I was scared. He pressed the .45 harder into my forehead and then, remarkably, I thought of Chad Everett on the television show *Medical Center.* It was popular back then. There was an episode where he had to deal with a similar situation. The advice he gave on TV was "to keep the gunman talking." I didn't know how to do that. So I started talking. What followed was pure creation.

I told him how he reminded me of my father (which he didn't), and then, I launched into several loosely related monologues I remembered from the television show. There were a lot of father-son conflicts between brash young Chad Everett and his dad, the head surgeon, James Daly. There were a lot of speeches about responsibility, the sanctity of life, and the dangers of infection while visiting a hospital.

I told my prospective murderer that my dad was a little taller than he was. He was a doctor. I was never smart enough to be a doctor. I thought that disappointed him. In fact, I was always a disappointment. It seemed like nothing I ever did was good enough for him, nothing I ever wanted was right enough for him. He saw me as a nothing, a loser. I almost summoned up tears as I said all I ever wanted was for my dad to love me. But we always fought. I just wanted to sit down with him for once and tell him what he meant to me and how I looked up to him.

I was talking faster than a horserace announcer on Mexican TV. I plunged from one monologue into another. The man still had the gun pressed into my forehead.

I kept talking. I asked him why love had to be so hard. Why couldn't a father and a son sit down at the table and just say, "You're fine the way you are, and I love you."

What made the surreal so real was that while I was telling the amazing and quite fabricated story of my father, I was looking out the big front window of the store. Outside in the parking lot I saw police running back and forth, crouching down, carrying rifles and wearing bulletproof vests. I saw a television news truck in the parking lot with the back of a newscaster doing a report live from the scene. I heard a helicopter bearing down from above. An ambulance pulled up. The back doors flew open and paramedics unloaded a stretcher and a body bag. And while I was talking, I was thinking, "Hey, stretcher. Body bag. One of them is for him. One of them is for me. I wonder which it will be?"

After forty-five minutes of nonstop blather, I felt the adrenaline start to wear off. I knew I was in trouble. He still had the gun on me. In this situation flop sweat could be fatal. I heard a voice in my head say, "Stephen. It's time to do something else." So I did. Escape seemed impossible so I did the only thing I could think to do in the moment. I invited the man over for dinner.

I recognize that this was not a particularly good plan. I said, "Excuse me, do you know what time it is? I have to get back and start dinner. Hey, are you doing anything now? I mean, we're having a good discussion, we're getting all of these things worked out. Why don't you come over? We'll have some chicken, drink a glass of wine, eat the mangoes. Let me give you my address." I realized I didn't have a pen or paper. "Do you have a pen on you?" I asked.

In what would be unbelievable in a movie, the man, still holding the gun to my forehead, reached for a ballpoint pen in his shirt pocket. He handed it to me. I took the pen. I tore off a bit of the brown paper bag that held the mangoes and started to write. Unfortunately, I was so tired and so scared that I wrote down my real address. I handed it to him.

Out of the whole ordeal I remember the next moment being the scariest. After I gave him my address, I told him I had to go and get the chicken in the oven. I pushed my cart past him. He stepped aside and then I felt him stick the gun into the back of my head. The voice inside me said, "Don't turn around, don't turn around, whatever you do, don't turn around." I didn't. I kept walking. Eyes front. I had no idea what would happen next.

I didn't know it but a SWAT team had sneaked into the back of the store a half an hour before, sometime during my *Medical Center* monologues. They crept down the aisles adjacent to us and had positioned their rifles at us through the food the whole time. Ahead of me there was a display of Pepsi at the end of the aisle. The voice in my head kept telling me, "Get around the Pepsi. Get around the Pepsi and you can run."

I didn't have to. As I rounded the corner, the SWAT team jumped over the huge shelves of food and tackled my potential dinner guest. They had him hog-tied in eight seconds. He had ties on his ankles, knees, arms, and hands. They carried him out of the store on their shoulders like he was a roll of carpet.

I walked with my shopping cart in the deserted store to the deserted check out counter and waited patiently with my wallet in my hand. A policeman walked up to me and said, "Hey, buddy. You can just go." I left.

I got home. Beth said, "Well, where were you?"

I said, "I was just held hostage at gunpoint."

She said, "Well, it took a long time."

"I know. I know. It does. The hostage thing takes time. I'm starving."

That night we ate our chicken and mangoes, and I will always remember that day as the only time I left a store without paying for my groceries.

As time has passed from that day so long ago, I realize it was important for another reason. Like my mother said in the car after I gave my report on Moses Austin, "You always should know who the man is that tells you things." Even though I never saw him, I think he was in the store with me that evening. I think he whispered advice to me and reminded me about Chad Everett. And somewhere between the mangoes and an invitation to dinner, in a blinding flash of darkness, he told me the light I was looking for was somewhere beyond the Pepsi.

25.

___

IT'S NOT MY DOG

I THINK IT'S safe to say that animals didn't fare too well in our neighborhood during my childhood, which spanned from the early 1950s to the mid-1960s. They had a lot to deal with. There were no leash laws, so dogs were constantly run over. Everyone owned a gun, so dogs and cats were frequently shot. Some of my neighbors owned multiple animals, so there was animal-on-animal violence. Some of the local animals were victims of all three scenarios, like Charlie Harp's dog, Kookie.

Kookie lived across the alley. He was a Chihuahua mix that over the course of a year was shot, run over by a pickup truck, and kicked by a horse—leaving him with three legs and one eye. In the best of times, Kookie was an irritating dog. He always yapped whenever you got in or out of your car. But his string of injuries and his ridiculously slow demise by subtraction demoralized everyone in our family, especially Mom. She would stare out the patio window and watch him hobble around yapping and attempting to chase cars driving down our alley. She would shake her head and look at me. I would never be able to tell if she was going to laugh or cry, and she would just utter one word, "Terrible." There was a particularly painful period when

Charlie's family got a rooster for some reason. The rooster would chase Kookie around the backyard and peck his rear end.

But as bad as that was, there was a worse scene down the block. A couple of houses from us lived the Dodges. Mr. Dodge was a full-blooded Indian who performed in movies, in Westerns. He could ride a horse at full speed and shoot a bow and arrow. If you are a fan of the Western, you are familiar with the work of Mr. Dodge. His daughters Debbie and Donna were also talented. They sang and danced and did a hobo act. There was talk that they were going to be on *The Ed Sullivan Show.*

However, their coexistence with the animal kingdom was misguided. They acquired a dog, a duck, and a horse. Kept together in their small backyard, these three animals created an ecological nightmare. The horse ate every blade of grass and every leaf on their tree, turning the yard into a moonscape. The duck sat on the horse's back to avoid the dog. The dog barked at the duck, constantly. It became a real-world textbook of the Catastrophe Theory, which states that order can be maintained only to a certain point of stress. Then all bets are off.

The rubber band snapped one rainy day after school. The horse was shot by a passing motorist, thus enabling the dog to eat the duck. White feathers covered the yard. It was like a deleted scene from *Saw III.* Police investigated but to no avail. It was a drive-by.

On top of all this brutality, Billy Hart and I formed the Dangerous Animals Club and made regular forays into the woods with jelly jars, broomsticks, and chemicals to bring the animal kingdom to its knees. In the end, the animal kingdom won, but you can still make a case that it was a dangerous time to be an animal in our part of the world.

But despite this climate of abuse, I developed a strong attachment to animals. Perhaps too strong. When I was five, I went to preschool at a place called Story Book Playhouse. One morning our teacher called Mom up and told her she had to come to the school and talk to me for disciplinary reasons. I was not participating in the tap-dance part of the class because I claimed I had turned into a rabbit and rabbits don't dance.

The teacher told me I had to join the others. I recall sitting on the bench in a catlike pose, resting on my knees and elbows and squinching my nose. She told me once again I could join the others or be punished. I told her I couldn't understand her because she spoke English and rabbits can't talk.

When Mom arrived, I was hopping around. I had further transformed by pulling out a long grocery receipt that I took from the car and kept in my pocket. I started eating it. The teacher confronted Mom and started talking in low, urgent tones. Occasionally, the teacher would point in my direction and Mom would look at me with a concerned expression on her face as she saw me hopping around. I only heard the mumbled words "rabbit," "not listening," and "sassing me."

I knew even at the age of five that the only offense that had any traction was "sassing." "Sassing" was such a gray area. It was only defined by the grown-up who heard it. "Sassing" could or could not be a hanging offense, depending on Dad's mood after work.

Mom nodded to the teacher and walked over and sat down with me. She asked why I wasn't listening. I told her that I was a rabbit and couldn't tap-dance. Mom said whether I danced or not I shouldn't eat the grocery receipts from the A&P. The ink was bad for me. I told her the ink was the best part. Mom shook her head and told me that rabbits don't eat paper, goats do. If I kept it up I could turn into a goat. I looked at Mom with fear that I had begun yet another unexpected transformation. I liked being a rabbit.

I began to dream about rabbits. I imagined I was walking in the woods and I came upon two lost bunnies. I told them that I had a home hidden in the trunk of a tree. I took them there. I opened a secret door and brought the rabbits inside. I gave them a bowl of water and a plate of fried chicken. The rabbits thanked me for my kindness and then started gnawing on the drumsticks.

I have never been able to explain the rabbit period of my life. I have often heard that imitation is the sincerest form of flattery. I'm not sure I have ever bought that. I believe imitation may be the sincerest form of regret.

A lot of the ways we live and react come from seeds planted in childhood. This idea is not new. It's an idea that's in just about every country-western song. Country music is the final repository of a good idea before civilization drops it. It's why a good country song can always make you cry. It reminds you of something you never should have forgotten.

But the seeds that are planted in us as children are amoral. It is our free will that gives them meaning. For example, the animals in our neighborhood. The seeds of neglect and cruelty were planted in me. But it was my choice as to whether they became the ideas I would embrace or reject. These seeds, like the tides, work powerfully but often invisibly, waiting for someone or something to bring them full force into our lives. One of those tides turned for me in 1983.

Beth and I got back from a camping trip to Havasu Falls, an offshoot of the Grand Canyon. We were gone for about a week and were exhausted. We had never camped before and had to buy a tent, sleeping bags, air mattresses, canteens, camping utensils, backpacks, and flashlights. Basically we paid about $1,500 a night to sleep on the ground, but we weren't eaten by bears so I guess we broke even. We had a friend watch our house for a couple of the days we were gone.

We returned late in the afternoon, tired, dirty, and in need of a bath. We dumped our backpacks in the living room, opened the doors and windows, happy to be home. The only thing that marred our return was what appeared to be a dead dog in the backyard. Besides the awfulness of seeing the body, it was a mystery as to how the dog got there, as the yard was enclosed.

Our suspicions rested on our housesitter. We called her and got a confession. She said she was having a party in our absence when a sick, starving dog came up through the woods and collapsed in the driveway. She felt sorry for it. To a point. She carried it into the backyard and gave it the remains of a deli platter. The dog tried to eat some roast beef and pastrami. It tried to drink a margarita. But in the end it was too weak and keeled over. Nobody at the party wanted it. She didn't have the heart to move it. That was a week ago.

I nudged the dog with my foot. Nothing. Beth told me I would have to call the city to cart the dog away. I had no idea whom to call. I wanted a hot bath. I didn't want to deal with a carcass. I went inside to look up the dead dog division of the city of Los Angeles. While I was thumbing through the Yellow Pages, I looked outside at the corpse in our backyard and lo and behold the corpse was looking back at me. We made eye contact before it dropped its head back to the ground.

I called to Beth and went out to investigate. She came running and we both took a closer look. We came to the conclusion that whether sick or starving, the dog was near death. Beth told me to be careful. It wasn't our dog. If we fed it, it would be.

"That's crazy," I said.

Beth said, "Trust me. It doesn't matter how nasty a dog is. If you feed it—it will be yours. That's the rule. Dogs think with their stomachs. You've never had a dog. You don't know what you're getting into."

Beth was right. I didn't know anything about dogs. I never had a dog except for about twenty minutes when I was seven years old. It was a grim childhood event. Our family had two pet snails. Mom thought it would be a good strategy to occupy my time with a normal pet. She got dibs on a cocker spaniel puppy. She brought it home, we fed it, we named it Honey, we talked to it in baby talk, we petted it, we poked at its sides ever so gently, causing it to vomit on the kitchen floor.

Unfortunately, Dad witnessed the event. He said something along the lines of "Get that damn dog out of here." So Honey was here and gone. That was the extent of my experience handling a dog.

Beth left me there to ponder while she went to take a bath: to feed or not to feed. I had the first flash of memory of the Dodges' backyard and that starving horse and that poor duck. I couldn't help myself. I went inside to see if we had any food in the fridge. The only thing there was part of a leftover turkey sandwich. I put it on a plate and went out back with a bowl of water, put it by the dog, and went inside.

I took a hot shower and climbed into bed. Beth was reading. Without looking up from her book she asked, "You feed it?"

I confessed. "Turkey sandwich."

"It's your dog," she said.

I got defensive. "It's not my dog. Anyway, I don't think it will live until morning. How about this, tomorrow, if it's alive, I will take it to the vet and let them treat it and send it out for adoption. They do that sort of thing all the time."

Beth was unconvinced. "Okay. But that dog is not staying here. It's the dirtiest, ugliest dog I've ever seen."

"I know. I know. It's horrible and it stinks. I'll get rid of it." I turned off the light and went to sleep praying that the Grim Reaper would visit our backyard that night.

The Grim Reaper let me down. The next morning it was still breathing, so it was off to the vet. I put the dog on my lap and headed down the hill. I looked down at this thing of filthy matted fur that had the stench of death about it and thought it couldn't be any worse. But once again, I was wrong. The dog groaned, and then let loose with a diarrhea explosion.

I erupted with a torrent of expletives directed at the dog as I did figure eights down Laurel Canyon Boulevard. When I gained control of the car, I pulled over and rolled down the windows for air. The dog looked up at me in utter humiliation. I looked back and felt guilty. I told her, "Don't worry. It's all fine. Ten more minutes and I check you into the nice vet man and it is *arrivederci*, baby." I stopped off at a 7–Eleven and got a big cup of water and tried to wash off my pants and the dog. It made it worse. We still stunk, and I looked like I had the accident.

We did not win any fans in the waiting area of the clinic. Between the stains and the stink, most pet owners gave us a wide berth. I was called up to the reception desk. The nurse asked me what was wrong with my dog. I explained, "It's not my dog. I found it and it needs to see the doctor."

The woman looked at me without a glimmer of humor or hope and said, "What's your dog's name?"

I explained again, "It's not my dog so I don't know its name. It may not even have a name."

The nurse said, "For treatment, we need to know the name of your dog."

I became more intense. "It's not my dog."

"Whose dog is it?"

"I have no idea."

"Well, we can't see a dog unless you own it and it has a name."

There was something Kafkaesque about the bureaucratic cloud hovering over the pet clinic. But I had something Gregor Samsa didn't have. I had a MasterCard. It worked wonders in the dog registration process.

The nurse ran the card through the machine and said, "There you go, but I will need the name of your dog."

I gave in and said, "Pooch." She smiled and looked at my credit card.

"Pooch Tobolowsky."

"Yes, yes, ma'am. Thank you."

She took the dog away from me and made a face of sheer revulsion. They would have to clean the dog before the doctor saw it so I would be billed for a bath as well.

I left the dog in their competent hands. I drove home with the windows rolled down thinking I would probably have to sell the car and burn my clothes. I jumped in the shower. Beth came in and said I had a phone call. It was the vet. He wanted to talk to me about Pooch Tobolowsky. Beth was not pleased. I stepped out of the shower and wrapped a towel around my waist. I ran to the phone with Beth calling to me, "I told you if you fed that dog you would own it."

The doctor explained that Pooch would need to be on an IV for about ten days. They needed to put her on vitamin therapy. She was so dirty that they couldn't just wash her, but they had to shave her. In the process they discovered she was covered with small tumors that would have to be removed. The doctor told me I was looking at several hundred dollars and even at that he couldn't guarantee the dog would live. He wanted to know what my decision was: treat Pooch or put her down.

The Ghost of Kookie the Chihuahua hobbled in front of me. I was uncertain of the dividing line between kind and cruel, but in the end, I pushed aside any reasoned debate and just said, "Treat her."

Ten days later I went back to the vet. I signed the credit card bill for $600 and the nurse called back for Pooch Tobolowsky. I gasped when after a few minutes the assistant came out with a shaved dog covered with scars and stitches from numerous surgeries. But when she saw me she leapt from the assistant's arms and ran helter-skelter across the floor of the waiting room and jumped into my lap. She started licking my face furiously and crying.

The doctor came out and told me she still couldn't eat dog food. I would have to cook a mixture of sautéed hamburger, egg, and rice five times a day. She could probably eat that. I said if she didn't, I would. The vet wanted to see her again in two weeks.

We got back to the house and Pooch was ecstatic. She was home. She dashed across the backyard and barked at the invisible squirrel by the tree. Beth heard us and came outside. She saw Pooch's buzz cut highlighted with fresh stitches and green antibacterial ointment and she started laughing. "Oh my God. Now she really is the most hideous dog on earth."

I said halfheartedly, "Beth, we can take her back to the clinic for their pet adoption day."

Beth laughed even harder. "Are you kidding? No one in their right mind would want this dog. It's horrible. It's like a Frankenstein dog."

Pooch ran over to Beth and almost knocked her down. She started licking Beth. Beth fell on her back in the grass laughing and Pooch jumped on her and continued with the affection offensive. If nothing else, Pooch embodied the joy of being alive.

THE NEXT WEEK I spent most of my waking hours in the kitchen cooking rice and simmering hamburger. This dog food could have won *Iron Chef America*. Pooch would watch me through the back door. I asked Beth if she thought we could let Pooch inside.

Beth explained that there are two kinds of dogs: outdoor dogs and indoor dogs. Pooch was an outdoor dog.

That proclamation lasted about three hours. Pooch snuck in behind me during one of my many trips from the kitchen to the dog bowl. Once inside Pooch ran roughshod over everything: barking, jumping on furniture, knocking things over. Beth said now that the dog had come into the house, we would have to teach it behavioral rules. A squirt bottle was the only way.

I went to the gardening store and asked the woman if she had anything I could use on a dog. She gave me a bottle that would shoot several sprays ranging from a fine mist to a long-range stream. I set the bottle for stun and came home. I filled it with water and waited for the first infraction. It came after about sixty seconds. Pooch started barking at the invisible squirrel in the backyard. She started leaping against the back door in response to nothing. I shot the dog with the spray bottle. She stopped, turned, and looked at me. I shot her again. She loved it. She thought I had come up with a novel method of hydration. So she would come up to me for an occasional drink.

After ten days it was time to go back to the clinic to get Pooch's stitches removed and a follow-up visit with the doctor. I waited for about twenty minutes. The vet came out to see me. He had a strange look on his face. He said, "Stephen, can you come back to my office?" I felt uneasy. I didn't even know veterinarians had offices. I walked back to a little room with a desk, some textbooks, family photos, and a poster on the wall of the life cycle of the tapeworm. The doctor went right up to his X-ray viewer and turned it on. There was a strange image of what I assumed was a dog. The doctor took his pen and used it as a pointer and began, "Stephen, I'm sorry. I need to show you why your dog is going to die."

Die? My brain went blank. I heard his words but couldn't feel a thing. He said that the malnutrition had kept her spine from developing as it should have. One of her disks was swelling. Sooner or later the disk would create enough pressure to cripple her. Eventually it would kill her.

I asked, "How long?" The doctor looked somber. "Soon. Eight weeks. Ten weeks. All you can do is keep Pooch comfortable. Try to keep her calm. Come back in a couple of months. If she is in any pain, we can put her down."

I was in shock. I shook his hand, collected the dog, and started home. She was in my lap. I rolled down the window so she could stick her head into the breeze. The wind blew back her ratty-looking bangs. She stuck her tongue out so it was flapping in the wind. I broke down and started to cry. I pulled the car over, much to Pooch's surprise, and I wailed like I had never done in my life. That's when I knew she was my dog.

After about three minutes, I collected myself and continued home. I carried Pooch out of the car so she wouldn't bound over to Beth. I placed her on the ground. She ran over to the tree and started barking at the invisible squirrel. Beth asked me how she was. I sat down in the yard and told her the sad story of our dog and Beth began to cry and held on to me for comfort. Pooch ran around us joyously, unaware of the source of our grief.

I have noticed in my life that even the most casual relationship with an animal is capable of eliciting powerful emotions. You can know a person for years and not be moved by them, but their cat is another story.

We took a breath, got up, and went inside. We left the door open so Pooch could follow. We walked back to the bedroom. Pooch trotted behind. We opened the door to the dog-free zone and Beth lifted Pooch up and set her on the bed. Pooch couldn't believe her good fortune. She spun in circles and snuggled down between us. "If she only has a few weeks with us, then she should be happy," Beth said.

The next morning, I decided that in her remaining time Pooch

THE DANGEROUS ANIMALS CLUB

should see the world. Every morning we went off in a different direction exploring the wilds of the Hollywood Hills.

At night Pooch nuzzled in between Beth and me. She took over the entire bed. We slept on the periphery. But every time we felt like we were going to fall off the edge, we thought of Pooch's final days. Her comfort came first.

We neared the date of the final visit to the vet. That day we walked from the top of our mountain to the bottom. We sat by a creek and I fed Pooch Poochburgers and we shared a drink from a canteen. We walked back up the mountain. I told Beth we were leaving for the doctor. She hugged me and kissed Pooch, and we headed off to the clinic.

We arrived and our doctor was waiting for us. I handed over Pooch. He said he would check her out. He would get me before they did anything drastic.

My dear friend Bob told me that we spend the first part of our lives choosing who we want to live with and the last half choosing who we want to die with. For whatever reason, Pooch found me. She gave me the opportunity of making the dream I had as a little boy—the dream with the rabbits—come true. She was lost. We brought her into our secret home in the woods; I gave her water and a turkey sandwich.

The doctor interrupted my rabbit reverie. He came out looking concerned and asked me to come back with him. We went into his office and he pointed to Pooch's X-rays. He said, "I can't explain it. Pooch is cured. The spine is normal. The disks are normal. I've never seen anything like it."

"She's going to live?"

"That's right. Her blood work is perfect. Her muscles are no longer atrophied. Whatever you did, you did it right."

I thought for a moment and then it hit me. "Good God. We walked. Every day. All the time. Up and down the Hollywood Hills."

"Well, all of the exercise did it. She's lucky she found you."

"I can take her home?"

"Take her home. She's all yours."

We rode home with the car window down and the wind tousling her ears and tongue. We got home. I told Beth the news.

Beth was overjoyed. We hugged each other until we realized that we now had a dog that had no discipline at all and slept in the middle of the bed. But there was nothing to be done but grab the squirt bottle in case she got thirsty at night and be grateful that she was still with us and would continue to be with us for a long, long time.

26.

DON'T ARGUE WITH THE ROAD

I RECENTLY VISITED my dad in Dallas. Mom passed away about three years ago. Dad is almost blind. He said if there was anything I wanted to keep from the old days, I should look around and take it. I went on a treasure hunt. I found a dinosaur I made from clay in first grade. It resembles a brontosaurus with a thyroid condition. I found the complete works of Shakespeare I got from a girlfriend my senior year of high school. I found a book on werewolves I bought when Beth and I lived in the flea apartment on McFarlin. That had to be thirty-three years ago.

I found photo albums I made in college. Polaroids of Beth when we first met. Pictures of friends I hadn't seen in decades. Pictures of my broken foot in Illinois and of my first apartment in Los Angeles where the ants almost ate me alive.

I found speech tournament awards my mom kept from my debate years in high school. Reviews from every play I was ever in. I was thrilled with every discovery and heartbroken that it had been so long since I had thought about them.

It's never the photo. It's the moment. The feeling of the cascade of time pushing you forward and the instant when you said to your mom or dad, or your girlfriend, or your sister holding the family cat, "Hold it, right there!"

We no longer lived in our childhood home, but I still slept on my childhood bed, the bed I had since I was fourteen. It no longer had the necessary structural integrity for a good night's sleep. It would either tilt to the right or the left depending on where your weight was distributed. There was no rest on this bed, but there was a sense of accomplishment in the morning if you managed to ride the balance point like a kid standing on the middle of a teeter-totter. They always advertised these mattresses as lasting a lifetime. Mom and Dad intended to put them to the test.

My first night home this trip I was determined to look at my art history notes from college that Mom had kept for me. I discovered my little bed had no sheets. Dad had gone to bed so I went on another hunt with far lower expectations. I checked a closet in the hall that seemed like it could be the final resting place for any number of things, including sheets and blankets. It was.

I found some trophies I had won for debate. I found pillows my mother said she had gotten from her mother, who brought them from her mother in Europe. I found my brother Paul's favorite green blanket. It was all so nothing and all so precious.

I found my sheets. I lifted them from the top shelf and there, underneath them, was the huge, white family Bible I bought when I played Jesus in *Godspell*. The one I had taken to Illinois over thirty years ago. I hadn't seen it or thought about it since. I used it to hold my window open at the apartment where Beth and I lived on Green Street. I know it sounds disrespectful. It probably was, but the fresh air was important and valued, especially on a muggy, Indian summer day. I remembered on slow mornings, out of boredom, I would open the Bible up at random and see if anything made sense to me.

I have no idea how the Bible ended up under the sheets. In her final years Mom was losing more and more of her memory due to Alzheimer's. She could have put it up there and forgotten about it.

I took the Bible to bed with me that night. I wanted to look it over for traces of memories more than insight. I turned once again to the story of Joseph. I found where I left off three decades ago. Joseph is thirty years old, give or take. He is the second most powerful man in all of Egypt. His brothers have come in search of food. They don't recognize Joseph. He recognizes them. He messes with their heads. He eventually breaks down into tears and embraces his family, telling them not to punish themselves over the way they treated him. His hardships have placed him here in Egypt in a position of power where he could save them and be an instrument of "astonishing deliverance."

That's where we left off. Now Joseph gives his brothers a bounty of food to take back home and here is where we come up to another one of those strange moments in the Bible. His final bit of advice to his brothers is what? Out of everything he could say at such a dramatic and lifesaving juncture, his final words are "Go, and don't fight on the road."

For a second it sounds like he's talking to children in the backseat of the station wagon on a car trip. But it's not just me who thought this seemed like an odd thing to say. He hasn't seen his brothers in almost twenty years. After his triumph over adversity, he reaches out to save them in a time of famine: "Don't fight on the road." This comment has been examined by dozens of scholars for the last two thousand years. What does Joseph mean?

There are several interpretations. Rashi, a great French rabbi and commentator from the eleventh century, said that the word "fight" really meant "be agitated" or "be fearful." Because the brothers had so many riches and food with them, if they acted nervous in any way, they could draw the attention of thieves. Joseph was warning them to act casually on the way back home.

Another commentator suggested it was a long trip. He was telling his brothers not to be afraid, that there was a sort of divine protection watching over them. Another suggested Joseph wanted to warn his brothers not to continue to blame each other for what they had done to him in the past. If they did, they wouldn't pay attention to the dangers and demands that lay in front of them. These are all good and interesting. But there is another I became enamored of from a Chasidic rabbi in the late eighteenth century. He argued that the line was mistranslated.

In Hebrew, the meanings of words are changed by letters added to the beginning and end of that word. Here we have the word *derech*, which means road. You add a *bet* (Hebrew for *B*) in front of it: *ba derech*, and you have something that can be translated as "on the road." It doesn't have to mean that. On occasion a *bet* at the beginning of a word can also mean "with." Now the sentence would read, "don't fight with the road." Strange. And one further change: *derech* doesn't have to mean "road." It can also mean "path" or "way."

Now the meaning has changed from "don't fight on the road" to something like "don't argue with the path." Maybe Joseph wasn't giving advice as to how to act on the journey. Perhaps he was describing the journey itself. Not travel tips, but a far more sweeping vision of how to live your life: don't fight with the path.

In my life and the lives of those I have loved, the path is something impossible to trace. It has never been predictable. It has never been easy. But in a strange way it has always been planned.

Here is a fairy tale. A real one. A real story of the path. It was 1973. It was my final year at SMU. One of the irascible characters in our school, the rough, gruff, Mississippi-born, Army-trained, shaggy-blond-haired graduate student Lanny Flaherty announced he was leaving us. He landed a lot of great parts, wrote some great term papers on Anton Chekhov, but he had had enough of school and was headed to New York City to take his shot at being what he wanted to be, a Broadway actor.

As I think back, Lanny could have been the first person we knew who broke from expectations and went his own way. If I were to play the "where and when" game of where and when we learn life lessons, it could have been Lanny's decision to leave school that led me to my decision to leave Illinois two years later without finishing the masters program.

Like everything Lanny did, it happened fast. He was "packing up and leaving in a couple of weeks." It was the talk of the drama department. Lanny announced that there would be a "good-bye/help-me-clean-up-my-damn-apartment" party the next Saturday night.

The entire drama school showed up. People came bearing beer and marijuana. The music was cranked up on the stereo. We packed up the yellow Datsun with all of his worldly belongings. We emptied out the fridge, we scrubbed the bathroom, we hauled and swept and threw away, and as the sun began to rise, we began to cry. Everyone lined up that dawn to kiss and hug Lanny good-bye. Even this big, gruff bear of a man's cheeks started flushing as the waves of love and loss washed over him.

We walked down to the street and watched as Lanny squeezed his way into the front seat. He turned to us in that beautiful light of the Texas dawn and waved a final farewell. My former roommate Jim McLure put his arm around my shoulder and watched Lanny go. Even Jimmy was a little teary as he said, "He's the first." I looked over to Jim as he continued, "We're crying now but it's something we're all going to have to do someday. If you don't leave, it means you never started."

It was a double whammy for me: Jim's words and the image of Lanny's Datsun rounding the corner. He was gone. That was it. He was on his way to another life. We looked back to the now empty apartment waiting for its next tenant.

A week later, I was walking across campus to my literature class. There was Lanny Flaherty striding out of the student center. I did a double take. Lanny was back! Apparently, he got to New York, decided that he didn't want to stay "in that godforsaken place," and turned around and came back to Dallas. Now he was looking for another apartment, and he'd let us know when he was going to have a "move-in/let's clean-the-place-up" party.

If the story ended there, it could be a good B plotline of a sitcom, but it didn't.

Two weeks after Lanny's return, James Earl Jones and company came to use space at SMU to rehearse a Broadway-bound production of *Of Mice and Men*. All of us actors hoped to catch sight of the man. The director of *Of Mice and Men*, Ed Sherin, spoke to us at Conference Hour and caught sight of Lanny Flaherty. Lanny's crusty, Southern character struck Ed as perfect for the play. Ed asked Lanny to read for him. Lanny did and was cast immediately.

Lanny Flaherty was back in his Datsun on his way back to New York, now a working actor on Broadway.

And as in all good fairy stories, Lanny lived happily ever after. As an actor he performed in a string of Broadway shows and, as a writer, he wrote the last play in which the great Henry Fonda performed. I was struck by the new irony in Jim McLure's observation, "If you don't leave, it means you never started."

———

As perplexing as the Bible can be, nothing can outdo science when it comes to proposing theories that can make you redefine the meaning of the word "What?!"

I always found books on science great to take on a movie shoot. You never know how long you will have to sit in your trailer. There is nothing worse than getting pulled away from a great novel at the wrong time. It's best if you have something that reads in short bursts, like Charles Dickens or books on physics.

With Dickens there is always a good place to stop. With physics books there's never a good place to start. You only have to read a couple of sentences before you're brought to a complete standstill. Nice and quick.

Here is one of my favorites. In quantum physics there is a particle called a tachyon. The tachyon, theoretically, travels faster than the speed of light, meaning that it can arrive somewhere before it has left.

Pause to absorb this idea.

But there's more. If the principle of special relativity is true—that to the observer nothing travels faster than light—it means that for the tachyon to exist, it must travel back into the past to appear to comply with natural laws.

You can think about this idea for days and days and not figure it out. I have been thinking about it for years. I have come up with one possible way that the tachyon may exist. Every day. In the form of memory. In a nonlinear way, you travel back into the past even though you are traveling forward at the same time. In a real sense you have arrived before you have left.

It is also a heartening principle for those of us who appeared to be going nowhere in our lives. Had I known about the tachyon back then, I could have imagined that in some theoretical universe, Beth and I had arrived at a new destination, even though it looked as though we were starting over again.

She came out to Los Angeles after doing the Lincoln show in Illinois, after our one year of graduate school. We moved into a real house with a real backyard where I tried to grow real zucchini. I had a job doing children's theater with Twelfth Night Repertory Company and Beth was back to the same place she was in Dallas, with no real job that suited her. Instead of working as a waitress, she was now working as a temp in a dog food factory.

But here was the difference. It was a slender thing, but now she had the revelation. The revelation from the evening we read Claudia Reilly's play: the revelation that she would write. And from that idea, she wrote.

She was writing a screenplay called *The Moonwatcher*, which drew on her experiences over the last summer. She still carried around those tattered spiral notebooks where she jotted down ideas and drew pictures of witches on broomsticks.

We had several friends from Dallas who were also actors. We decided that we should band together and do plays to keep our souls alive, or, if that failed, we could get together and get stoned, drink beer, and talk about banding together to do plays to keep our souls alive. We often settled for option two.

Enter Fred Bailey. Bailey was a fellow SMU alum. He also provided something every group of actors always needs and usually forgets. A play. He was a writer. He had the tools to turn all of that drunken potential energy into a kinetic production. It turned out to be the catalyst we needed. Bailey wrote fun, exciting plays. He was also a great director.

He also had recognition. Fred had won the prestigious Actors Theatre of Louisville's Great American Play Contest with his Vietnam-era play *The Bridgehead.* This almost guaranteed that the major newspapers in Los Angeles would review our productions. If we got lucky with a show, it could mean casting directors and agents would see us, and we could be on the road to real careers. There was also something intangible Fred brought to our group: the energy of the possible.

It was the opposite of the Twitter psychology: that the more followers you have, the more valid you are. We had validity because we felt we had something to say, and Bailey provided that something. We rehearsed in backyards and barns. We all chipped in money to make the sets, costumes, and the theater rental happen. But in the end, the most powerful contribution we made was with our time.

When I was addicted to cocaine several years later, a dealer told me something important. He said addiction is not just made up of the time you spend getting high. It is also made up of the time you spend thinking about drugs, earning money to buy drugs, and driving around trying to find drugs.

The man was not a friend, but that night in the alley behind a restaurant, he made me see the world differently. Our life isn't necessarily measured by what we accumulate, but how we spend our time. There is a pressure to value achievement by focusing on the finish line. I often think more praise should be bestowed on those who make sure we're starting at the right place. That was Fred Bailey.

Bailey took us to a true starting line where everything we wanted in our past and everything we hoped for in the future came together. It focused our energy in such a way that the topics of our weekend parties weren't about how we couldn't get agents and how we didn't have careers, but what our next show would be.

It was an environment of excitement. It was during this charged period that what appeared to be a personal tragedy hit Beth. Her grandfather in Mississippi got lost in the woods. Beth got the phone call and burst into tears. Everyone expected the worst. He was an old man. The search parties had turned up nothing. But in a couple of days he was found. He was healthy and in good spirits. He even joked about it. But it was after this event that Beth's spiral notebooks came out with purpose.

After a few months of taking notes, Beth started writing a play. She pulled out her old electric typewriter and started turning pages of scribbles into characters and dialogue. The process didn't call a lot of attention to itself. Because our little group was so focused on the creative rather than the endgame, everybody was writing something.

After a few days, Beth had a stack of typed pages on the dining room table. She still hadn't finished, and she still didn't have a title, but she asked me if I could read it to see if it was a complete disaster. I had learned my lesson with *Am I Blue* not to take Beth's trash-talking too seriously.

I sat in the rocking chair that evening and began to read. Nothing I had experienced with *Am I Blue* could have prepared me. Whereas *Am I Blue* was small and quirky, this play was massive. Beth's offbeat humor had turned into a startling voice. It could be funny and then tragic, often within the same line. It had the feel of a simple play about three sisters, but Beth revealed the universe in that simplicity.

Once again I had the feeling I was sitting in the presence of un-expected beauty. She handed me the sheets as she finished typing. We reached the end together. All I could do was hold her and cry. She asked me if I liked it. I told her it was great, simply great. She asked if I thought it was good enough for us to do as a production with our group. I said are you kidding? It was one of the best plays ever written. It's going to be on Broadway.

A few days later we had a read-through in our living room with our friends. The play had an amazing effect on the group of innocent bystanders. I don't think I ever remember hearing that much col-lective laughter, followed by stunned silence, and followed by tears. Afterward it was nuclear. Everyone was so excited. The only talk was when could we start rehearsals.

The play also needed a name. Beth called it *Old Granddaddy's Dying*, which I thought lacked curb appeal. Sharon Ullrick, one of our troupe, said that one SMU graduate, Jack Heifner, had success with his play *Vanities*. Maybe we could think of a snappy one-word title. She came up with *Crimes*. Everybody liked that, but it still didn't fit the grandness of the play. I came up with *Crimes of Passion*. It stuck.

We started rehearsals. Beth played Babe, I played Barnette. Sharon Ullrick, who was playing Meg, was the only person in our group who had an agent, Richard Bauman. She gave him the play to read. He didn't, but he did keep it on his desk. His friend was a literary agent in New York. Richard's custom was that whenever his friend came to town, he would hand him a pile of scripts for him to read on the long flight back.

As it happened, the top script on the pile was *Crimes of Passion*. One afternoon a strange man named Gilbert Parker called. He had just landed at Kennedy International Airport and wanted to talk to Beth. He asked her if he could help her with her play. Beth looked at me with huge eyes and shrugged her shoulders and said, "Sure."

At the time none of us knew that Gilbert Parker was one of the biggest literary agents in the country. He had worked with the Curtis Brown Agency, where he dealt with Tennessee Williams and Lillian Hellman. Now he was with William Morris where he represented the top playwrights on Broadway.

Gilbert mentioned that the name of the play would have to be changed. Ken Russell was directing a movie called *Crimes of Passion*, and we didn't want the two to be confused. I suggested to Beth that we could call it *Crimes of the Heart*. She liked the sound of it, and that became title number four.

This was the beginning of a road that led Beth, like Fred Bailey, to winning the Great American Play Contest in Louisville. It was a good news/bad news situation. The bad news was that we had to cancel our little production in Hollywood. The good news was that now our little group could boast of having two of the best writers in America.

The road led to a limited Off-Broadway run at the Manhattan Theatre Club, where Beth enjoyed moderate success until Gilbert called up and told her she had been nominated for the Pulitzer Prize.

We celebrated for about a week straight. It was joyous. We couldn't believe where the road had led. In retrospect you could trace that not getting cast at SMU led to taking a playwriting class. Waitressing at Pepe Gonzalez Mexican Restaurant led to leaving Texas and going to Illinois, which led to being inspired by Claudia Reilly. We left Illinois and came to Los Angeles and the words of Jim McLure come back again: "If you don't leave, it means you never started."

Beth won the Pulitzer Prize for *Crimes of the Heart*. It opened on Broadway and ran for over a year. It was made into a movie. Beth was nominated for a Tony and an Academy Award for writing. But to me, one of the sweetest memories I have of this amazing tale of success is that out of nowhere, opening night on Broadway, Claudia Reilly came to see the play of her old schoolmate. I don't think Claudia ever knew the influence she had on Beth.

At intermission on opening night, Claudia ran to congratulate Beth. They screamed and hugged. Claudia looked like Claudia, dressed in black with her beret and boots and sharply cut blond hair. Beth looked like Beth in her ragamuffinish attire. Several women came up and pushed Beth away to talk to Claudia, because Claudia looked like a Broadway playwright.

One woman turned to Beth and said, "Excuse us, honey, we know Beth's family from Mississippi." They surrounded Claudia and started heaping praise on her for her play. Claudia smiled and nodded, taking it all in, and then she said, "I'm just letting you keep talking so I can watch your faces when I tell you what you just did."

The road eventually led to many lucrative contracts, one of which was writing the novelization of *Crimes of the Heart*. That's the book form of the movie. Beth was writing another play at the time and didn't want the job and asked Gilbert if she could offer the book deal to someone else. "Certainly, as long as they can write," Gilbert said.

Beth gave the job to Claudia Reilly. And so in another unpredictable turn in the road, the season of misdirection that led to graduate school in Illinois, that led to Beth being inspired to write by Claudia, now led to Claudia getting her first professional writing job from Beth.

And my mind comes back to the tachyon, the little particle that may or may not be real. It is invisible to us all. It travels faster than the speed of light so that it arrives before it departs. Perhaps the tachyon is a scientific accounting of what we call destiny—and the secret that Joseph tried to reveal to his departing brothers.

ACKNOWLEDGMENTS

To my wife, Ann, for the countless hours, the love, the crises weathered at every stage of our lives together—including this book.

To Cedering Fox, for being the first to kick me in the pants years ago to write my stories, and for giving me a forum to tell them.

To Robert Brinkmann, for making *Stephen Tobolowsky's Birthday Party* happen.

To David Chen, for his friendship, counsel, and inspiration in creating *The Tobolowsky Files,* a whole new world for my stories on that thing we call the Internet.

To Jeff Hansen, for bringing my stories to the world of radio.

To Ben Schwartz, for reaching out and helping my writing become reality, for no other reason than kindness.

To Sarah Silverman, for her generosity and support at the beginning of this project.

To Rabbi Jonathan Jaffe Bernhard
Rabbi Deborah Silver
Rabbi Elianna Yolkut
Sarah Har-Shalom
For their inspiration and insights on Judaism that are with me every hour of every day.

To Jud Laghi, for giving my stories a chance to reach the printed page.

To Ben Loehnen, for helping me, with humor and brilliance, to finish the project.

And to my wife, Ann, because you are the first and the last.

ABOUT THE AUTHOR

Stephen Tobolowsky is an actor and writer living in Los Angeles with his wife and two sons.